The Rock Climber's Exercise Guide

The Rock Climber's Exercise Guide

Training for Strength, Power, Endurance, Flexibility, and Stability

Eric J. Hörst

FALCON®

Guilford, Connecticut

To my original training partner and life hero,
Jeff Batzer.

FALCON®

An imprint of Globe Pequot
Falcon, FalconGuides, and Chockstone are registered trademarks and Make Adventure
Your Story is a trademark of Rowman & Littlefield.
Distributed by NATIONAL BOOK NETWORK
Copyright © 2017 by Eric J. Hörst
Photos by Eric J. Hörst unless otherwise credited

British Library Cataloguing-in-Publication Information available

Library of Congress Cataloging-in-Publication Data available

ISBN 978-1-4930-1763-8 (paperback)
ISBN 978-1-4930-1764-5 (e-book)

∞™ The paper used in this publication meets the minimum requirements of American National Standard for Information Sciences—Permanence of Paper for Printed
Library Materials, ANSI/NISO Z39.48-1992.

Climbing-
Specific
Training

Training Programs

Injury Prevention

General
Training

Training Principles
and Self-Assessment

Performance Nutrition

Contents

The author climbing the classic Young Girl (5.13a), Wild Iris, Wyoming. JONATHAN HÖRST

Acknowledgments

The idea for *The Rock Climber's Exercise Guide* came from the many climbers who urged me to write a book focusing solely on physical training. Given the wealth of positive feedback on my previous books, I decided to accept this challenge and spend a year exercising my fingers on a keyboard. I hope that I meet or exceed the expectations of these climbers, and I thank all those folks who have encouraged me.

My deepest gratitude goes out to all the climbers I have worked with or talked training with over the years, whether in person, by phone, or over the Internet. It's this interaction that inspires and energizes me to spend frequent late nights and weekends writing climbing books at the expense of many a good night's sleep and the occasional missed weekend of climbing. Similarly, I am grateful for the climbing companies that continue to support—and enhance—my endeavors both on the rock and as a performance coach and author. Foremost I must thank Nate and Pam Postma and everyone else at Nicros, Inc. You guys are such a big part of my various training projects, and I tremendously enjoy working with you all! Likewise, I thank the supportive crew at La Sportiva for keeping me climbing in the best shoes on the planet. Ditto to my friends at Maxim Ropes, DMM/Excalibur, Organic Climbing, Friction Labs, and Kuhl.

The process of creating this book begins and ends with all the good folks at Falcon and Globe Pequot. Many thanks to the editors and designer and anyone else who, unbeknownst to me, has helped enhance this book in some way. And what would this book be without the many beautiful instructional photos? Shooting these photos was a major production for me, and I appreciate everyone who contributed both in front of and behind the camera. Thanks to Chadd Gray, Jessica and Geoff Britten, Dana Bleiberg, Laura Mae Hornberger, Jessica Rohm, Mark Himelfarb, and Crystal Norman for lending your talents to this project. Many thanks also to Earth Treks, Spooky Nook Sports, Philly Rock Gym, and Vertical Endeavors for allowing me to shoot instructional photos on your great climbing walls!

Above all I am thankful for my wife, Lisa Ann, for her unconditional love, support, and understanding of the long hours it takes to write these climbing books. Similarly I cherish the help and support of my two rope-gun sons, Cameron and Jonathan—I truly value our time training and climbing together above all else! And to my parents: I am blessed to have you in my life and still following my climbing over the past forty years!

Kyle O'Meara on The Bleeding (5.14a/b), Mill Creek, Utah. SAVANNAH CUMMINS

Introduction

Effective training for climbing is as different from other sports' training programs as vertical departs from horizontal.

Since you are holding this book in your hands, I trust you already know firsthand that climbing is a rigorous physical sport that will test your strength, power, endurance, flexibility, and stamina. Elevating climbing performance therefore demands that you enhance your capabilities in each of these areas, as well as elevate your technical and mental skills. While there are numerous books available that touch on these subjects, there has been no comprehensive exercise book for climbers—until now.

The Rock Climber's Exercise Guide is the ultimate manual for climbers who are looking to improve their physical prowess. Regardless of your age, ability, or sports background, this book will empower you to develop and engage in a supremely effective training program. And as you progress as a climber, *The Rock Climber's Exercise Guide* will guide you in modifying your program for long-term benefits that will keep you upwardly mobile for many years to come.

Without a doubt, piecing together an optimal exercise program for yourself is like solving a complex and completely unique puzzle. The fact is that the vast majority of climbers do not train optimally—in fact, some of the workouts I've observed over the years arguably provide no benefit on the rock! I have therefore written *The Rock Climber's Exercise Guide* to take you through all the essential steps of effective training, from self-assessment to program design to proper execution of dozens of important exercises. In addition I have tried to avoid going unnecessarily deeply into exercise

science or describing esoteric training practices, with the goal of crafting a streamlined, content-rich book filled with practical how-to information. The bottom line: There is no more complete instruction available short of me working with you one-on-one as your personal performance coach.

The Rock Climber's Exercise Guide is divided into four parts containing thirteen chapters total. Part I provides an overview of the core principles of effective training, as well as the most detailed self-assessment worksheet ever devised for climbers. Accurate self-assessment is an essential precursor to developing a comprehensive program that will really work for you. Like a prism, this forty-question assessment will separate out all the areas that influence your climbing performance, thus revealing your true limiting constraints and empowering you to target them with training.

Parts II and III provide the most complete array of training-for-climbing exercises ever assembled in a single book. Chapters 3, 4, 5, and 6 cover all aspects of general conditioning, including warm-up and flexibility exercises, entry-level strength training and weight-loss tips, essential antagonist and stabilizer exercises, and more than a dozen fabulous core-training exercises. Chapters 7 through 10 then delve into the rich area of climbing-specific training. With a narrow focus on training the finger and pulling muscles, there are individual chapters dedicated to training limit strength, power, strength/power-endurance, and aerobic endurance. If you are serious about becoming a stronger climber, these are your go-to chapters!

In the final section, part IV, you will learn how to assemble a comprehensive training program that works. Based on the results of your self-assessment, chapter 11 will guide you in selecting and combining exercises from throughout the book to make up your weekly training program. Workout schedules are provided for beginner, intermediate, and advanced ability levels, so this book will remain your companion for effective training as you climb your way up the grading scale! In chapter 12 you will find what I hope is enlightening and inspiring information on optimizing training for youth, women, and over-50 climbers—three groups that I view as especially gifted at climbing. Chapter 13 then wraps things up with coverage of three important subjects—ironically, topics overlooked by many climbers—including the power of performance nutrition, the importance of rest days and planned breaks from climbing, and the secrets to avoiding injury.

As you read *The Rock Climber's Exercise Guide*, you may occasionally come upon unfamiliar muscle groups, scientific terms, or climbing lingo. Flip to the back of the book for a glossary of terms and anatomy photos showing all the major muscle groups.

Before we dive into a sea of great training-for-climbing exercises, I must stress once more that excellence in climbing demands more than muscle and might. While increasing your physical capabilities is absolutely essential, so is developing excellent technique and steadfast mental skills. Vow to work constantly on all three aspects of the climbing performance triad—physical, mental, and technical—and I guarantee that you will perform beyond your expectations and succeed in reaching your goals and beyond. Now let's get training!

PART I

Climbing-
Specific
Training

Training Programs

Injury Prevention

General
Training

**Training Principles
and Self-Assessment**

Performance Nutrition

Natalie Duran throwing down Visor (V6), Black Mountain, California. DAVE CEPEDA

Principles for Effective Training

The key to climbing stronger is not necessarily training harder, but training smarter. Premeditating your workouts and acting in accordance with the principles of effective training are the essence of smart training.

Effective training for climbing is as different from other sports' exercise programs as vertical departs from horizontal. No matter your previous sports experience, you can probably forget much of what you learned about physical conditioning. Consider that it is leg strength and power that generally matter most in field and court sports, while exceptional cardiovascular conditioning and stamina are required for endurance sports such as running and biking. By contrast, the physical constraints of rock climbing relate mostly to arm and finger strength, upper-body power, and a high level of anaerobic endurance. Consequently, getting in shape for climbing requires a highly distinct and unique exercise program.

Workouts for many traditional sports involve weight training to build strength and mass, which in turn yields more force and inertia for engaging the opponent. In climbing, however, you might view gravity as the lone opponent, and excessive body mass and lumbering, inefficient movement plays to her favor. Therefore, a climber's training program must be designed to produce greater relative strength (strength-to-weight ratio) rather than aiming to develop absolute strength at the expense of excessive muscle mass gains.

As a rough blueprint, the prototypical climber's physique should resemble the sculpted, powerful upper body of a gymnast merged with the lean lower body of a distance runner. Of course, we each possess unique DNA, and we all will come to climb at a high level with somewhat different looking body builds. Trust that by committing to an intelligent, long-term training program, your physique will gradually morph into its best shape for optimal climbing performance.

The goal, then, of this chapter is to arm you with the basic knowledge needed to design and execute the most effective training-for-climbing program. First, you will learn about the unique physical demands of climbing, including the specific roles that strength, power, endurance, and stamina play. Next, we'll take a look at the purposes of general and sport-specific training, and examine the role of the three energy systems that fuel your training and climbing. The chapter concludes with a look at nine guiding principles of effective training. The degree to which you abide by these principles will ultimately determine the quality of your results.

Training for the Vertical Athlete

As a vertical athlete you are faced with many physical, technical, and mental challenges that come together into a complex matrix to be solved. In climbing near your limit, it's often difficult to determine which one of these performance-limiting constraints is holding you back. Consider that mental stress can trigger physical tension such as overgripping the rock or holding your breath, just as poor technique or a missed foothold can cause the

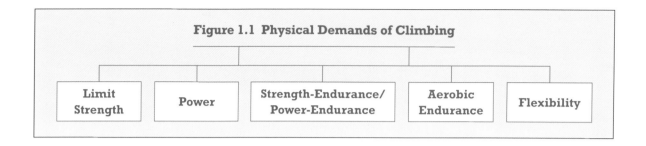

Figure 1.1 Physical Demands of Climbing

| Limit Strength | Power | Strength-Endurance/ Power-Endurance | Aerobic Endurance | Flexibility |

needless muscling of a move and a high burn rate of energy. The best climbers, of course, gradually refine their mental and technical abilities in order to move with utmost precision and fuel economy. So while elite climbers often appear to be tapping into some superhuman level of strength, what you can't readily see is the many years—often decades—they spent developing their exceptional climbing skills and mental acumen.

The key distinction here is that achieving excellence in climbing requires a commitment to work on all facets of the game—improving technique, refining mental skills, and increasing your level of physical conditioning. Many climbers make the mistake of concentrating only on physical training. It's the premise of *The Rock Climber's Exercise Guide* that while physical training is important, you must also be dedicated to improving mentally and technically if you are ever to reach your full potential. Let's take a look at each of these topics.

Physical Demands of Climbing

The raw physical demands of climbing vary dramatically from route to route and with advancing grades of difficulty. While a beginner-level climb might be doable for an out-of-shape novice, an elite-level climb may require Herculean strength such as the capability to do a one-arm pull-up or climb 100 feet of overhanging rock without a rest. For the purposes of developing an effective training program, it's important to distinguish five types of physical demands (see figure 1.1).

LIMIT STRENGTH

Limit, or maximum, strength is fundamental to increasing almost all the physical capabilities required to improve your climbing. As you might expect, limit strength is the maximum force you can generate in a single all-out effort such as crimping on a minuscule handhold or pulling hard through a strenuous move. While such limit strength is only utilized on the most physical of climbing moves, it is very influential in determining your levels of power and endurance. The importance of training limit strength cannot be overstated—it is fundamental to advancing your climbing ability.

Ironically, exercises for building crucial limit strength are overlooked by many climbers. Popular body-weight exercises and the act of climbing do not build it, so there are big gains in limit strength awaiting most climbers. Effective limit-strength training utilizes brief, high-intensity contractions to compel neural adaptations and hypertrophy (climbing-specific muscles only). Chapter 7 will reveal several excellent limit-strength training exercises including fingerboard hangs, weighted pull-ups, uneven-grip pull-ups, and more.

POWER

Power is the application of force with velocity—think of it as explosive strength—as in popping a deadpoint, making a fast pull and reach, or throwing a lunge. The rate of force development in the finger flexor muscles as you engage a handhold is another measure of power often referred to as "contact strength." Power is a product of limit strength and the ability to rapidly activate a high percentage of fast-twitch muscle fibers. Therefore, power (and contact strength) will increase with gains in limit strength and from explosive exercises that increase and synchronize muscle fiber recruitment. For example, speed-oriented exercises such as gym rope sprints, power pull-ups, one-arm lunging, and campus training are all valid for training power since they all demand rapid neuromuscular recruitment.

STRENGTH-ENDURANCE & POWER-ENDURANCE

When climbers talk about endurance, they are usually referring to anaerobic endurance local to the forearm and pull muscles, not the aerobic endurance needed for a long-distance run or full day of climbing (which I prefer to call "stamina"). In climbing, your anaerobic endurance is tested during sustained sequences involving repeated powerful arm moves and successive gripping of small holds requiring near maximum strength. For many climbers, failure on a route often seems to come down to a lack of forearm endurance—although you must always consider whether inefficient movement and fearful thoughts might be causing accelerated energy drain—and so improving strength/power-endurance is a common training goal.

Strength- and power-endurance, then, relate to how long the muscles can produce high, but sub-maximal, power output despite intermittent occlusion of local blood flow (and subsequent cellular hypoxia and metabolic acidosis) caused by repeated near-maximal contraction of the finger flexor and arm muscles. A rapid decrease in anaerobic energy production will take place between 30 seconds and 2 minutes of sustained difficult exercise, depending on power output levels and a person's anaerobic capacity. Individuals with high anaerobic capacity will excel at climbing long, powerful sequences—despite a growing pump—lasting upward of 2 minutes without a rest, whereas a climber of similar technical ability but lesser anaerobic capacity will fail more quickly, perhaps in less than 30 seconds.

Training anaerobic capacity tends to be painful and grueling, but doing the right amount of this type of training is extremely important if your climbing goals include sending difficult rope-length routes or long, sustained boulder problems. Ironically, many climbers unknowingly overtrain in this way due to their "pump lust"—a need to climb and train every session to the point of a muscle-failing pump. An intelligent training program must also include dedicated sessions (and training phases) that focus on building limit strength and local aerobic endurance, since both also contribute indirectly to improving anaerobic endurance.

The bottom line: Training strength/power-endurance will get you pumped, as you engage in repeated efforts of fatiguing high-intensity exercise. The adaptive payoff of said training is primarily biochemical (improved cellular buffering of $H+$, an increase in anaerobic enzymes, and tolerance of other metabolic by-products), although there are also gradual, long-term circulatory adaptations. Toward this end, your go-to exercises, as detailed in chapter 9, include fingerboard repeaters, pull-up intervals, Frenchies, campus board ladder laps, and bouldering 4x4s, among many others. Last but not least, there's interval training—the gold standard for building anaerobic capacity—which you can conduct in a number of ways, including the classic protocol of climbing difficult terrain for 30 to 90 seconds separated by equal or longer rest periods.

AEROBIC ENDURANCE

Aerobic endurance (or what I often call "stamina") is the capacity to engage in sustained exercise for several minutes and intermittent activity for several hours or even all day long. For the vertical athlete, there's an important distinction between climbing-specific aerobic endurance and generalized aerobic capacity. Let's take a look at each.

Climbing-specific aerobic endurance relates to the capacity of the finger flexor and pulling muscles to generate ATP via the aerobic pathway—an extremely important process for route climbers! Not only is the aerobic pathway the dominant energy system for sustained climbing of 2 or more minutes, but ATP-CP resynthesis between hand grips and during rests is an aerobic process. Improving local (forearm/arm) aerobic endurance, however, requires a long-term commitment to training in just the right way to glean the exceedingly slow adaptations of increased mitochondria and capillary density.

Effective training of the aerobic energy pathway via climbing is only possible if you set aside the desire to climb for performance (near your limit) and instead embrace the potentially boring process of climbing high volumes of moderate rock (or plastic). No matter if the climbing is done indoors or outside, this approach will naturally involve lots of submaximal climbing at varying intensities. The critical guideline to obey is that the climbing intensity never ascends deeply into the anaerobic zone, the hallmark of which is a deep muscle pump and shortness of breath. Ultimately, you want to find the margin of the anaerobic lactate zone and strive to climb mostly just below it (in the aerobic zone) while only occasionally crossing into the low end of the anaerobic zone. A light to moderate forearm pump is fine and desirable; however, a flaming pump, heavy breathing, and a growing sense of losing control is a clear sign you've climbed too deep into the anaerobic zone. By keeping your perceived exertion and exercise intensity between 5 and 8 (see figure 1.2), you can rest assured that you're getting it right. See chapter 10 for specific exercises.

Generalized aerobic capacity—full body stamina, if you will—is a most important attribute if your preference is multipitch, big-wall, or alpine climbing. Furthermore, research has shown that sport climbers possessing a higher level of generalized aerobic conditioning recover more quickly at mid-climb rests than climbers who do not partake in any nonspecific aerobic training.

There are two approaches to generalized training. The first and most effective strategy is to regularly log long days on the rock. Since this may not be possible for the weekend-only climber, engaging in traditional aerobic activities such as jogging, trail running, or mountain biking a few days per week is a beneficial substitute. Either way, a crucial stamina-training guideline is that exercise sessions must regularly push beyond what you are accustomed to. Do this two or three days per week, and you will soon be able to outlast almost any partner on the rocks.

Figure 1.2 Training Zones for Rock Climbers

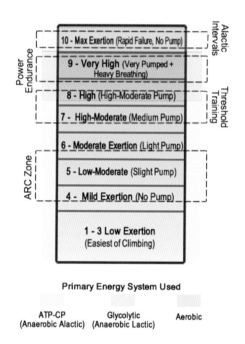

Effective climbing-specific aerobic training must be performed between 5 and 8.5 on the rating of perceived exertion. Chapters 7 through 10 will detail specific protocols for training maximum strength and alactic power, power/strength-endurance, and local and generalized aerobic endurance.

FLEXIBILITY

While you may never need the extraordinary suppleness of a gymnast or dancer, proficiency at climbing does demand sufficient flexibility to execute fundamental techniques without undue stress or effort. Most important is lower-body flexibility as needed to stem, high-step, and hip turnout, although shoulder mobility is important for some advanced indoor and outdoor climbing movements.

Fortunately, climbing is an excellent active stretching routine in and of itself. Climb three or four days per week and you will gain more functional flexibility. You can further increase flexibility with supplemental stretching exercises performed as part of your warm-up and cool-down ritual. As you will learn in chapter 3, all climbers can benefit from a few minutes of stretching and other warm-up activities. That being said, flexibility is rarely a limiting constraint on the rock, so it need not be the focus of intensive, time-consuming training. The majority of your training program should concentrate on the physical demands of strength, power, endurance, and stamina.

Figure 1.3 Climbing Performance Pie

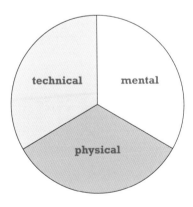

Perhaps more than any other sport, rock climbing requires equal mastery of the physical, mental, and technical domains.

Technical and Mental Demands

The physical demands of climbing are obvious, while the technical and mental demands are often more subtle—yet highly complex and even elusive for some climbers. While they are beyond the scope of this book, I would be remiss if I didn't stress the importance of all three aspects of what I call the Climbing Performance Pie (see figure 1.3). In working with hundreds of climbers over the years, I've observed that many were actually further ahead in their physical capabilities than they were in their technical and mental abilities (despite their belief to the contrary). This may or may not be your situation, and it's often quite difficult to discern your limiting constraints. This is where a self-assessment test (see chapter 2) or climbing coach comes in handy.

In summary, a training-for-climbing program will be most effective only if it addresses your greatest weakness, whether physical, mental, or technical. For most climbers, the optimal program will include some training and drills in all three areas. Consult my books *Learning to Climb Indoors* (beginners) and *Training for Climbing* (intermediate and advanced climbers) for comprehensive instruction on developing your mental and technical skills.

Types of Physical Training

There are two types or categories of exercises: nonspecific (generalized) and climbing-specific. Depending on your level of experience and conditioning, you may want to perform mostly generalized training, mostly climbing-specific, or a combination of the two.

Generalized Training

The goal of general training is to develop all-around fitness and the base level of strength needed to learn climbing moves and skills. Novice climbers will benefit from a period of generalized training ranging from a few months to a year or two, depending on their level of fitness. A well-designed program will help improve cardiovascular fitness and stamina, optimize body composition through a reduction of percent body fat, and build strength in all the major muscle groups including the pull muscles that are so crucial to climbing. Such a generalized training program should be executed two or three days per week in addition to climbing once or twice a week. More information on general conditioning exercises and beginner-level programs is found in chapters 4 and 10, respectively.

Periodic general conditioning is also useful for advanced climbers. A few weeks of general strength training is beneficial after an extended layoff or at the beginning of a preseason training program. Furthermore, it is advantageous for intermediate and advanced climbers to engage in frequent generalized exercise of the antagonist and stabilizer muscles, which over time tend to fall out of balance with the agonist pull muscles. Just 15 to 30 minutes of antagonist-muscle training, twice per week, will improve muscular balance and lower the risk of numerous upper-body injuries. See chapters 5 and 6 for a complete look at training the antagonist and stabilizer muscles.

Climbing-Specific Training

As the name implies, this type of training targets the muscles, movements, and skills that are specific to climbing movements. Because the forearm and upper-arm muscles are the most common physical constraint while climbing, a well-designed climbing-specific program will use a variety of exercises to target these muscles in ways that are very similar to their use in climbing. Exercises such as pull-ups, weighted pull-ups, one- or two-arm lock-offs, hanging knee lifts, and front levers are all valid as climbing-specific training. And, since the fingers are the weakest link to the rock, it's crucial to engage in a variety of exercises to improve contact grip strength and endurance. A fingerboard, campus board, System Wall, and small

home bouldering wall all provide highly specific and, thus, supremely effective training. Chapters 7 through 10 provide encyclopedic detail on dozens of climbing-specific exercises.

A Primer on Energy Systems

Contraction of muscle fibers is powered by ATP, a high-energy phosphate derived from the breakdown of carbohydrates, fats, and proteins. There are three distinct pathways by which ATP is synthesized: anaerobic alactic, anaerobic lactic, and aerobic. While all three energy systems contribute to ATP production at any given moment, just one or two energy systems tend to dominate depending on the duration and intensity of muscle contraction (see figure 1.4). An optimally effective training-for-climbing program must include exercises and training phases that target all three energy systems.

Correctly designing and executing a climbing-specific training program, then, requires a basic understanding of bioenergetics. Toward this end, let's briefly examine each energy system and the role it plays in climbing.

Figure 1.4 Muscular Energy Production

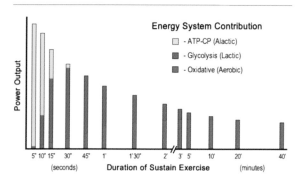

Brief, maximal muscular action is fueled by ATP-CP. After about 12 seconds, anaerobic lactic energy production becomes the primary energy source. Exercise lasting longer than 2 minutes depends mostly on aerobic energy production, although power output is only a fraction of maximal.

ATP-CP (Anaerobic Alactic)

The ATP-CP system, also known as the anaerobic alactic energy pathway, provides rapid energy for brief, intense movements such as a few hard pull-ups, a powerful lunge, or a maximal contraction of the finger flexors. In maximal exercise the stored supply of ATP and CP (creatine phosphate) will diminish in just 10 to 12 seconds, thus resulting in a drop in power output as the glycolytic (anaerobic lactic) system takes over as the primary source of ATP production. This explains why it's virtually impossible to perform your maximum campus training movements for more than about 10 seconds.

A strong anaerobic alactic energy system is important in climbing because it's called upon to produce the maximum power output needed for a crux move, lunge, or to sustain a maximal finger grip for a few seconds. Fortunately, depleted creatine phosphate stores can recover quickly during submaximal climbing and brief rest periods. What's interesting—and relatively unknown among coaches and athletes—is that creatine phosphate resynthesis is an aerobic process. Therefore, a strong aerobic energy system will support a high rate of creatine phosphate resynthesis—important for climbing intermittent near-maximal moves separated by only a few easier moves or a brief marginal rest.

The bottom line: Your level of aerobic conditioning plays an important role in your ability to do repeated bouts of anaerobic alactic–fueled exercise or maximal moves. Recent research has confirmed this concept in showing that the finger flexor muscles of elite climbers use (and replenish) oxygen at a higher rate than non-elites, and that aerobic-trained climbers (who engaged in regular unspecific aerobic activity such as running) recovered faster than climbers who did no generalized cardiovascular training.

Glycolytic (Anaerobic Lactic)

Sustained high-intensity exercise (or climbing) lasting between about 12 seconds and 2 minutes is principally powered by the anaerobic lactic energy pathway (see table 1.1). The process of fast glycolysis can rapidly regenerate ATP in an oxygen-free (anaerobic) environment, which is the common state of the forearm flexor muscles during high-intensity isometric contractions (as in sustained gripping of difficult holds) and the large muscles of the arms and back when pulling many successive hard moves without rest. Muscle contractions of as little as 15 percent of maximum voluntary contraction (MVC) begin to impede blood flow, and contractions of more than 50 percent of MVC completely occlude blood flow, so it's easy to understand why the anaerobic lactic energy system is so often called upon in climbing.

Common hallmarks of a hardworking anaerobic lactic energy system are muscular pain, the "pump," a growing shortness of breath, and increasing fatigue (and drop in power output) between 30 seconds and 2 minutes. At about 60 seconds into sustained near-maximal climbing, the anaerobic lactic system begins to fade quickly, and by 2 minutes the aerobic energy pathway becomes the dominant source of ATP, thus compelling a sharp drop in power output.

Table 1.1 Energy Systems

Energy System	Energy Source	Duration of Steady-State Exercise	Power Output
Anaerobic Alactic	ATP-CP	1–12 seconds	Very High
Anaerobic Lactic	Muscle Glycogen	12 seconds–~2 minutes	High
Aerobic	Fatty Acids, Glycogen, Lactate	2 minutes–~2 hours	Low to Moderate

The choking off of the anaerobic energy pathway between 45 seconds and 2 minutes of sustained, difficult exercise is due to the metabolic by-products of the anaerobic splitting of glucose to create ATP. Although a complex process (and still somewhat controversial), we know that the anaerobic metabolism of glucose generates a number of by-products including pyruvate and hydrogen ions (H+), which are generated at a rapid rate, along with lesser amounts of other metabolites such as inorganic phosphate, reactive oxygen species, and ammonia. While all these metabolites may contribute to fatigue, it's rapidly increasing H+ concentration that most threatens homeostasis.

This increasing intracellular acidosis (due to H+ production) is likely the cause of the muscle burn you feel; more critical, however, rising acidosis hampers the function of glycolytic enzymes, which results in a sharp drop in anaerobic energy production. Fortunately, there are intracellular buffers that can consume H+ (for a short time) and slow the rising tide of acidosis. Interestingly, the metabolite pyruvate is one such buffer, as one molecule of pyruvate can attract two H+ to create lactate. Even more fascinating is the fact that lactate can pass into nearby slow-twitch fibers and be used as fuel for aerobic metabolism. The bulk of the lactate, however, exits the cell into the blood and circulates to the liver (to be converted back into glycogen), to the brain or other organs to support local energy production, or to other muscles where it can be used for aerobic energy production. This helps explain why aerobically trained climbers can recover more quickly between bouts of strenuous (anaerobic) climbing.

Aerobic

Sustained activity lasting longer than 2 minutes relies primarily on the aerobic (with oxygen) pathway, as energy produced via the anaerobic alactic and lactic systems quickly wanes. This transition to aerobic energy production is evidenced by the marked drop in power output due to the slower rate of ATP synthesis via the aerobic energy system. Fortunately, the only metabolic by-products of the aerobic system are CO_2, water, and heat—therefore, lower-intensity aerobic activity can continue for as long as oxygen and energy substrate are available (primarily muscle glycogen and fatty acids) and heat can be removed from the working muscles. Interestingly, the lactate produced by anaerobic glycolysis is another fuel source for aerobic energy production, and therefore lactate is a kind of molecular "holding tank" that bridges the anaerobic and aerobic energy systems.

The Basic Principles of Conditioning

Knowledge of the basic principles of physical training empowers you to design a workout program that will be both maximally effective and time-efficient. While you may be familiar with a few of these principles from previous sports training, I urge you to consider how each principle can be uniquely applied to your training-for-climbing program.

Warm-Up

The importance of a warm-up period is one of the few things that virtually all coaches and trainers agree upon. Five to 15 minutes of light aerobic activity followed by a few minutes of foam rolling and mild stretching will increase the temperature and range of motion of the working muscles, as well as spread synovial fluid throughout the joints. The benefits of these adaptations include increased musculotendon function, improved joint articulation, and decreased risk of injury.

Individualization

This could also be called the snowflake principle, since it highlights that no two climbers—or their optimal training programs—are the same. The best training program for you will target your specific weaknesses, address past or present injuries, provide sufficient time for recovery, and be structured to provide the greatest output for the available training input. Since there is no other climber quite like you, there is no other climber's conditioning program that you'd want to copy—doing so will provide less-than-optimal results and might even get you injured. *The Rock Climber's Exercise Guide* will help you design the optimal program for you!

Specificity

The principle of specificity may be the most important of all for climbers to heed. It simply states that the more specific a training activity is to a given sport—muscle group, workload, velocity and pattern of movement, posture, and range of motion—the more it will contribute to increasing performance in that sport. For an exercise to produce meaningful gains in functional strength and endurance for climbing, therefore, it must be markedly similar to climbing. Obviously, exercises that involve actual climbing motions (bouldering, fingerboard pull-ups, HIT workout, and such) are the most specific and will have the greatest transfer to climbing performance.

Effective training must also target the specific muscle fiber type and energy system most used in your preferred style of climbing. For instance, hard bouldering draws largely on fast-twitch muscle fibers and the ATP-CP energy pathway, so you want to favor brief, high-intensity exercises that target these constraints. Longer traditional or sport climbs, however, typically demand extended and alternating use of fast- and slow-twitch muscle fibers fueled predominantly by anaerobic glycolysis and the aerobic energy pathway. To specifically train these systems, you must frequently train with higher-repetition exercises, incorporate interval-training protocols, climb for mileage, and even do some generalized aerobic training.

Progressive Overload

This granddaddy of training principles states that in order to increase functional capacity for exercise, it is necessary to expose the neuromuscular and cardiovascular systems to a level of stress beyond that to which they are accustomed. You can achieve this overload by increasing the resistance and intensity, volume, and speed of training, or by decreasing the rest interval between successive sets. The best method of creating overload depends on the outcome you desire from your training program. To excel in bouldering, for example, you'd want to create overload by increasing resistance and exercise intensity to build maximum strength and power. A roped climber would be more interested in developing local endurance and, thus, should create overload both by increasing exercise volume and by reducing rest intervals between exercise sets. Finally, a big-wall or alpine climber in need of greater stamina should train at a lower overall intensity and create overload by increasing total daily exercise volume.

Optimal Sets, Reps, and Rest Intervals Between Sets

While one set per exercise may be sufficient for a general conditioning program, it's widely accepted that performing multiple sets per exercise is needed to develop higher levels of strength and power. Well-conditioned climbers engaging in an off-season strength-training program may benefit from doing six or more sets of certain sport-specific exercises such as pull-ups, campus training, fingerboard hangs, and such. However, two or three sets are ideal as supplemental in-season training performed in addition to actual climbing.

The optimal training load (resistance), the number of reps and sets, and the rest interval between sets depends on the desired training outcome. Warm-up sets and stabilizer-muscle training (e.g., rotator cuff, wrist extensions, and scapular stabilizers) are best performed with a relatively modest resistance that allows fifteen to twenty-five repetitions. Similarly, antagonist-muscle exercises need only be performed at a moderate resistance with ten to twenty reps per set. For the purposes of developing climbing-specific strength and power, however, a much higher workload (in some cases five to ten sets) is needed to produce beneficial results on the rock.

The length of rest between sets can similarly be managed to produce optimal training adaptations. A 3- to 5-minute recovery period is best when training for strength and power. A much shorter rest period—30 seconds to 2 minutes—is optimal when training for improved local endurance.

Exercise Order

Every workout should, of course, begin with a warm-up period that gradually progresses from general to climbing-specific exercise. Once all the muscles have been warmed and "turned on," the next segment of your workout should involve actual climbing—practicing new moves, working hard boulders, rope climbing, and such—since being mentally and physically fresh is important for developing and reinforcing efficient motor and movement skills. Only upon completion of your climbing should you move on to targeted supplemental exercises such as pull-ups, fingerboard work, campus training, and hypergravity training. Follow

these activities with stabilizer and core training, and conclude with some foam-rolling and stretching to jump-start the recovery process.

Any extensive antagonist-muscle training, supplemental free weight work, or aerobic exercise is best performed on a rest day from climbing. As you'll learn in chapter 5, there's no need to train the antagonists more than twice per week. Some climbers, however, may wish to do aerobic training on two to four days per week, while also climbing three or four days and taking one full day of rest per week. The only way to schedule all this (and get one day of complete rest per week) is to do a couple of split workout days—that is, days in which you do a morning and late-day workout. The most effective way to split workouts is to do an aerobic session as early in the morning as possible and then the climbing workout in the late afternoon or evening. Scheduling 6 to 8 hours rest between the split sessions is essential, and it's important to always train general endurance early and strength/power late in the day—you'll get suboptimal results the other way around.

Periodization

Periodization is the practice of varying workout focus, structure, intensity, and length every few days or weeks in order to maximize the training effect. If you do not use periodization, long-term

Figure 1.5 The Supercompensation Cycle

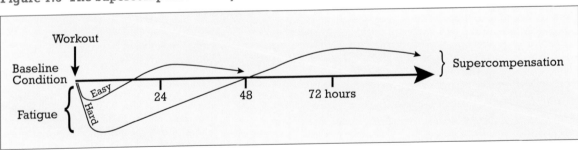

Recovery and supercompensation from a light workout may take as little as 24 hours, whereas it can take 72 hours or more to fully recover from a severe workout or day of near-maximal climbing.

consequences include a plateau in performance, boredom, and an increased risk of overtraining and injury. By training and climbing in the exact same ways and on the same schedule week after week, you are at risk of these undesirable outcomes. You can best employ periodization by planning your workouts ahead of time on a calendar or notebook, so that training focus and climbing preference change every few weeks. You can also incorporate a training mesocycle such as the 4-3-2-1 Cycle or a Daily Undulating Periodization (DUP) scheme (as described in chapter 11).

Recovery

Muscular adaptations occur between, not during, workouts. Sufficient rest and healthy lifestyle habits (proper nutrition, adequate sleep, and the like) are fundamental to maximizing physiological adaptations to exercise. Depending on the intensity and volume of the training stimulus, the recovery process, known as supercompensation, typically takes anywhere from 24 to 72 hours (see figure 1.5). For example, it might only take one day to recover from a high volume of low-intensity activity like climbing several easy routes or an aerobic workout, whereas it often takes two or three days (sometimes more) to recover completely from a lengthy high-intensity workout such as climbing many routes near your limit or intensive training of maximum strength and power in the gym.

Muscle soreness and stiffness provides a rough estimate of recovery—if your muscles are sore, you have not recovered completely from your previous workout or day of climbing. Furthermore, a sense of lethargy and lack of high-end strength and power often signals lingering central nervous system fatigue, despite muscles that feel recovered (free of soreness).

The importance of this principle cannot be overstated, since training too often—frequently climbing sore or tired—will eventually lead to a decline in performance and possibly injury. This is known as the overtraining syndrome, and it's unfortunately quite common among highly motivated climbers. Ironically, overtraining is the ultimate bad investment because it will eventually lead to a decrease in strength and performance—the opposite of the intended outcome!

Detraining

Upon cessation of strength or endurance training (or frequent climbing), recent functional gains begin to erode in as little as seven days of rest. Local endurance diminishes more quickly than strength, and noticeable loss of endurance is likely after just seven to ten days away from climbing. Research has shown that half the mitochondria (and aerobic enzyme) gains from four weeks of training can be lost in as little as a week, and all is lost in five weeks of inactivity. Regaining the one-week loss of mitochondria content will take up to four weeks of endurance training. Realizing the remarkable plasticity of mitochondria—and how quickly you'll lose your endurance—should be enough to compel you to go climbing once or twice per week! Fortunately, strength gains don't diminish as quickly—two weeks away from climbing or the gym may yield no remarkable loss in strength, although slacking much longer than this surely will.

Andrew Hunzicker redpoint-ing his first 5.14a, Mr. Yuk, at age 52! Smith Rock, Oregon.
NATHAN GERHARDT

Self-Assessment and Goal Setting

Accurate self-assessment is an essential precursor to developing an uncommonly effective training program.

The effectiveness of your training-for-climbing program will be directly related to how well it targets your true weaknesses. For a beginning climber, weaknesses usually center on lack of climbing skill, poor economy of movement, and lack of strength and endurance. More experienced climbers, however, tend to have specific areas of weakness, such as poor footwork, fear of falling (or failure), or inadequate finger strength and power. Of course, there are many other skills and personal attributes that may be limiting your performance, and as a rule it gets more difficult to identify the limiting constraint as you advance in ability. Furthermore, your weaknesses change as you grow as a climber—so your limiting constraints are actually a moving target!

Regular self-assessment is a powerful tool to determine your true weaknesses so that you can accurately design a training program that works. On a micro scale, it's important to self-assess after every climb by asking yourself, *What could I have done better?* Some technical and tactical flaws aren't always self-evident at the moment of the climb—this is where a video review of your ascent can provide an enlightening detached perspective.

Perhaps the best analysis of the current state of your climbing will come from an experienced climbing coach. If you're lucky enough to have a veteran coach at your gym (or nearby), by all means engage him or her!

Another useful tool for evaluating all aspects of your climbing game is a self-assessment test. A well-designed assessment will break down the spectrum of your climbing performance into specific elements, thus highlighting your strong and weak areas.

This chapter presents you with an eight-part self-assessment that targets the critical areas of climbing experience, technical skills, mental skills, general and climbing-specific fitness, injury risk, nutrition, and lifestyle. Each part consists of five questions worth a total of 25 points. Compare your scores in each part to identify the two or three areas most holding you back—these would be the lowest-scoring parts of the assessment. Similarly, survey your answers question by question to identify specific weaknesses that should become the bull's-eye of your training program.

In taking this assessment, it's best to read each question once and then immediately select an answer. Don't read anything into the questions, and resist the common tendency to cheat up on your scores. Circle the answer that most accurately describes your current abilities and modus operandi.

Evaluate Your Climbing Experience

1. How long have you been climbing?

    1—less than six months
    2—six to twelve months
    3—one to four years
    4—five to ten years
    5—more than ten years

2. On average, how many days per month do you climb (both indoors and outdoors)?

    1—one day or less
    2—two or three days
    3—four to eight days
    4—nine to twelve days
    5—more than twelve days

3. How many different climbing areas and gyms have you visited in the last year?

    1—just one
    2—two to four
    3—five to nine
    4—ten to fifteen
    5—more than fifteen

4. How many of the following styles of climbing have you been active in over the last year: bouldering, roped gym climbing, outdoor sport climbing, follow trad climbs, leading trad climbs, big walls?

    1—one
    2—two
    3—three
    4—four
    5—five or six

5. How many of the following types of climbing have you engaged in over the last three months: slab climbing, face climbing, crack climbing, overhanging face climbing, pocket climbing, roofs?

    1—one or two
    2—three
    3—four
    4—five
    5—six

Analysis

Add up your scores for each question and record your total score here: _____. Use the scale below to assess your level of climbing experience.

    23–25: You are well on your way to mastery!
    20–22: Your experience is above average.
    15–19: Your experience is average.
    10–14: Your experience is limited or narrow in scope, but huge gains await you given a commitment to climb more often and explore new types of climbing.
    5–9: As a novice climber you possess tremendous potential to improve. A regular schedule of climbing and a willingness to stretch your boundaries will yield rapid gains in ability.

Set Goals

Review the questions on which you scored 3 or less, then set a specific goal for improvement in each area. Write down what actions you plan to take and a time frame for attaining this goal. For example, if you scored 3 or fewer points on question 3, you could set a goal to visit ten new climbing areas in the next year.

Set goals for broadening and deepening your experience: _____
_____
_____
_____
_____
_____
_____
_____
_____

Evaluate Your Technical Skills

1. My footwork and overall technique deteriorate during the hardest part of a climb.

    1—almost always
    2—often
    3—about half the time
    4—occasionally
    5—seldom or never

2. Cracks, slabs, and roofs feel hard for the grade compared with a similarly graded face climb.

    1—almost always
    2—often
    3—about half the time
    4—occasionally
    5—seldom or never

3. I have difficulty finding mid-route rest positions and shakeouts.

    1—almost always
    2—often
    3—about half the time
    4—occasionally
    5—seldom or never

4. On the typical climb, I feel like much of my body weight is hanging on my arms.

    1—almost always
    2—often
    3—about half the time
    4—occasionally
    5—seldom or never

5. On overhanging routes and roofs, I have difficulty finding the optimal body position or keeping my feet from cutting loose.

    1—almost always
    2—often
    3—about half the time
    4—occasionally
    5—seldom or never

Analysis

Add up your scores for each question and record your total score here: _____. Use the scale below to assess your level of technical skills.

23–25: You possess excellent technical skills!

20–22: Your technical skills are above average.

15–19: Your technical skills are near average; however, the next level is attainable given a focused effort to improve in weak areas.

10–14: You possess some fundamental flaws in climbing technique. Make improving your technique a top priority. Consider employing a coach to provide technical instruction and tips for improvement.

5–9: You are at the beginning of the learning curve. With a consistent schedule of climbing, you will see rapid gains in ability.

Set Goals

Review the questions on which you scored 3 or less, then set a specific goal for improvement in each area. Write down what actions you plan to take along with a time frame for attaining this goal. For example, if you scored 3 or fewer points on question 1, make it a goal to constantly focus on your footwork and to resist the tendency to muscle through difficult moves.

Set goals for improving your technique: _____

_____
_____
_____
_____
_____
_____
_____
_____
_____
_____
_____
_____
_____

Evaluate Your Mental Skills

1. I visualize myself successfully climbing the route before I leave the ground.

    1—seldom or never
    2—occasionally
    3—about half the time
    4—often
    5—almost always

2. I get anxious, tight, and hesitant as I climb into crux sequences.

    1—almost always
    2—often
    3—about half the time
    4—occasionally
    5—seldom or never

3. I miss hidden holds or blow a known sequence.

    1—almost always
    2—often
    3—about half the time
    4—occasionally
    5—seldom or never

4. I make excuses for why I might fail on a route before I even begin to climb.

    1—almost always
    2—often
    3—about half the time
    4—occasionally
    5—seldom or never

5. When lead climbing a safe route, I push myself to the complete limit, and if I fall, I fall trying.

    1—seldom or never
    2—occasionally
    3—about half the time
    4—often
    5—almost always

Analysis

Add up your scores for each question and record your total score here: _____. Use the scale below to assess your level of mental skills.

    23–25: You possess excellent mental skills!
    20–22: Your mental skills are above average.
    15–19: Your mental skills are near average; however, significant gains are attainable given a commitment to mental training.
    10–14: Your limited mental skills are an Achilles' heel that's sabotaging your climbing performance. Desire and discipline to improve in this area will yield huge breakthroughs in climbing ability.
    5–9: Your weak mental skills will improve rapidly given a regular schedule of climbing and a willingness to stretch your boundaries and challenge your fears.

Set Goals

Review the questions on which you scored 3 or less, then set a specific goal for improvement in each area. Write down what actions you plan to take along with a time frame for attaining this goal. For example, if you scored 3 or fewer points on question 1, commit to the goal of inspecting and visualizing every route before leaving the ground.

    Set your mental-training goals: _____

_____

_____

_____

_____

_____

_____

_____

_____

_____

_____

Evaluate Your Level of General Fitness

1. How many pounds (body fat or excessively bulky muscles) do you estimate you are from your ideal climbing weight?

    1—more than 20
    2—10 to 20
    3—5 to 10
    4—just a few
    5—zero

2. How far could you jog (modest-paced steady running) without stopping?

    1—less than 0.5 mile
    2—0.5 mile to 1 mile
    3—1 to 2 miles
    4—3 to 5 miles
    5—more than 5 miles

3. How many pull-ups can you do in a single set?

    1—women: one or none, men: fewer than five
    2—women: two to four, men: five to nine
    3—women: five to nine, men: ten to nineteen
    4—women: ten to twenty, men: twenty to thirty
    5—women: more than twenty, men: more than thirty

4. How many push-ups can you do in a single set?

    1—women: two or fewer, men: fewer than five
    2—women: three to six, men: five to fifteen
    3—women: seven to fifteen, men: sixteen to twenty-five
    4—women: sixteen to twenty-five, men: twenty-six to forty
    5—women: more than twenty-five, men: more than forty

5. How many abdominal crunches can you do in a single set using the technique shown on page 64?

    1—fewer than ten
    2—ten to twenty
    3—twenty-one to forty-nine
    4—fifty to seventy-five
    5—more than seventy-five

Analysis

Add up your scores for each question and record your total score here: _____. Use the scale below to assess your level of general fitness.

23–25: You possess excellent general fitness!

20–22: Your general fitness is above average.

15–19: Your general fitness is near average. Improvement in this area will facilitate better movement and improved stamina and reduce injury risk.

10–14: Your general fitness is below average and is undoubtedly limiting your climbing ability. See chapter 4.

5–9: You possess poor general fitness. It's paramount that you improve in this area before engaging in a regular schedule of climbing. See chapter 4.

Set Goals

Review the questions on which you scored 3 or less, then set a specific goal for improvement in each area. Write down what actions you plan to take along with a time frame for attaining this goal. For example, if you scored 3 or fewer points on question 1, set a weight-loss goal and commit to a regular schedule of aerobic activity.

Set your general fitness goals: _____

_____

_____

_____

_____

_____

_____

_____

_____

_____

Evaluate Your Climbing-Specific Fitness

1. On overhanging routes with large holds, I pump out quickly and need to hang on the rope.

   1—almost always
   2—often
   3—about half the time
   4—occasionally
   5—seldom or never

2. I have difficulty hanging on small, necessary-to-use holds.

   1—almost always
   2—often
   3—about half the time
   4—occasionally
   5—seldom or never

3. I find it difficult to hold a lock-off with one arm when I let go to advance the other hand.

   1—almost always
   2—often
   3—about half the time
   4—occasionally
   5—seldom or never

4. Given a marginal mid-climb rest, I can shake out and recover enough to complete the route.

   1—seldom or never
   2—occasionally
   3—about half the time
   4—often
   5—almost always

5. My maximum bouldering ability is:

   1—V0 or V1
   2—V2 to V3
   3—V4 to V6
   4—V7 to V9
   5—V10 or above

Analysis

Add up your scores for each question and record your total score here: _____. Use the scale below to assess your level of climbing-specific fitness.

   23–25: You possess excellent climbing-specific fitness!

   20–22: Your climbing-specific fitness is above average.

   15–19: Your climbing-specific fitness is near average; however, a program of targeted training will quickly elevate you to the next level.

   10–14: Your climbing-specific fitness is a major constraint in climbing performance. If you are an intermediate or advanced climber, vow to increase your commitment to this type of training. If you are a novice, however, continue general training for another year or so before beginning climbing-specific training.

   5–9: You possess a poor level of conditioning. Engage in a general training program for at least one year before initiating a climbing-specific training program.

Set Goals

Review the questions on which you scored 3 or less, then set a specific goal for improvement in each area. Write down what actions you plan to take along with a time frame for attaining this goal. For example, if you scored 3 or fewer points on question 5, make it a goal to go bouldering more frequently to benefit from the targeted training it provides.

   Set your climbing-specific fitness goals: _____

_____

_____

_____

_____

_____

_____

_____

Evaluate Your Injury Risk

1. I perform a warm-up activity and some stretching before climbing or training.

    1—seldom or never
    2—occasionally
    3—about half the time
    4—often
    5—always

2. I climb hard on three or more consecutive days.

    1—every week
    2—often
    3—a couple times per month
    4—once per month
    5—seldom or never

3. When climbing, I experience elbow, shoulder, or finger pain.

    1—almost always
    2—often
    3—occasionally
    4—infrequently
    5—never

4. I engage in regular training of the antagonist and stabilizer muscles.

    1—never
    2—infrequently
    3—a few times a month
    4—once or twice a week
    5—twice a week, religiously

5. I stop climbing or end a workout prematurely if I experience unusual joint or tendon pain.

    1—never
    2—infrequently
    3—about half the time
    4—often
    5—always

Analysis

Add up your scores for each question and record your total score here: _____. Use the scale below to assess your potential risk of injury.

23–25: Congratulations: Your injury awareness and risk mitigation practices make you less susceptible than average to a climbing injury.

20–22: Kudos to you, too, for doing what it takes to reduce injury risk.

15–19: You are at near-average risk of a climbing injury. Just a small commitment to warm-up activities, planned recovery, and antagonist/stabilizer-muscle training will significantly lower your risk.

10–14: You are at above-average risk for overuse or acute climbing injuries. Strive to be more proactive with injury prevention.

5–9: You are at high risk for an injury while training or climbing. Review each question to determine what actions you can take to lower your risk.

Set Goals

Review questions on which you scored 3 or less, then set a specific goal for improvement in each area. Write down what actions you plan to take along with a time frame for attaining this goal. For example, if you scored 3 or fewer points on question 4, commit to training your antagonist and stabilizer muscles twice per week.

Set goals for decreasing your risk of injury: ____

_____

_____

_____

_____

_____

_____

_____

_____

_____

_____

Evaluate Your Nutritional Habits

1. How often do you eat breakfast?

    1—never
    2—weekends only
    3—three days a week
    4—five days a week
    5—every day

2. How often do you eat fast food or fried food?

    1—four or more days per week
    2—two to three days per week
    3—once a week
    4—once or twice per month
    5—less than once per month

3. On average, how soon after a workout or the end of your climbing day do you consume some carbohydrate and protein?

    1—more than 3 hours
    2—2 to 3 hours
    3—1 to 2 hours
    4—30 minutes to 1 hour
    5—within 30 minutes

4. How many servings of fruits and vegetables do you consume per day?

    1—zero or one
    2—two
    3—three
    4—four
    5—five or more

5. How often do you plan out your meals ahead of time for the purpose of eating for performance and optimal recovery?

    1—seldom or never
    2—once per week
    3—two or three days per week
    4—four to six days per week
    5—every day

Analysis

Add up your scores for each question and record your total score here: _____. Use the scale below to assess the quality of your nutritional habits.

    23–25: You possess excellent nutritional habits!

    20–22: Your nutritional habits are above average.

    15–19: Your nutrition is near average, but improving your habits will boost your energy, stamina, and recovery times.

    10–14: Your diet is below average. Strive to eliminate this constraint on your climbing performance and recovery ability by improving dietary surveillance throughout the week.

    5–9: Your poor nutritional habits are both a health risk and a constraint on climbing performance. Make it a priority to make permanent changes in this area—it will improve your quality of life as well as your climbing.

Set Goals

Review questions on which you scored 3 or less, then set a specific goal for improvement in each area. Write down what actions you plan to take along with a time frame for attaining this goal. For example, if you scored 3 or fewer points on question 3, make it a high priority to consume some protein and carbohydrate within the first hour after training or climbing.

    Set your nutritional goals: _____

_____

_____

_____

_____

_____

_____

_____

_____

_____

_____

Evaluate Your Lifestyle and Discipline

1. How many days per week do you engage in a physical activity such as climbing, training, or another sport?

    1—one
    2—two
    3—three
    4—four
    5—five

2. On average, how many hours of sleep do you get each night?

    1—less than five
    2—five to six
    3—six to seven
    4—seven to eight
    5—more than eight

3. How often do you pig out eating and drinking with little restraint?

    1—three or more days per week
    2—twice per week
    3—once per week
    4—once or twice per month
    5—seldom or never

4. Do you smoke?

    1—yes, a half pack or more per day
    2—yes, but only a few smokes per day
    3—yes, but not daily—only a few times per week
    4—I quit
    5—I've never smoked

5. When you set goals or begin a workout program, how often do you follow through to successful completion?

    1—seldom
    2—occasionally
    3—about half the time

    4—often
    5—almost always

Analysis

Add up your scores for each question and record your total score here: _____. Use the scale below to assess your lifestyle and level of self-discipline.

23–25: You are a highly disciplined individual and well on your way to climbing mastery!

20–22: Your discipline is above average and a real asset to your climbing.

15–19: Your discipline is near average. Try to identify one or two areas in which you can strive for improvement.

10–14: Your below-average discipline is a constraint on your climbing. If you are serious about climbing better, resolve to adjust your lifestyle and subordinate less important activities.

5–9: Your lifestyle and lack of discipline are definitely holding you back. Determine your priorities, and make the lifestyle changes needed to elevate your score to 15 or above.

Set Goals

Review questions on which you scored 3 or less, then set a specific goal for improvement in each area. Write down what actions you plan to take along with a time frame for attaining this goal. For example, if you scored 3 or fewer points on question 2, determine what low-value activities (such as socializing, watching TV, or surfing the Net) you might reduce or eliminate to allow for more sleep each night.

Set your lifestyle and discipline goals: _____

_____

_____

_____

_____

_____

_____

_____

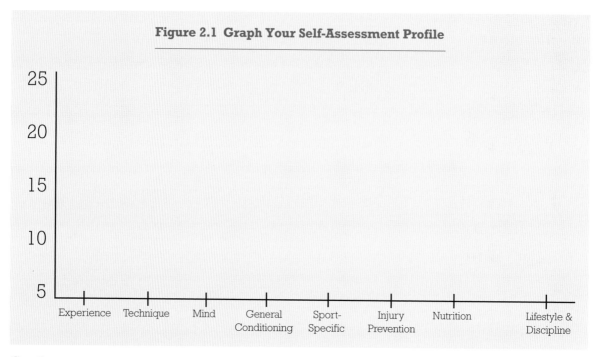

Figure 2.1 Graph Your Self-Assessment Profile

Creating your assessment profile. Upon completing and scoring this full self-assessment package, it's beneficial to plot the results to obtain a graphical profile. Using figure 2.1, draw bar graphs according to your score in each part of the package. Take note of your three shortest bars. These low-scoring areas likely represent the greatest constraints on your climbing performance.

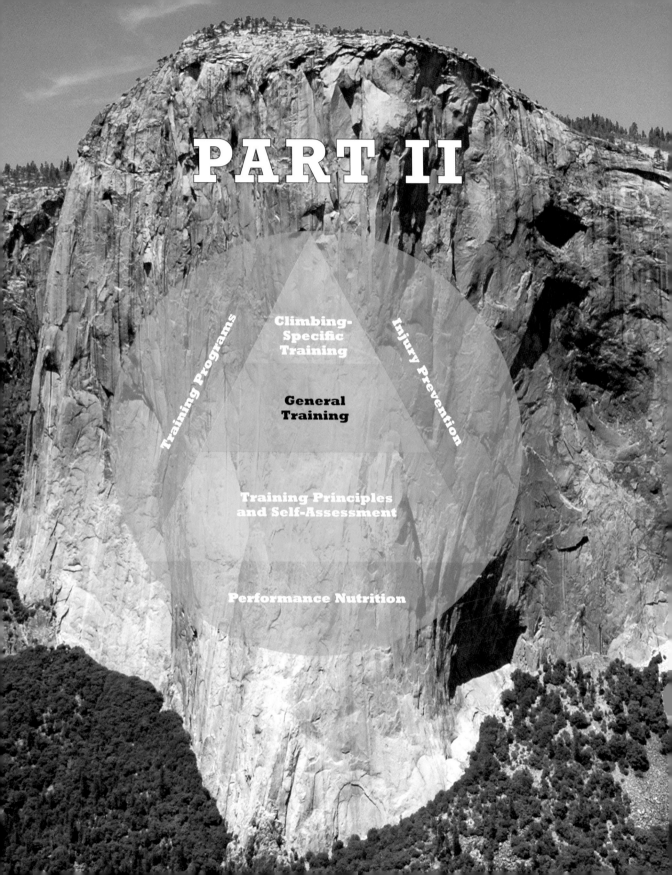

PART II

Climbing-Specific Training

Training Programs

Injury Prevention

General Training

Training Principles and Self-Assessment

Performance Nutrition

Samantha Caligiuri on *Kyberspace*
(5.13a/b), Ten Sleep Canyon, Wyoming.
ERIC HÖRST

Warm-Up, Mobility, and Flexibility Exercises

Given that movement is the very essence of the vertical dance we call climbing, there should be no debate that warm, flexible muscles and mobile joints will facilitate smooth, efficient movements and enhance performance.

While strength and endurance are common constraints on difficult climbs, it's rarely apparent that lack of flexibility is a limiting factor. But just because it's not apparent doesn't mean it's not a very real factor affecting your performance. Let me state in no uncertain terms that possessing a moderate functional level of flexibility and engaging in a preclimb warm-up will enhance performance, albeit in a number of subtle ways that you may not recognize.

Consider that movement is the very essence of the vertical dance we call climbing. From this perspective, there should be no debate that warm, flexible muscles and mobile joints will facilitate smooth, efficient movements. Furthermore, warm muscles function better both in terms of force production and through a lessening of inherent resistance in the antagonist muscles that oppose the prime movers. Finally, there's the payoff of reduced injury risk and increased rate of recovery. Given all these benefits, why would any climber not engage in a routine of warm-up and mobility activities before every workout or climbing session? It should be as obvious a thing to do before climbing as chalking up and tying into a rope!

Gleaning the benefits of warm-up and flexibility training does not require a large time investment or much energy. As little as 10 to 20 minutes per day will provide all the benefits listed above. This chapter will arm you with more than thirty highly effective warm-up, mobility, and stretching exercises for your fingers, arms, shoulders, neck, torso, hips, and legs. You can maximize your results by performing every stretch in this chapter—in the order they are presented—and by following the stretching guidelines provided in the "Tips for Safe and Effective Flexibility Training" sidebar on page 46.

Warm-Up Activities

There are several warm-up activities that you should engage in before moving on to the mobility and stretching exercises. The best strategy is to begin with a general warm-up activity to increase heart rate and body temperature, after which you can perform some of the arm and torso movements to warm individual muscles and spread synovial fluid through the joints. Do this and you'll be ready to execute the highly beneficial foam rolling and stretching exercises detailed in this chapter.

General Warm-Up

The first and most important step of the warm-up process is to engage in a brief period of light aerobic activity. While 5 minutes of steady, light exercise is sufficient for increasing blood flow and core temperature, many climbers discover that they perform better after 10 to 15 minutes of aerobic activity. Many climbing gyms are equipped with a stationary bike, rowing machine, treadmill, or elliptical trainer, all of which are ideal for the purpose of a general warm-up. You could also go for a short run, jump rope for 5 minutes, or do one hundred jumping jacks—all good alternatives if you are training in a home gym. Upon breaking a light sweat, you can move on to the specific warm-up movements described below.

Finger Curls and Massage

This warm-up movement is the most important for climbers, because it warms the many joints of the hands and helps increase circulation to the forearm muscles. Always perform finger curls before engaging in any forearm stretching.

1. Stand with your arms relaxed by your sides.
2. Close your hands to make a relaxed fist, and then quickly open your hands and fan out the fingers as if trying to flick water off your fingertips.
3. Continue for thirty to forty repetitions. Use a pace that allows about two repetitions per second.
4. Now perform a minute or two of massage on both sides of your fingers and hand—this will encourage blood flow and help warm the tendons and tendon pulleys.

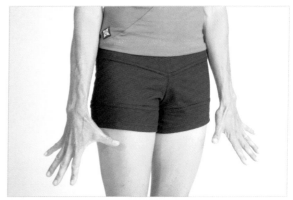

Finger curls.

Wrist Circles

This motion warms the wrist joint and increases circulation to the forearm muscles.

1. Stand with your arms by your sides.
2. Make a relaxed fist with both hands, and then circle your hands through a comfortable range of motion for ten repetitions.
3. Switch directions and perform another ten wrist circles.

Wrist circles.

Arm Circles

This movement warms the shoulder joints and increases circulation to the muscles of the shoulders and arms. Do these before you engage in any of the following upper-body flexibility exercises.

1. Start with your arms out to the sides and parallel to the floor.
2. Begin moving your arms in small circles. Gradually increase the size of the circle until you feel slight tension in your shoulders—go no larger with the circles than this.
3. Use a moderate pace, so that each circle takes about 1 second to complete.
4. Complete ten or more circles, then switch directions and perform another ten circles.

Safety note: Do not wildly whip your arms or swing them in any way that hurts your shoulders. Strive for a smooth, gentle motion throughout.

Arm circles.

Arm Scissors

This is an excellent movement for warming up the many large muscles of the chest, shoulders, and upper back.

1. Start with your arms out to the sides and parallel to the floor.
2. Begin moving your arms forward until they pass across each other in a scissor-like motion. Stop the motion at the point the arms cross each other at about a 90-degree angle.
3. Immediately reverse direction and move your arms back out to the sides until they pass just beyond the plane of your body. Cease the motion at the first sign of tension in your shoulders.
4. Continue this scissor-like motion for a total of twenty to thirty repetitions. Use a modest pace that takes 1 to 2 seconds per rep.

Safety notes: Do not swing your arms wildly, and don't force the range of motion beyond comfortable limits.

Arm scissors.

Shoulder Shrugs

This movement is wonderful for releasing tension from the often tight muscles of the neck, shoulders, and upper back. When done properly, you will feel a stretch at the top and bottom of the movement.

1. Stand with arms relaxed by your sides and your head straight.

2. Raise your shoulders up toward your ears, rolling them slightly backward at the top of the movement.

3. Lower your shoulders back to the starting position and then press them toward the floor.

4. Continue this up-and-down shrug motion at a slow, controlled pace, taking about 2 seconds per repetition.

5. Perform a total of fifteen to twenty shrugs.

Shoulder shrugs.

Neck Circles

This movement will further warm up and relax the many small muscles of your neck.

1. Stand with your arms relaxed by your sides and your head straight.

2. Start by dropping your chin to your chest, then begin a slow, gentle clockwise movement that takes about 2 seconds per complete circle.

3. Do ten circles, then change direction to perform ten head circles in the counterclockwise direction.

Safety notes: Do not race through this movement, and don't force an unnatural range of motion. It's important to only move your head in a circular motion and not in a front-and-back nodding motion.

Neck circles.

Hula Hoop

This is a great movement for loosening your hips and back joints.

1. Stand with your feet shoulder width apart. Let your arms hang loosely by your sides—or you can place them on your hips.

2. Flex slightly in your knees and begin rotating your hips in a circular motion, as if you're playing with a hula hoop. Maintain a nearly still head and shoulders throughout.

3. Continue for 10 seconds, then switch directions and rotate for another 10 seconds.

Hula hoop.

Back Roll

This final movement improves spine flexibility and warms the abdominal and lower-back muscles.

1. Sit with your knees bent and feet flat on the floor.

2. Extend your arms forward and grab your knees. Relax through your arms, but try to maintain good sitting posture.

3. Pull your knees toward your chest and roll backward until your shoulders touch the floor. Immediately rock back up to the starting position, striving for smooth, steady movement throughout the range of motion.

4. Continue for fifteen to twenty repetitions.

Safety note: Err on the side of rolling too slowly through the range of motion. You never want to do fast, ballistic warm-up movements.

Back roll.

Foam Rolling for Mobility and Self-Myofascial Release

Use of a foam roller—and other tools for soft tissue management—is one of the more exciting and useful developments in sports training in recent years. While the simplicity of the following exercises may tempt you to pass on them and advance to the flexibility exercises, I implore you not to! For me, it took just a few days of use to become addicted to my foam roller and Armaid device—I now use them daily, no matter if it's a training day or a recovery day, and I even pack them on all my climbing trips.

Detailed below are several techniques to increase blood flow before training; loosen stiff, cold muscles; and, most important, hunt out and destroy tight, painful trigger points. Each provides a self-massage and myofascial release that will make a real difference in terms of subjective feelings of muscle function and actual mobility by increasing circulation, releasing trigger points, and perhaps encouraging fascial remodeling. Make foam rolling and Armaid use a daily habit (as I do) and you will improve mobility, climb better, recover faster, and lower your risk of certain overuse injuries such as medial and lateral epicondylitis.

Upper Back and Shoulder Roll

This may be the single most important foam rolling exercise for a rock climber, as it addresses the many hard-working muscles of the upper back and shoulders, as well as improves thoracic extension—important to combat the round shoulders and forward head lean known as "climber's posture."

1. Begin with the foam roller under your upper back and your arms across your chest in a hug position.

2. With your knees bent and feet flat on the floor, slowly roll up and down along the thoracic spine. Pause for 15 to 30 seconds on any painful spots (trigger points) you locate in your trapezius and rhomboids.

3. Next, tilt about 30 degrees to each side—still with your arms across your chest—and roll along the latissimus dorsi and up across the posterior deltoid and infraspinatus. Again, dwell for a half minute or so on any sore or tight spots.

4. Finally, return to the neutral position and extend your arms overhead. Keeping your elbows locked and maintaining butt contact with the floor, slowly roll up and down along the thoracic spine. This is excellent for improving thoracic extension and addressing the posture issues and shoulder strains common among climbers.

Upper back and shoulder roll.

Lower Back and Glutes Roll

The muscles of the lower back and buttocks are common hiding spots of tightness among climbers. Anyone who spends large amounts of time sitting (commonly with a flexed lumbar spine) will find lower back rolling to be surprisingly therapeutic. Rolling lower onto the gluteal muscles of the buttock may be similarly pleasurable. Many climbers discover extremely tight gluteus medius muscles (located on the sides of the buttocks, just below the hip)—this isn't surprising, since it's the gluteus medius that produces external thigh rotation when the knee is flexed (as it is in just about every climbing move).

1. To address the lower back, position the foam roller perpendicular to the lumbar spine and roll slowly up and down along the often tight erector spinae muscles.

2. Add a slight roll to each side and you'll likely find soreness in the quadratus lumborum (QL). The QL connects the pelvis to the spine, and it's a common source of lower back pain.

3. To address the gluteus maximus, assume a sitting position with your rear end on the foam roller, legs extended straight to the front and arms extended behind you. Now slowly roll just a few inches in each direction; relax your gluteus and allow the roller to smash deep into the muscle.

4. To release the often tight gluteus medius, however, you'll want to bend one leg and then lean to the opposite side—roll just a few centimeters up and down and side to side and you'll quickly locate the trigger point. Dwell there for a minute and feel the tightness release.

Lower back and glutes roll.

Hip Flexors and IT Band Roll

The hip flexors and iliotibial (IT) band are two more common tight spots to address with a foam roller. If you spend much time in the sitting position, then you'll surely discover that you have tight hip flexors that will hurt (in a good way) when addressed with a foam roller.

1. Assume a prone position with the foam roller under your hips and only your toes and forearms contacting the floor. Now roll just a few centimeters up and down along the hip flexors (front of your upper thigh and pelvis).
2. Tilt slightly to the side to attack the hip flexors only on that side—this will double the pressure (more painful), but yield even more of a release. Dwell for up to a minute on each group (side) of hip flexors.
3. Next, proceed to rolling the IT band, along the outside of each leg. Lie on your side with the foam roller under the upper outside of one leg. You'll need to support much of your weight on the floor-side forearm and position the other leg for balance. Now slowly roll along the outside of the leg, tracking the roller from just below the hip to just above the knee.

Hip flexor and IT band roll.

Pectoral Stretch and Rhomboid Release

This final foam roller exercise provides a nice stretch of the pectoral muscles. The pecs are a commonly tight muscle among climbers (and others who regularly sit hunched over a computer keyboard), and long-term tightness often leads to the hunched-shoulder posture and dysfunctional movement patterns.

1. Lie on your back with the foam roller aligned down your spine. Rest hands and elbows at your side, and use as needed for balance.

2. Relax and allow your shoulders to droop toward the floor.

3. Take a few seconds to breathe, and then try to deepen the relaxation so the shoulders droop even closer to the floor. Hold this position for 10 to 20 seconds.

4. Now place your arms in a goalpost position, with palms facing upward and forearms parallel to the floor, and slowly slide your arms up and behind your head and then back down to your side. This movement will stretch the entire pectoral muscle and help mobilize the rhomboids and lower trapezius.

Training tip: Consider having a partner assist the stretch by gently pressing down on your shoulders. Lie on the foam roller with your feet flat on the floor and your arms resting by your side.

Pectoral stretch and rhomboid release.

Pronator "Pin and Stretch"

The pronator teres is but a small muscle in the upper forearm, but for a climber it's one of the hardest-working muscles.

1. Before you address the pronator teres, you need to precisely locate this small muscle—do this by extending an arm straight to the front and making a tight fist while you pronate the hand completely (as if pouring water from a jug). The pronator teres will bulge on the inside of the elbow just beyond the boney medial epicondyle.

2. Now relax your fist and, using the thumb of the opposite hand, press deeply into the pronator muscle (the "pin") and hold for 30 seconds.

3. Repeat the "pin" again with your thumb, but this time slowly pronate and supinate your hand to achieve a deeper massage and stretch of the pronator. Alternatively, use an Armaid on your pronator, as it provides even better leverage than using your thumb.

Training tip: If you find the pronator muscle to be chronically painful, it's a signal you must not ignore. Temporarily reduce your pull-up training, and use this "pin and stretch" exercise and the pronator exercise (see page 77) several days per week as corrective measures.

Pronator "Pin and Stretch."

Wrist Extensors "Pin and Stretch"

The finger and wrist extensor muscles of the lateral forearm are another common problem spot, especially among climbers who are chronic crimpers. Persistently tight extensor muscles often develop painful knots and trigger points at one or more locations from the middle lateral forearm up to within about 1 inch of the boney lateral epicondyle. While daily forearm stretching of the extensor muscles is essential (page 41), addressing these tight muscles with an Armaid will lessen tension, release trigger points, and ultimately reduce your chance of someday developing lateral tendinosis. Here's how to do it.

1. Using an Armaid (or your thumb), probe the soft tissue of the lateral forearm to locate any sore spots—when you find one, apply steady pressure and hold for 30 seconds.

2. Next, "pin and stretch" this trigger point by making a fist and flexing your wrist as you apply increasing pressure on the sore spot.

Training tip: Climbers with numerous trigger points on the lateral forearm would be wise to invest at least 5 to 10 minutes per day addressing these developing problem spots.

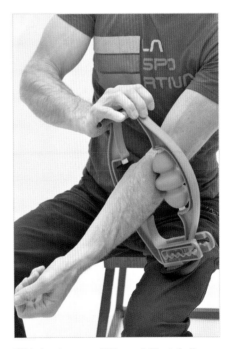
Wrist extensors "Pin and Stretch."

Warm-Up, Mobility, and Flexibility Exercises **39**

Upper-Body Stretches

Climbing places high demands—and sometimes potentially injurious levels of stress—on the many muscles of your arms, shoulders, chest, and back. To begin climbing without first thoroughly warming and mobilizing these upper-body muscles is, thus, foolish and tempts injury. Use the following nine stretches to best prepare these muscles and joints for peak performance and injury avoidance.

Finger Flexors Stretch

This is the most basic stretch for climbers, since it works the forearm muscles that enable finger flexion and your grip on the rock. Perform the stretch in the two positions described below.

1. Stand with arms relaxed by your sides.
2. Bring your arms together in front of your waist. Straighten the arm to be stretched and lay the fingertips into the palm of the opposite hand. Position the hand of the stretching arm so that it's oriented palm-down with the thumb pointing inward.
3. Pull back on the fingers of your straight arm until the stretch begins in your forearm muscles. Hold this stretch for about 20 seconds, being sure you keep your elbow locked throughout.
4. Release the stretch and turn your hand 180 degrees so that your stretching arm is now positioned with the palm facing upward and the thumb pointing outward.
5. Again using the opposite hand, pull the fingers back until a stretch begins in the forearm muscles. Hold for 20 seconds.
6. Repeat this stretch, in both positions, with your other arm.

Finger flexors stretch.

Finger Extensors Stretch

This important yet often overlooked stretch targets the numerous extensor muscles of the lateral forearm, as well as the commonly sore and tight brachioradialis muscle. These muscles are especially strained when crimping with a chicken-wing arm position, and so daily stretching (and Armaid use) is essential for lengthening the tissues and releasing tension that can eventually contribute to lateral epicondylitis.

1. With nearly straight arms, cross your hands in front of your body and interlace your fingers, palms together.
2. While maintaining mild tension throughout the length of both arms, pull with one hand to flex the wrist of the other hand until you feel the stretch develop in the finger/wrist extensors along the outside of the forearm.
3. Hold the stretch for about 20 seconds and then pull with the other hand to create a stretch along the other arm.
4. Perform the stretch twice on each arm.

Finger extensors stretch.

Finger Isolation Stretch

This isolation stretch, along with massage of the fingers and hands, is very effective for warming up your precious digits. Work through this sequence one finger at a time.

1. Either sitting or standing, bend one arm at the elbow to position the hand to be stretched at chest level with the palm facing inward.
2. Curl your fingers about three-quarters of the way, but do not close your hand or make a fist.
3. Place the thumb of your other hand across the fingernail of the finger to be stretched.
4. Now position your index finger (of the free hand) under the finger near the hand knuckle.
5. Gradually apply pressure with your thumb to further close the bent finger and to push it back toward the back of the hand and forearm. Stop when you feel mild tension in the joints.
6. Hold this stretch for 20 seconds. Release the finger for a few seconds and repeat the stretch for another 10 to 20 seconds.
7. Repeat this process with all eight fingers.

Safety notes: Stop immediately if you experience any pain. Also, do not use this stretch on a recently injured finger or if you have any finger knuckle pain.

Finger isolation stretch.

Finger Split

Here's another good stretch to do before your fingers start levering off pockets or twisting in finger cracks.

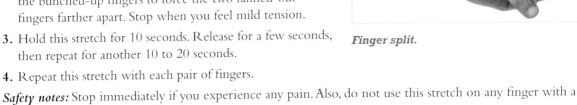

1. Either sitting or standing, bend one arm at the elbow to position your hand thumb-up at chest level. Keep your hand in a straight, neutral position and fan the fingers wide open.

2. Bunch up the fingers of the other hand and place them between two of your fanned-out fingers. Gradually expand the bunched-up fingers to force the two fanned-out fingers farther apart. Stop when you feel mild tension.

3. Hold this stretch for 10 seconds. Release for a few seconds, then repeat for another 10 to 20 seconds.

Finger split.

4. Repeat this stretch with each pair of fingers.

Safety notes: Stop immediately if you experience any pain. Also, do not use this stretch on any finger with a recent ligament or joint injury.

Posterior Shoulder Stretch

This important stretch addresses the shoulder capsule and, in particular, stretches the infraspinatus and trapezius.

1. While in a standing position, bring one arm across your chest until the hand rests on the opposite shoulder. Importantly, you must have your elbow bent (around 90 degrees) and maintain a shoulder back position—do not roll your shoulder forward.

2. With the other hand, grasp behind the bent elbow from below. Pull on the bent elbow until you feel tension in the shoulder and upper back.

3. Hold the stretch for 10 seconds. Release the stretch for a few seconds before repeating for 20 seconds more.

4. Repeat the stretch with the other arm.

Posterior shoulder stretch.

Rotator Cuff Stretch

The towel (or dowel) stretch is a great exercise to help improve the flexibility and range of motion of your shoulder, and it's a must-do before every climbing and training session. Specifically, this exercise involves internal rotation and shoulder extension of the arm that's in the bottom position (thus stretching the external rotators), while it places the other (top) arm in external rotation and shoulder flexion.

1. Roll up a towel and hold one end above and just behind your head, then grab the other end of the towel with the opposite hand (palm facing backward) behind your back.
2. Pull up on the towel with the top hand until you feel a light to moderate stretch—hold this position for 10 to 20 seconds.
3. Perform the stretch two or three times on each side.

Rotator cuff stretch.

Scalenes Stretch

The scalene muscles are located in the lateral neck, originating from the cervical vertebrae and inserting onto the first and second ribs. The scalenes bend the head to the side, flex the neck forward, and lift the first rib. Tight scalenes can affect the brachial plexus network of nerves (causing transient tingling of the arm/hand and covertly affecting motor control), impede subclavian arterial flow (especially during overhead air movements), and hamper proper breathing and blood oxygenation. A slumping posture (over a computer or steering wheel) and the common climbers' round-shoulder/head-forward posture are both indicative and causative of tight scalenes. There are a few easy ways to stretch the scalenes with a simple head tilt, but the essential requirement for each is to anchor the first rib to prevent it from elevating.

1. In a standing position (as in warming up at the crag before climbing), you can best anchor the first rib by holding a towel (or the end of your climbing rope) over the upper shoulder of the side to be stretched (see photo).

2. Tilt your head away from the towel (or rope) to create the stretching of the scalenes. Think of lowering your ear toward the top of your shoulder; do not bend your head forward.

3. Hold the stretch for five slow, deep belly breaths.

4. Perform the stretch twice on both sides.

Do this stretch daily—at work, school, home, and the gym—and you will likely discover some long-term benefits (improved breathing and arm function) in addition to the short-term release of local tightness and stress.

Alternate stretch: Sitting in a chair with good posture (push your chest out), you can anchor the first rib by sitting on one hand or grabbing the bottom of the seat, then gently tilt your head toward the opposite shoulder until you feel the stretch.

Scalenes stretch.

Anterior Shoulder, Chest, and Biceps Stretch

This exercise provides a global stretch to improve shoulder mobility and, specifically, shoulder extension. This stretch is my personal favorite for the upper body, because it addresses all my common tight spots—the biceps, pectorals, and shoulders.

1. Sit on the floor with feet flat and knees bent about 90 degrees. Position your arms just behind your hips with the elbows straight, palms flat on the floor, and fingers pointing back.

2. Slowly walk your hands away from your hips until you feel mild tension in your shoulders, pecs, and biceps. Hold this position for 20 seconds. Be sure to keep your shoulders back (do not let them roll forward)—thinking about extending your lumbar spine and pushing your chest forward will provide a nice stretch into the pectorals.

3. Walk your fingers back a bit farther to enhance the stretch. Hold this position for 20 to 30 seconds before releasing the stretch.

Anterior shoulder, chest, and biceps stretch.

Latissimus, Shoulder, and Triceps Stretch

This stretch will improve range of motion and shoulder mobility in the overhead, externally rotated arm position common to most climbing movements.

1. Stand erect with arms overhead and bent at the elbows.

2. Grab one elbow and gently pull it toward the back of your head until you feel a stretch in the back of the upper arm. Hold the stretch for 10 seconds.

3. Release the stretch for a few seconds and then perform a secondary stretch for about 20 seconds. You can extend this stretch down through the latissimus dorsi muscle by leaning slightly sideways in the direction of the pull.

4. Repeat the stretch with the other arm.

Latissimus, shoulder, and triceps stretch.

Tips for Safe and Effective Flexibility Training

- Always engage in 5 to 10 minutes of jogging, jumping jacks, easy climbing, or foam rolling before beginning flexibility training. Stretching a cold muscle can lead to injury.

- Stretch in a slow, gradually progressive manner. Stretching should produce mild discomfort, but never sharp pain.

- Perform a primary stretch of 10 to 20 seconds. Release the stretch for a few seconds before performing a secondary stretch for 20 to 30 seconds.

- Direct slow, deep breathing throughout the stretch. Inhale through your nose and exhale through your mouth.

- Maintain a neutral back position—neither rounded nor hyperextended—to maximize the stretch and avoid injury.

- Limit extensive "gain" stretching to the legs and hips. Be conservative in stretching the shoulders.

- Using foam rolling in conjunction with stretching will have a synergistic effect. Roll first, stretch second.

- Refrain from excessive stretching of the forearm flexors prior to climbing, since this may affect the nervous system in a way that reduces your maximum strength and power for up to 1 hour. Favor light stretching, Armaid use, and sports massage prior to performance climbing.

Lower-Body Stretches

While leg strength is rarely a limiting factor in rock climbing, lack of lower-body flexibility can be, at times, a limitation. For example, dihedrals and overhanging routes often require the ability to stem widely between holds, while steep face climbs often demand high steps and hip turnout to optimize center-of-mass positioning and reduce weighting of the fingers. A modest level of flexibility is an asset on such climbs; in fact, limber, nimble legs and hips will help facilitate smooth, efficient movement on all routes regardless of type and grade. Why not, then, spend 10 to 15 minutes stretching the large and commonly taut muscles of the lower body? Following are eight useful stretches to put to work beginning today!

Buttocks and Lower Back Stretch

This stretch will improve hip flexion and help facilitate high-stepping.

1. Lie flat on your back with both legs straight.
2. Bend one leg, grasp it behind the thigh or around the upper shin, and pull it toward your chest.
3. Hold the stretch for 10 seconds, then release it for a few seconds.
4. Pull the thigh toward your chest again for a secondary stretch of about 20 seconds.
5. Repeat with the other leg.

Buttocks and lower back stretch.

Hamstring Stretch

The hamstring muscles along the back of the thigh are chronically tight in many climbers, thus restricting stem and high-step movements. Daily use of this stretch will yield significant improvement.

1. Lie flat on your back with one leg straight and the other bent slightly.
2. Lift the straight leg upward, grab it behind the thigh or calf, and pull gently forward until you feel the stretch down the back of your leg.
3. Hold this stretch for 10 seconds, then release it slightly for a few seconds.
4. Pull the leg once again for another 20- to 30-second stretch. Be sure to maintain a straight leg all the while.
5. Repeat with your other leg.

   Alternatively, loop a fitness band over your foot and regulate the stretch by pulling on the band.

Hamstring stretch.

Piriformis Stretch

The piriformis muscle lies deep beneath the gluteal muscles and assists in lifting and rotating the thigh laterally. In climbing, you use this muscle to position your foot on a hold that's up and out to the side. If you have trouble reaching out your foot to engage distant edges, a tight piriformis is likely part of the problem. The piriformis stretch may also provide some relief for individuals experiencing mild sciatica.

1. Kneel on the floor with your hands positioned under your shoulders.

2. Shift your upper-body weight onto your arms, so that you can reposition your legs as follows.

3. Move one leg in front of you, keeping the knee sharply bent so that the heel is positioned near your groin.

4. Slide the other leg backward until it's straightened out behind you. The kneecap should be facing down to the floor while the sole of your foot faces up toward the ceiling.

5. Use your arms to align your torso over the center of your bent leg. Lower your hips toward the bent leg to increase the stretch. Hold this position for 10 seconds, then raise your hips slightly to release the stretch for a few seconds.

6. Lower your hips once more for a secondary stretch of 30 to 60 seconds. Most people feel a pleasant stretching deep within the gluteal muscles.

7. Repeat with your other leg.

Safety notes: Perform this stretch with caution and ease up at the first sign of any pain in your knees, hips, or lower back. This stretch may be inappropriate for individuals with a history of knee injuries.

Piriformis stretch.

Adductor Stretch

This wall stretch is one of the very best lower-body stretches for climbers. Lying on the floor eliminates strain on the lower back and allows you to relax and let gravity do the work. Wearing socks can reduce friction between your heels and the wall, helping maximize your range of motion.

1. Lie on the floor with your buttocks about 6 inches from a wall and your legs extending straight up the wall, with a 90-degree bend at your hips.
2. Slowly separate your legs by sliding your heels out to the sides. Concentrate on relaxing throughout your body, and allow gravity to extend the split until you feel mild tension in your legs and groin. Hold this position for 10 to 20 seconds.
3. Now split your legs a bit farther apart; if needed, press on your thighs to apply some downward pressure to extend the stretch. Hold this position for 30 to 60 seconds.
4. Try to extend the split a bit farther and hold for another minute or so.

Adductor stretch.

Groin Stretch

This stretch, also known as the Froggie or Butterfly, is excellent for improving hip turnout. Flexibility gains from this stretch will allow you to move your center of mass in closer to the wall—more over your feet—on near-vertical climbs.

1. Sit upright with your legs flexed and your knees out to the sides so that you can bring the soles of your feet together.
2. Grasp your ankles and rest your elbows on the insides of your thighs.
3. Press down with your elbows to apply light pressure on both thighs until you feel mild tension in your groin and inner thigh. Hold this stretch for 10 seconds, then release it for a few seconds.
4. Apply pressure for a secondary stretch of 20 to 30 seconds.
5. Next lie flat on your back while keeping your feet together.
6. Relax and allow gravity to pull your knees toward the floor for another minute or two.

Groin stretch.

Hip Flexors and Quadriceps Stretch

The hip flexor muscle group is commonly tight, not only because of the critical role they serve in running, hiking uphill, and lifting the legs in climbing, but also because they can readily shorten during extended periods of sitting. This makes the hip flexors, including the powerhouse psoas, a prime muscle group to target with foam rolling and stretching. Here's how to do it.

1. Kneel on the floor with one leg forward and bent at near 90 degrees, while the other leg is nearly straight and extended behind you.

2. Resting your hands on the knee for balance, shift your hips forward while maintaining a flat or slightly extended spine—this should create some tension in the hip flexors atop the straight leg. Hold this position for 10 seconds, and then raise your hips slightly to release the stretch for a few seconds.

3. Now shift your hips forward again and, if you can maintain balance, extend your arms straight overhead. This will enhance the stretch and perhaps elicit a "pop" from the lumbar zone. Hold the stretch for 30 seconds.

4. Release the stretch and then flex your rear leg so that you can grab it with the opposite hand.

5. Now do a final stretch in which you both shift forward and pull gently on the rear foot. This will provide an excellent stretch of the quadriceps.

Hip flexors and quadriceps stretch.

Calf Stretch

There are many ways to stretch the calf muscles of the lower leg, so there's no reason not to give these hard-working muscles a few stretches throughout the day.

1. Elevate the front part of the foot on a small step or other object.
2. Keeping your heel on the floor, lower your hip level and flex your knee forward to elicit a good stretch. Hold the stretch for 20 seconds, then release it for a moment.
3. Resume the stretch for another 30 seconds or so.
4. Repeat the stretch with the other leg.

Calf stretch.

High-Step Stretch

This final lower-body stretch is very sport-specific and will leave you ready to go climbing. The high leg position and erect posture produce a deep stretch in your buttocks, adductors, and lower back that will help facilitate more effortless high-stepping.

1. Stand along the front of a table, high stool, or at the gym a tall plyometric box, and position your feet about shoulder width apart and turned out to the sides.
2. Lift one leg—as in high-stepping—and place the sole of that foot atop the table or chair with the foot pointing out to the side, as if it were edging on a foothold.
3. Slowly rock over your high foot until you feel a stretch in your buttocks, groin, and lower back. Hold this for 10 seconds, then shift your weight back to center to relax the stretch for a few seconds.
4. Slowly shift your weight back toward the high leg to stretch for another 20 seconds.
5. Repeat with the other leg.

Safety notes: Do not use a table or chair higher than your hip level. A table of normal height—between 26 and 32 inches high—works best for most individuals. Cease stretching if you feel any unusual pain in your groin, lower back, hips, or knees.

High-step stretch.

Torso/Core Stretches

Whether you know it or not, the muscles of your core are at work with every climbing move you make. This group of muscles surrounds your torso from the shoulders, chest, and upper back down along your abdomen and spine to near your pelvis, hips, and lower back. This chain of muscles maintains proper posture, produces body tension, and transfers power and torque from upper to lower body, and vice versa. The importance of properly warming up and stretching these muscles should be obvious to any serious climber.

Obliques Stretch

This is an excellent first stretch for the core muscles of the torso and, in particular, the external obliques.

1. Stand with your feet shoulder width apart.
2. Bend your arms directly overhead. With each hand, grip the opposite elbow.
3. Lean slowly sideways until you feel mild tension along the side of your trunk. Bend at the waist while remaining still below the waist. Don't lean forward or backward, only sideways.
4. Hold this stretch for 10 seconds, and then return to the starting position for a few seconds.
5. Perform a secondary stretch for another 20 seconds.
6. Repeat this stretch on the other side.

Obliques stretch.

Abdominal Stretch

While strong abdominals that can stiffen on demand are highly coveted, it's equally important to be able to quickly relax the abs and extend the torso. Most people find it relaxing and pleasurable to stretch the abdominals and extend the spine before and following a workout.

1. Begin in a prone position with your arms bent and palms flat on the floor next to your shoulders.

2. Slowly press your shoulders away from the floor until you feel mild tension in your abdominals. Keep your legs and pelvis in contact with the floor for the duration of this stretch—it helps to contract your buttocks in order to maintain the position and reduce stress on your lower back.

3. Hold the stretch for 10 seconds, and then return to the starting position for a few seconds.

4. Press up for a secondary stretch of 20 to 30 seconds. Relax and allow the curve of your spine to extend up through your upper back and neck. Look forward, but not up toward the ceiling.

Safety note: Do not be overly aggressive with this stretch—proceed with caution, especially if you have a history of back problems. Stop immediately if you experience any pain in the lower back.

Abdominal stretch.

Obliques, Hips, and Back Stretch

Climbing contorts your body along three axes: front-to-back, side-to-side, and rotationally along a vertical axis. This stretch will help prepare your body for the torso-twisting, hip-turning, drop-kneeing movements that are ubiquitous during indoor and sport climbs.

1. Sit erect on the floor with one leg straight and the other bent and crossing over your opposite knee.
2. Slowly turn your body toward the side of the bent leg until you feel mild tension in your lower back, your hips, and the side of your torso. Maintain a level head position and fix your eyes on the wall to the side of your bent leg.
3. Hold the stretch for 10 to 20 seconds, and then return to the starting position for a few seconds.
4. Perform a secondary stretch for 20 to 30 seconds. If needed, you can increase the stretch by levering your elbow against the thigh of the bent leg.
5. Repeat the stretch in the other direction. Be sure to switch leg positions.

Safety note: Use caution in performing this or any rotational stretch. Stop immediately if you experience pain in your hips or spine.

Obliques, hips, and back stretch.

Lisa Ann Hörst redpointing Good Luck Jonathan (5.12a/b), Ten Sleep Canyon, Wyoming. ERIC HÖRST

Basic Training and Weight Loss

*Since there is no other climber quite like you,
there is no other climber's training program that
you'd want to copy. You possess unique strengths
and weaknesses, experience, genetics, and goals,
so your optimal program will be unlike that of
any other climber.*

Important note: You may skip this chapter if you
scored 20 or greater in the "Level of General Fitness" portion of chapter 2's self-assessment test.

Developing movement skills and enjoying a day
of climbing requires a certain base level of physical fitness. For example, if you cannot climb several
beginner-level routes without incurring significant
fatigue, then poor general fitness is a primary constraint that will limit your potential to improve as a
climber.

One benchmark of general fitness for climbing is your strength-to-weight ratio, or how well
you can perform specific exercises at your current
body weight. Measurements of this ratio include
how many pull-ups and push-ups you can perform
and, to a lesser extent, how fast and far you can run.
Obviously, excessive body fat is a liability, whereas
well-trained yet not excessively bulky muscles are
an asset. Good cardiovascular conditioning is also
advantageous, because it enhances recovery ability
and overall resistance to fatigue while you train and
climb. Improving in all these areas is the focus of
this chapter.

If you scored less than 20 points in the "General Fitness" portion of chapter 2's self-assessment,
then it's best to begin your training-for-climbing

journey with a period of general conditioning.
In this chapter you will learn several effective
body-weight exercises to perform a few days per
week at home or at the gym after climbing. These
basic training exercises are not particularly specific to climbing; however, they are a good starting point if you are somewhat out-of-shape and
just getting into climbing. As an alternative to the
body-weight exercises, we'll also examine the use
of circuit training with exercise machines or free
weights.

The chapter concludes with a review of the
important subject of body composition and weight
loss. In terms of increasing strength-to-weight ratio,
training to reduce excessive body fat or muscle mass
is as valid as—and perhaps more easily achieved
than—increasing muscular strength. It's important
that all climbers consider both sides of the strength-
over-weight fraction, and then train to improve in
both areas.

Body-Weight Exercises

In chapter 2 you assessed your level of general
conditioning using several body-weight exercises
as metrics. These same exercises are also your tools
for improving general physical fitness. Perform the
following exercises three days per week, either at
home as part of a training day or at the climbing
gym at the end of your session. Retake the general
conditioning self-assessment (in chapter 2) every
three months and modify your training program as
follows:

- Upon reaching a score of 15 points, begin to introduce some of the climbing-specific training exercises contained in part III of this book.

- With a score of 20 or greater, you can cease basic training and focus exclusively on climbing-specific training activities.

Pull-Up

The pull-up is the most universal exercise used by climbers, and it should be a staple of your general fitness-training program. Perform your pull-ups on a bar, the bucket hold of a fingerboard, or on a set of free-hanging Pump Rocks. Use the next two exercises (aided pull-ups and the lock-off and lower) if you are unable to do at least eight pull-ups.

1. Mount the bar or board with your hands in a palms-away position (the way you usually grip the rock) and about shoulder width apart.

2. Pull up at a relatively fast rate in order to reach the top position in 1 second or less. Pause at the top for just a moment, and then lower yourself to a 2-second count. Subvocalize: one thousand one, one thousand two.

3. Upon reaching the bottom position, immediately begin your next pull-up.

4. Continue in this fashion until you can no longer perform a complete pull-up.

5. Do three to five sets with a rest interval of at least 3 minutes between sets.

6. As your pull-up strength improves, begin to vary the distance between your hands to better simulate the wide range of hand positions you'll encounter in climbing.

Training tip: To properly active your rotator cuff and scapular stabilizers, try to bend the pull-up bar as you begin each pull-up. While the bar will surely resist your efforts to bend it, the act of trying to bend the bar is an excellent external cue to support proper execution of the pulling motion.

Pull-up.

Aided Pull-Ups

A conundrum for some beginning climbers is how to train pull-up strength if they can't do a pull-up! Fortunately, there are two highly effective exercises that will help you over this hurdle in a matter of weeks. The first strategy is simply to have a spotter hold you around your waist and lift a portion of your body weight so that you can do eight to ten less-than-body-weight pull-ups. Use this exercise three days per week, and soon you'll be doing pull-ups on your own!

1. Mount the bar or hangboard with your hands in a palms-away position, about shoulder width apart.
2. With the spotter standing behind you and holding you lightly around your waist, begin doing pull-ups. The spotter should provide help only on the upward phase of the pull-up.
3. Pause for a moment at the top, then lower to a slow 2-second count. The spotter should let go during the down phase so that you are lowering full body weight.
4. Continue doing pull-ups in this manner until you reach eight to ten total repetitions.
5. Rest for 5 minutes, then perform two more sets.

Training tip: In beginning both the up and down phases of the aided pull-up, think about trying to bend the pull-up bar—this will help to properly activate your rotator cuff and scapular stabilizers.

Aided pull-ups.

Lock-Off and Lower

If you do not have a spotter available to help you (as needed for Aided Pull-Ups), you can similarly train your pull muscles by lowering through the down phase of the pull-up and just skipping the upward phase. Here's how.

1. Place a chair below the pull-up bar or hangboard and step up into the top position with your hands pulled in near your armpits.
2. Remove your feet from the chair and maintain a lock-off at this top position for 2 seconds before slowly lowering yourself to a 5-second count. Subvocalize: one thousand one, one thousand two, and so on, trying to sustain a slow descent that takes 5 seconds.
3. Upon reaching the bottom, straight-arm-hang position, step back up on the chair to reach the top again.
4. Hold another lock-off at the top position for 2 seconds before beginning another slow-motion descent.
5. Continue in this fashion for a total of five to ten repetitions. Stop the exercise if you can no longer lower yourself at a slow, controlled rate. Never allow yourself to drop uncontrolled into the straight-arm position.
6. Perform a total of three sets with a 5-minute rest between sets.

Push-Ups

This popular gym-class exercise is actually a great exercise for climbers to use in strengthening their shoulder and chest muscles. Performing two sets of standard push-ups, two or three days per week, will help prevent some of the shoulder injuries that climbers commonly experience.

1. Lie facedown on the floor with your arms bent and your hands flat on the floor near your armpits.
2. Stiffen your torso muscles just enough to create body tension so that you can maintain a straight body position as you begin your push-ups.
3. Push up to the straight-arm (top) position, and immediately return to the bottom position.
4. Without pause, continue the up-and-down motion at a brisk pace that takes just 1 to 2 seconds per repetition. No resting between reps!
5. Continue until you can no longer push up to the top position. If you are able to do more than twenty-five reps, increase the difficulty by moving your hands a few inches closer together for the next set and for future workouts. The most difficult way to do push-ups is with your hands overlapped directly below your sternum.
6. Perform one or two more sets with a 3- to 5-minute rest between sets.

Beginner's note: If you cannot perform at least ten push-ups in the manner described above, you should then do the push-ups with your knees remaining on the floor to lower the resistance. In a few weeks you'll gain enough strength to do at least the first set with your knees off the ground.

1. Starting position.

2. Ending position.

Bench Dip

Dips are an excellent exercise for strengthening the triceps, deltoids, pectorals, and the many smaller stabilizer muscles of the upper body. Of course, the dip motion is similar to that of pressing out a mantle move on the rock, so you have double the reason to perform this exercise two or three days per week. Most health clubs have apparatuses similar to the parallel bars for performing dips, but at home you'll need to be a little more creative. For general conditioning I advocate using the bench dip, but I suggest that you progress to dipping on a set of free-floating Pump Rocks or gymnastics rings (see page 93 in chapter 5) as you advance in ability.

If you haven't done dips before, you will discover that they are surprisingly difficult. Initially, strive to do two sets of six to twelve repetitions, with the long-term goal of fifteen to twenty reps. To further increase the difficulty of this exercise, you can elevate your feet by resting your heels on the edge of a chair positioned a few feet in front of you.

1. Begin by sitting on the edge of a bench or sturdy chair, your feet flat on the floor. Securely grip the edge of the bench with the palms of your hands pressing on the top of the bench at hip width.

2. Press down with your hands and lift your rear end off the bench. Walk your feet a foot or two forward so that your hips shift to a position a few inches in front of the bench.

3. Slowly lower your hips toward the floor by bending your arms. Stop when your arms are bent at a 90-degree angle, then immediately push back up to the top position.

4. Continue this up-and-down motion at a steady pace that takes just 1 to 2 seconds per repetition.

5. Return to the seated position on the bench when you feel that you can no longer control your motion or complete another dip. Rest for 3 to 5 minutes.

6. Perform one or two more sets with an additional 3- to 5-minute rest between sets.

Safety note: Never lower yourself below a 90-degree arm position.

1. Starting position.

2. Ending position.

Side Squat

This body-weight exercise is highly effective for training many of the lower-body muscles you use in climbing. Perform fifteen to thirty repetitions and I'm sure you'll begin to feel a burn in your quadriceps. The Side Squat also works the glutes, adductors, abductors, hamstrings, and the muscles of your calves. Fortunately, body-weight squats will strengthen your leg muscles without adding bulk—important for climbers.

1. Stand with your feet a bit more than shoulder width apart. The farther apart they are, the harder this exercise will be.
2. Bend your arms slightly and hold them just in front of your hips. You'll need to subtly shift your arms to maintain balance while performing this exercise.
3. Slowly bend your left leg and begin shifting your center of gravity to the left as you lower yourself over your left foot.
4. Now press back up with your left leg to return to the starting position. Maintain a straight right leg throughout this down-and-up motion.
5. Immediately begin another repetition with the same leg. Continue for fifteen to thirty repetitions, or stop when you can no longer control your downward motion.
6. After a brief rest, perform a set with your right leg doing the squatting motion.

1. Starting position.   *2. Ending position.*

Hip Thrust–Floor Version

This version of a hip thrust is a good entry-level exercise for strengthening the posterior chain muscles (spinal erectors, glutes, and hamstrings)—all important for anti-flexion core stiffening on overhanging climbs.

1. Lie on your back with your arms out to the sides, your legs bent at about 90 degrees, and your feet flat on the floor and about shoulder width apart.
2. Press down simultaneously with your feet and shoulders to lift your hips and lower back off the floor—thick about contracting hard with your gluteal muscles. Push your hips toward the ceiling as far as comfortably possible.
3. Hold the top position for 1 second, then return to the starting position.
4. Continue this motion for ten to twenty reps (hard).
5. Rest for 3 minutes before performing a second set.

1. Starting position.   *2. Ending position.*

Elbow Plank

There are many ways to plank, but the elbow plank is the most basic and popular. While this is a decent total core exercise, it primarily targets the anterior core muscles (abdominals).

1. Assume the plank position with only your toes and your forearms touching the floor. Your upper arms should be perpendicular to the floor.
2. Maintain a straight line from your head to your toes. Don't let your hips sag, nor rise.
3. Concentrate on contracting all the muscles of your core. Hold this position for 30 seconds to 1 minute.
4. Do three sets with a 1-minute rest in between.

Maintain a straight line, from head to toes.

Abdominal Crunch

Chapter 6 provides a detailed look at strengthening the important core muscles of the torso. As an ice-breaker, let's examine the most basic exercise, the abdominal crunch—a safer, more effective version of the traditional sit-up we all learned in grade school.

1. Lie on the floor with your legs bent at about 90 degrees and your feet flat on the floor. Cross your arms over your chest or place your hands behind your head (harder), but do not interlace your fingers behind your neck.

2. Now lift your shoulder blades off the floor and exhale as you "crunch" upward. The range of motion is small—the goal is to lift your upper back off the floor, but not to ascend the whole way as you would in old-school sit-ups.

3. Continue this up-and-down motion at a brisk pace that takes just over 1 second per repetition—but don't go so fast that you are bouncing off the floor!

4. Perform as many crunches as possible. Your long-term goal should be fifty to seventy-five reps.

5. Rest for 5 minutes, then execute a second set. As your conditioning improves, you can perform a third set as well.

Safety note: When performing crunches with hands behind your head, it's important never to pull on your neck or head.

1. Starting position.

2. Ending position.

Circuit Training

If you have access to a health club or well-equipped climbing gym, you can engage in a circuit-training program as an alternative to the body-weight exercises described above. The goal of your circuit training is not to lift maximally heavy weights or to build big muscles—don't get drawn down that path!—but instead to simply acquire enough muscular strength to climb regularly, learn skills, and reduce injury risk. You can gain all these upsides from a modest time investment of about 45 minutes, three days per week. Per chapter 3, engage in 10 to 15 minutes of warm-up activities beforehand, and then conclude your workout with about 20 minutes of aerobic activity. This 90-minute workout represents an excellent general conditioning program.

The accompanying sidebar lists the primary circuit training exercises to perform—ask an instructor for help should you be unsure how to do a specific exercise or uncertain how to set up or adjust a specific machine. Initial workouts will require a little experimentation to find the right training weight for you on each machine. The ideal weight will allow you to perform ten to fifteen repetitions before reaching muscular failure—I do not advise using the standard health-club, bodybuilding protocol of doing eight to ten repetitions. Upon finding the correct exercise weight on each machine, stick with it until your newfound strength enables you to crank out more than twenty reps. Upon reaching this benchmark, simply increase the weight 5 to 10 pounds for future workouts. Consider keeping a written record of your weights and reps so you can track your improvement.

After three months of circuit training, it's time to retake the general conditioning self-assessment in chapter 2 and modify your program accordingly:

- If you reach a score of 15 points, then you can begin to introduce some of the climbing-specific training exercises contained in part III of this book.

Circuit Training Exercises

Perform two sets of each exercise listed below. Select a weight that produces muscular failure in ten to fifteen repetitions. Execute each exercise slowly and without stopping in the middle of a set—continuous muscular tension throughout the entire set is critical for maximizing the training effect. Count one thousand one on the upward phase of each repetition and one thousand one, one thousand two on the way down. Take a 1- to 2-minute rest between sets.

1. Bench Press
2. Shoulder Press
3. Pec Fly
4. Lat Pull-Down
5. Upright Rows
6. Triceps Extension
7. Biceps Curl
8. Leg Press
9. Leg Extension
10. Leg Curl
11. Rotary Torso
12. Abdominal

- Score 20 or more points and you can cease circuit training in favor of exclusively climbing-specific training activities.

Weight-Loss Strategies

If you've ever hiked with a heavy pack or carried someone on your back, you've experienced the negative effects of increased weight on physical performance. Conversely, a reduction in percent body fat or unnecessary muscle mass will have a profoundly positive effect on performance. As mentioned earlier, strength-to-weight ratio is the best single metric of your climbing fitness. While much of this book focuses on increasing strength, we must also examine the other side of the coin: reducing weight.

First, I must state that I am an advocate of slow, reasonable weight loss. Crash dieting in pursuit of a gaunt, ultraskinny physique not only is dangerous but will ultimately have a negative effect on your climbing as well. A reasonable weight-loss target is to achieve a percent body fat of between 6 and 12 for men, or 8 and 16 for women. If you're not sure how you measure up, consider having your body fat tested at a local health club or university training center. Otherwise, use the simple pinch-an-inch method on your waistline. If the skin fold you pinch is an inch or greater in thickness, then you are definitely not in the optimal ranges listed above and will benefit noticeably from a reduction in percent body fat. A skin fold of 0.5 to 1 inch indicates body fat slightly above the optimal range and, thus, the need to lose just a few pounds. If you possess a skin fold of 0.5 inch or less, you are in the optimal range and not in need of weight loss.

Although myriad books have been written on this subject, the fact is that the prescription for weight loss is simple. Two principles represent the alpha and the omega of weight loss:

- To lose weight, your daily calorie intake must be less than your total daily calorie expenditure. Regardless of where the calories come from—fat, carbohydrate, protein, alcohol—your daily "net" must be negative. The best strategy is to both reduce caloric intake and increase daily expenditure.

- Diets don't work in the long term. Whether you diet for a week or a month, you will gain back all the weight when you go off the diet. Individuals who succeed in permanent weight reduction aren't really on a diet but have instead made fundamental changes in the way they eat that are permanent.

Let's examine the two sides of the weight-loss coin: reducing caloric consumption and increasing expenditure of calories.

Nutritional Surveillance

Nutritional surveillance consists of increasing awareness of what, where, when, and why you eat. The goal is to reduce empty calories consumed via junk foods, high-fat fast foods, and such, while maintaining steady consumption of protein and carbohydrate, as well as water- and fiber-rich fruits and vegetables. The ideal macronutrient caloric breakdown for a rock climber is 65 percent carbohydrate, 15 percent protein, and 20 percent fat. Consequently, you can dismiss the high-fat fad diets such as the Zone or Atkins—these are absolutely the wrong eating strategies for an athlete, whose primary source of energy is carbohydrate!

As an example, an active 160-pound male desirous of some weight loss might restrict his total dietary intake to around 2,550 calories per day (consuming up to 50 percent more calories on extremely active days). According to the 65/15/20 macronutrient profile for climbers, this would break down to about 415 grams of carbohydrate, 96 grams of protein, and just 56 grams of fat. Similarly, an active 130-pound female wanting to drop a few pounds might limit her total daily consumption to about 1,700 calories (up to 50 percent more on extremely active days), striving for a macronutrient breakdown of around 275 grams of carbohydrate, 64 grams of protein, and just 38 grams of fat. Upon achieving your desired climbing weight, gradually increase caloric intake to determine the level at which you can maintain a stable body weight. Of course, every individual has a unique basal metabolic rate and therefore different caloric needs—the values above are just sample estimates.

In striving to improve nutritional surveillance, it's important to begin reading food labels and to never eat anything without knowing the precise fat and calorie content. Remember that a gram of fat contains 9 calories, while a gram of protein and a gram of carbohydrate each contain just 4 calories. Therefore, it's your ability and desire to control fat consumption that will most readily make or break

Determining Your Caloric Needs and Weight-Loss Prescription

Your caloric needs are a function of your metabolic rate, body weight, and the amount and intensity of exercise you perform.

- If you have a slow metabolism, multiply your body weight (in pounds) by 12. The total is your daily "maintenance" caloric needs if no exercise is performed.
- If you have a midrange metabolism, multiply your body weight by 15.
- If you have a high metabolism, then multiply your body weight by 18.

Add 150 calories for each hour of low-intensity exercise; for example, an hour of walking at work or school burns about 150 extra calories per day. High-intensity exercise, such as climbing near your limit or running hard, can burn 600 calories or more per hour of sustained exercise. Therefore, 45 minutes of aggregate climbing time or trail running would burn approximately 450 calories above your basic metabolic rate.

As an example, a 160-pound person with a midrange metabolism who walks 1 hour per day and climbs a total of 1 hour in aggregate would burn: (160 x 15) + 150 + 450 = 3,000 calories on that day. Now calculate your approximate daily caloric needs using this method.

Determine a reasonable calorie deficit for producing weight loss.

For the 160-pound climber featured above, a modest caloric restriction of 15 percent below daily maintenance would yield a target value of 2,550 calories. Eating 2,550 calories per day while expending an average of 3,000 calories yields a 450-calorie deficit. Given the discipline to maintain this exercise and nutrition schedule for eight consecutive days, the result would be a 3,600-calorie deficit and a legitimate weight loss of just over 1 pound. It's important to note that a scale might register a weight loss of more than 1 pound, but any additional "loss" is water weight, which fluctuates up and down from day to day.

Determine the ideal amounts of each macronutrient given your daily calorie target amount. In the above example, a 160-pound climber wanting to restrict intake to 2,550 calories per day would want to consume roughly the following amount of each macronutrient.

Carbohydrate: 2,550 x 0.65 = 1,658 calories

1,658 calories / 4 calories per gram = ~415 grams of carbohydrate

Protein: 2,550 x 0.15 = 382 calories

382 calories / 4 calories per gram = ~96 grams of protein

Fat: 2,550 x 0.20 = 510 calories

510 calories / 9 calories per gram = ~56 grams of fat

your nutritional goals. The simplest step for dropping some unwanted pounds is to avoid high-fat foods, and in particular foods containing saturated fats and trans fats—start reading food labels and you may be surprised to see how many foods contain these killer fats. However, you do not need to stop

Running is one of the most
effective general conditioning
and calorie-burning activities.
MEREDITH JUNE COLLECTION

eating all dairy and animal products. Simply select the low-fat varieties such as skim milk (an excellent source of protein), grilled chicken or fish, and extra-lean cuts of steak. See chapter 13 for more tips on performance nutrition.

Aerobic Conditioning

The goal is to perform 20 to 40 minutes of an aerobic exercise that elevates your heart rate to between 65 and 85 percent of maximum. Calculate your maximum heart rate by subtracting your age from 220. For example, a 35-year-old has a maximum heart rate of 185 beats per minute; calculating 65 to 85 percent of this maximum rate prescribes an optimal training zone of 120 to 157 beats per minute.

You get maximum benefits from your aerobic exercise by maintaining a heart rate within this zone for the full duration of exercise. No matter the method, increase the intensity or speed of training if your heart rate is below this zone. Conversely, you should slow down (but not stop) immediately should your heart rate exceed the high end of the training zone. The easiest way to monitor heart rate is to take a 15-second count of heartbeats from your wrist, then multiply this number by four to get the 1-minute total. (Alternatively you can obtain a real-time heart rate measurement on the fly by using a chest-strap heart rate monitor, FitBit watch, or similar device.) Do this every 3 to 5 minutes during your aerobic exercise.

When it comes to aerobic exercise, running is by far the most effective method of incinerating fat and shrinking unwanted muscle. Don't worry about losing your climbing muscles—they will be preserved as long as you continue to climb regularly and consume at least 1 gram of protein per kilogram of body weight per day. Other popular aerobic activities such as mountain biking and the StairMaster may yield mixed results if your genetics are such that these activities result in larger, heavier leg muscles (not desirable for rock climbing). Swimming, brisk hiking, rowing, and the use of an elliptical trainer (or similar) are good alternatives if you can't run.

Frequency and length of aerobic training should be proportional to the magnitude of your weight-loss goal. For example, a 20- to 40-minute run, five days per week, would be an important part of your training-for-climbing program if you are significantly overweight. As you near ideal weight, however, just two or three 20-minute runs per week would be sufficient.

Guidelines for General Fitness Conditioning

- Concentrate on improving body composition and all-around fitness. Moderate aerobic training (such as running) and basic training exercises will effectively build base fitness.

- Frequent use of body-weight exercises, such as pull-ups, push-ups, dips, abdominal crunches, and planks, is essential. Supplementary weight training, two or three days per week, can be beneficial for individuals lacking base strength.

- Perform a modest amount of push-muscle training to maintain muscular balance, since the pulling muscles will steadily grow stronger as a result of climbing.

- Engage in regular stretching to improve flexibility and reduce injury risk.

- Climb two to four days per week to develop climbing strength. For the time being, resist the urge to engage in the high-intensity, sport-specific exercises commonly used by more advanced climbers.

Matt Fultz on Bronson's Arête (V9), Little Cottonwood Canyon, Utah.
GEORGE BRUCE WILSON

Antagonist and Stabilizer Training Exercises

"Stability before strength, strength before power"—make this your training mantra and you'll be training smarter—and soon climbing harder—than the mass of climbers!

Climbers naturally obsess over strength training of the gripping, pulling, and lock-off muscles, since they are the agonist or prime movers in climbing. Meanwhile the antagonist push muscles, which oppose the pulling muscles, and the many smaller stabilizer muscles of the wrist and shoulder are often dismissed as less important. The resultant lack of antagonist and stabilizer training among climbers is a contributing factor to many elbow and shoulder injuries that have become alarmingly common.

The antagonist muscles used in climbing include the pectorals (chest), deltoids (shoulders), and triceps (back of the upper arm). Important stabilizer muscles include the finger/wrist extensors (outside of the forearm), the scapular stabilizers (trapezius and serratus anterior), and the four muscles of the rotator cuff (teres minor, infraspinatus, subscapularis, and supraspinatus). Strength and flexibility in these muscles is fundamental to controlled, precise movement and for maintaining joint stability. Unfortunately, few climbers regularly train these antagonist muscles, while the agonist pull muscles get all the attention. Growing imbalance subsequently develops around the elbow and shoulder joints, thus affecting movement patterns and stability and, ultimately, increasing the risk of

injury. Outside of the fingers, the most common injuries among climbers are elbow tendinosis, shoulder subluxation, and rotator cuff and labrum tears. You now know why.

Unlike acute finger tendon injuries, many elbow and shoulder maladies are avoidable given a modest investment in stretching and training of the antagonist and stabilizer muscles. As little as 20 to 30 minutes, two or three days per week, is all that it takes to maintain muscle balance and reduce injury risk. This chapter is divided into three sections that detail exercises for the forearms, the rotator cuff and scapular stabilizers, and the larger push muscles of the chest and shoulders. I encourage you to include a broad selection of these exercises in your weekly conditioning program. As always, perform a general warm-up of light activity and mild stretching before engaging in this targeted strength training.

A final word of caution: Never train or stretch a freshly injured muscle, tendon, or joint. Pain in your fingers, elbows, or shoulders is a warning sign that something is wrong—cease climbing and training until you are pain-free. Also, it would be wise to consult a doctor if you have any doubts about the cause of the pain you're experiencing or if you are unsure of the best course of treatment and rehabilitation for an existing injury. See the "Suggested Reading" chapter for a list of useful references, including two excellent books on climbing injuries: *One Move Too Many* (Volker Schöffl, MD) is the definitive text written by a surgeon with more than twenty years' experience treating climbers, while *Climbing Injuries Solved* (Lisa Erikson, DC) presents a chiropractor's perspective with many self-help treatments for common injuries.

		Exercise	Page	Beginner	Intermediate	Advanced
Wrist & Forearm Stabilizers		Finger Extension Against Rubber Band	73	X	X	X
		Reverse Wrist Curls	74	X	X	X
		Wrist Extension Isometric	75		X	X
		Wide Pinch with Wrist Extension	76		X	X
		Pronators	77	X	X	X
		Reverse Arm Curls	78	X	X	X
Rotator Cuff & Scapular Stabilizers		Dumbbell Internal Rotation	80	X	X	X
		Dumbbell External Rotation	81	X	X	X
		Sling Trainer Ts	83	X	X	X
		Sling Trainer Ys	84	X	X	X
		Scapular Push-Ups	85		X	X
		Scapular Pull-Ups	86		X	X
		Shrugs	87	X	X	X
Antagonist Training (Push Muscles)		Tricep Pushdown	88		X	X
		Sling Trainer Pec Flys	89		X	X
		Shoulder Press	91	X	X	X
		Bench Press	92	X	X	X
		Dips	93		X	X

Wrist and Forearm Stabilizers

Relative to normal everyday use, no group of muscles works harder in climbing than the forearm muscles that produce finger flexion. Interestingly, the finger flexors can't grip the rock without the wrist being held in a fixed position by the extensor muscles of the lateral forearm. Given this perspective, you can see why a climber absolutely must do some training of these extensor muscles—unfortunately, many climbers don't, yet they do spend hours training the finger flexors with rigorous exercises like campus board training, fingerboard hangs, and hard bouldering.

An increasing imbalance between the finger flexors and finger extensors, and chronic tightness that often develops in the extensor muscles, can lead to pain and eventually tendinosis near the lateral epicondyle (bony outside part of your upper forearm). Traditionally referred to as "tennis elbow," this pesky climbing injury develops as a result of over-reliance on the crimp grip, frequent chicken winging of the arm, and disproportionately weak extensor muscles. Fortunately, you can reduce your risk of this injury by taking at least three rest days off (from climbing) per week, regular stretching and self-myofascial release of the extensor muscles, and disciplined thrice weekly finger/wrist extensor training. It's paramount to train the wrist in both a neutral and extended position, as well as in a wide-pinch-grip position—this is the single most overlooked and important position to train it. While you don't need to do all of the exercises every workout, at the minimum I suggest doing reverse wrist curls, wide pinches, and pronators. Do one set of these three exercises (with a light resistance) as part of your warm-up for climbing (or training), and then do two more sets with higher resistance toward the end of your workout.

Finger Extension Against Rubber Band

Okay, let me get this one out of the way first, as rubber-band finger extensor training is quite popular. Interestingly, use of a rubber band (or similar) to extend your fingers against is sufficient only for the purposes of warm-up, beginner strength training, and rehabilitation from injury. I recommend use of Powerfingers (see photo) to warm up before climbing and in advance of the more stressful finger extensors exercises. Extend your fingers against the Powerfingers (or a rubber band) for 15 to 25 repetitions. If strength training (rather than warming up), do a second and third set with higher resistance (Powerfingers come in five different resistances), although use of the wide pinch with wrist extension and reverse wrist curl exercises (covered next) is essential to develop the higher levels of extensor strength and wrist stabilization needed for high-end climbing

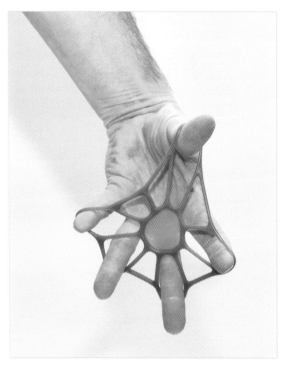

Powerfingers are an excellent tool for warming up and rehabbing the finger extensors.

Reverse Wrist Curls

This exercise is mandatory for all climbers to work the extensor muscles. Use this in conjunction with the forearm stretches provided in chapter 3 as part of your warm-up and cool-down ritual. Just as the name implies, this exercise involves curling a dumbbell upward with your palm facing down.

1. Set up with your forearm in a stable, horizontal position using a bench, table, or on your thigh (if sitting) and grasp the dumbbell with your hand overhanging the supporting surface.

2. Begin with the dumbbell in the top (fully extended) position and lower it to the neutral (straight wrist) position, then curl the dumbbell back to the top position.

3. Continue with slow, controlled reverse curls—at a rate of one repetition per second—until you reach the desired number of repetitions.

I recommend doing two sets with progressive resistance. For the first set select a weight that allows twenty to twenty-five repetitions, but stop the exercise before complete failure. Rest for 3 minutes before doing a second set with a heavier dumbbell that allows only ten to fifteen reps. Initially you may need to use only a 5-pound dumbbell; advanced climbers may need as much as a 20- to 30-pound dumbbell for their high-resistance set. Do some mild stretching of the extensors during each rest period.

Training tip: Anyone with elbow pain or recent history of lateral tendinosis should do only the negative phase of this exercise—that is, use your free hand to grab the dumbbell-holding hand and aid its return to the top position before doing the next negative (lowering) phase of the exercise.

1. Top position. 2. Bottom position with neutral wrist.

Wrist Extension Isometric

I love this exercise! You'll need a clock (with a second hand) in view or a timing app to train against. The setup is the same as in the reverse wrist curl, but you'll be using a lighter-weight dumbbell. The difference here is that there's no lowering phase—you'll simply hold the dumbbell in the up (over-extended position) for a long isometric contraction. Select a dumbbell light enough to allow an isometric hold in the over-extended position for 45 to 60 seconds. Do two sets on each arm with a 3-minute rest in between. Long term, strive to hold the over-extended position for a full 2 minutes. It'll feel good to do some stretching of the forearm extensors during the rest period.

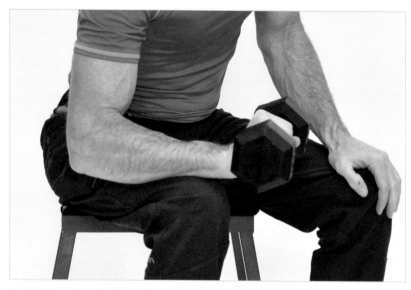

1. Hold the dumbbell stationary in the top position.

Wide Pinch with Wrist Extension

This novel exercise is absolutely essential, as it strengthens the extensor muscles with the fingers fully extended as in grabbing open-hand and wide pinch holds in climbing. It may seem like a minor distinction, but the wrist extensors function a bit differently when the fingers are straight (extended) compared with when they are flexed, as in crimping or holding a dumbbell. So it's important to do this exercise in addition to one of the previous.

While you may be able to find some kind of a pinch block on the Internet, you can easily kludge a rig by screwing together three short pieces of a 2x4. Another option is pinching a thick bumper weight plate. Anyway, the exercise is straightforward.

1. Stand upright with good posture and level shoulders.

2. Pinch the wood block or bumper plate with a straight arm and extended wrist; hold this position for 10 to 30 seconds.

3. Repeat the exercise on the other side.

4. Do three to five sets with at least 2 minutes rest in between.

Training tip: Initially, I suggest training for strength-endurance, which will require a light weight that allows a full 30-second hold. Longer term, consider using a heavier weight that allows only a 10-second hold.

Wide pinch with wrist extension. 1. Using a bumper plate. 2. Wood blocks.

Pronators

Arm-pulling movements naturally result in supination of the hand. If you perform a pull-up on a free-hanging set of Pump Rocks, you'll discover that your hands naturally turn inward, or supinate, as your biceps contract. Consequently, training forearm pronation is an important antagonist exercise for climbers to maintain muscle balance across the forearms. While a well-equipped gym may have a machine for training forearm pronation, most folks will need to find a creative training solution. My preference is using an ordinary 3-pound sledgehammer!

1. Sit on a chair or bench with your forearm resting on your thigh, your hand in the palm-up position.
2. Firmly grip a sledgehammer with the heavy end extending to the side and the handle parallel to the floor.
3. Turn your hand inward (pronation) to lift the hammer to the vertical position. Stop here.
4. Now slowly lower the hammer back to the starting position. Stop at the horizontal position for 1 second before beginning the next repetition.
5. Continue lifting the hammer in this way for twenty to twenty-five repetitions. Choke up on the hammer if this feels overly difficult.
6. Perform two sets with each hand.

Alternate exercise: You can train pronation with an exercise band. Hold one end of the band in your hand with the excess hanging out the thumb side of your palm. Anchor the other end of the band around your leg or foot, and rotate your forearm while keeping it parallel to the floor.

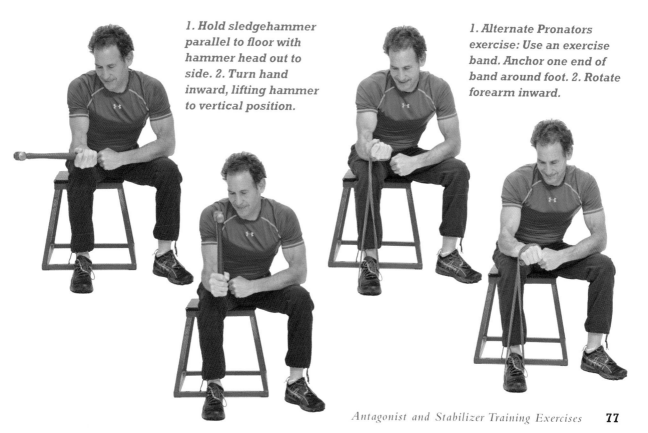

1. Hold sledgehammer parallel to floor with hammer head out to side. 2. Turn hand inward, lifting hammer to vertical position.

1. Alternate Pronators exercise: Use an exercise band. Anchor one end of band around foot. 2. Rotate forearm inward.

Reverse Arm Curls

The reverse arm curl is one of my favorite warm-up exercises. While it obviously activates the biceps, it more importantly demands an isometric contraction of the wrist extensors, and it calls the often overlooked brachioradialis into play to stabilize and assist in flexing the elbow. In elbow flexion the brachioradialis is most active when the hand is pronated, as in the majority of climbing moves—therefore strengthening the brachioradialis means a stronger wrist and a more stable elbow and forearm while gripping and pulling down on the rock. Do this exercise with a barbell or bent E-Z curl bar (shown), not with dumbbells.

1. Take an overhand grip, with elbows fixed at your side.
2. Curl the bar upward with the elbow joints fixed at your side throughout the exercise motion.
3. Continue for fifteen to twenty repetitions, being sure to contract your core, glutes, and spinal erectors throughout the duration of the exercise.

Training tip: I suggest doing one set with a light weight as part of your warm-up, and another moderately heavy set or two later in your workout.

With a palms-down grip (pronated forearms), curl the barbell upward while keeping elbows fixed.

Rotator Cuff and Scapular Stability Exercises

The rotator cuff is arguably the most stressed group of muscles in the body of a climber. While the forearms get all the attention—and pump—the rotator cuff and scapular stabilizers are the real heroes as a climber repeatedly pulls with his arms from a wide range of angles, both statically and dynamically applying force of varying intensity. Climbing on overhanging walls, at times with jumping, lunging, and campusing moves, challenges the small rotator cuff muscles to keep the humeral head in its place; similarly the scapular stabilizers must work hard to move the scapula into the proper position for each given arm position in climbing. Even in vertical climbing, the crimp grip and the chicken-wing arm position stress the rotator cuff, and not surprisingly, shoulder pathology will weaken your grip. Hence, dysfunction anywhere along the chain of force application—fingers, wrist, elbow, or shoulder—will negatively affect performance of the entire system.

If you still aren't motivated to train the rotator cuff and scapular stabilizers, roll this over in your mind: Weak rotator cuff muscles are a common, yet unrecognized, limiting constraint in your maximum pulling strength, lunging power, grip strength, and contact strength. So if you're a hard-training climber frustrated by a lack of strength/power gains on the rock, it may be that your central governor is limiting power output due to afferent feedback from your weak, unstable shoulder joints. This is why it's essential to *train stability before strength, and strength before power*—make this phrase your training mantra and you'll be training smarter than most other climbers.

Anyway, I trust you'll agree that the shoulder is a truly wondrous and remarkably dynamic joint, and, therefore, it's essential that you are proactive in training (and addressing weaknesses in) the many muscles involved. By using both the mobility

The steeper a route is, the greater the stress placed on the shoulder joint.

exercises detailed in chapter 3 and the stabilizer-muscle exercises that follow, you will improve movement patterns and function, even when climbing in a state of high fatigue (when injury risk is highest).

First, in this section I'll present two exercises to isolate and strengthen the four muscles that comprise the rotator cuff: the supraspinatus, infraspinatus, teres minor, and subscapularis. Next, I'll detail five exercises that work the supporting cast of muscles, including the upper, middle, and lower trapezius, rhomboids, and serratus anterior, that move the scapula into proper position for the multitude of arm positions and movements encountered in climbing. Consult the anatomy photos in appendix A to see the location of the muscles described in this section.

Dumbbell Internal Rotation

Of the four rotator cuff muscles, only the subscapularis contributes to internal rotation. The subscapularis does get substantial help, however, from the deltoids, teres major, latissimus, and pectorals—this helps explain why you are likely much stronger at internal rotation than external rotation. Still, you want to do this exercise twice per week since it (partially) isolates and strengthens the subscapularis.

1. Lie on your side with your bottom arm in front of your waist; place a rolled-up towel under your head to support your neck. Rest your other arm along your hip and upper thigh.
2. Hold a 10- to 15-pound dumbbell in the hand of your bottom arm, positioning this forearm perpendicular to your body.
3. Lift the weight up to your body and hold for a moment before lowering it back to the floor. The upper portion of your arm should remain fixed throughout the range of motion—think of the upper arm and shoulder as a door hinge that allows your forearm to swing "up and down."
4. Continue in a slow but steady motion for a total of twenty to twenty-five repetitions.
5. Do two sets on each side, with a 3-minute rest between sets.

Training Tip: Select a weight heavy enough to make you work, but not so great that you have to strain hard or compromise technique. Increase weight in 2- to 5-pound increments, as needed.

  Alternate exercise: Anchor an exercise band to a waist-high object and, while standing, grip the band and pull it across your body. The key is to keep your elbow and upper arm in a fixed position, and only move your hand and forearm across your body. Repeat this twenty-five times, adjusting resistance as needed by changing your distance from the anchor point. In my opinion such exercise band training, while good for rehab, doesn't cut it for serious training of the rotator cuff. Therefore, I recommend using the dumbbell exercises detailed here.

1. Start position. 2. Finish position. 3. Alternate exercise.

Dumbbell External Rotation

The infraspinatus and teres minor are the primary external rotators, although they get some help from the deltoids. Many climbers are surprised to discover that they have weak external rotators and thus may be able to use only about one-half as much weight as when doing the internal rotation exercise above. Strengthening the external rotators should be a high priority, as this will provide additional protection of the rotator cuff when grabbing the rock with the stressful above-the-head Gaston positions common to hard climbing.

1. Lie on your side with your bottom arm in front of your waist and a rolled-up towel under your head to support your neck. Alternatively, you can bend your bottom arm and use it as a headrest.

2. Hold a 5- to 10-pound dumbbell in the hand of your top arm. Rest the upper arm and elbow on the top side of your body, and then bend at the elbow so that the forearm hangs down over your belly and the weight rests on the floor.

3. Keeping your elbow and upper arm fixed, lift the weight upward toward the ceiling and stop as your forearm approaches a vertical position.

4. Return the weight to the starting position, and continue for twenty to twenty-five repetitions.

5. Do two sets on each side, with a 3-minute rest between each set. Increase weight in 2- to 5-pound increments.

Initially, you may need to use as little as 5 pounds. With long-term training, however, you should be able to improve to using a 10-pound dumbbell; especially fit climbers may be able to use up to 15 pounds. This is a difficult exercise, and using proper technique is essential for isolating the external rotators. Err on the side of using too little weight, rather than too much.

1. Start position.

2. Finish position.

Alternate exercise: If you don't have access to dumbbells, you can use an exercise band as an alternative training method. Stand with your arms bent at 90 degrees, elbows by your side and hands extending forward holding a taut exercise band with a palms-up grip. Now pull your hands apart while keeping your elbows fixed by your side—think about pinching your scapula together as you separate your hands. Adjust your grip on the exercise band to regulate tension. Do twenty repetitions.

1. Alternate start.

2. Alternate finish.

Sling Trainer Ts

This exercise targets the middle trapezius and rhomboids, the muscles that produce scapular retraction. This is a great exercise to combat (or correct) the common climbers' hunchback. You can do the Ts in a standing position with a sling trainer or prone on a bench.

1. Using a sling trainer, grasp the handles with straight arms extended forward and palms facing each other.

2. Now contract your core, glutes, and leg muscles, and lean backward to weight the sling trainer; you can also walk your feet slightly forward (farther forward is harder).

3. Maintaining a tight torso and straight arms, pull your hands apart until your arms are straight out to your side in a T position—think about squeezing your shoulder blades and pushing your chest out.

4. Slowly lower back to the starting position and continue for ten to twenty repetitions.

5. Rest for 3 minutes before doing a second set.

Alternate exercise: If you don't own a sling trainer, you can still train Ts in an effective way by assuming a prone position on a bench with your arms hanging straight down. Contract your core and glutes, and lift your straight arms out to the side until raised just above horizontal. Feel your shoulder blades come together, and actively squeeze them at the top position. Continue for twenty repetitions. You can progress to using very light dumbbells (a few pounds max).

Ts with sling trainer. 1. Starting position.

2. Ending position.

Sling Trainer Ys

This exercise is only slightly different from the Ts described above, but the Y motion specifically targets the lower trapezius. The lower traps produce scapular depression and rotation, which is essential to avoid shoulder impingement when doing overhead movements. Among climbers the lower traps are commonly a weak link (possibly revealed in the hunchback posture) and thus are a potential contributing factor to shoulder injury. If you frequently engage in campus training and lunge moves, then a strong mid and lower trapezius are vital for maintaining proper scapular position (to avoid trashing your shoulders).

1. Set up in the same way as in doing Ts, but the motion is up and slightly outward to form a Y.

2. Stop pulling when your arms come in line with your body—at this top position your arms should be just beyond shoulder width apart.

3. Be sure to contract your core, glutes, and legs to maintain rigidity throughout the range of motion. Think about drawing your scapula downward as you reach the top of the Y position.

4. Do two sets of ten to twenty repetitions with a 3-minute rest in between.

Alternate exercise: You can also do the Y exercise lying prone on a bench with just arm weight or a 1- or 2-pound dumbbell in each hand. Begin with your arms straight and hanging down under the bench below your face. With a stiff core and tight glutes, lift your straight arms up into the Y position with your hands just beyond shoulder width at the top position. Do two sets of ten to twenty repetitions with a 3-minute rest in between.

Ys with sling trainer. 1. Starting position.   *2. Ending position.*

Scapular Push-ups

The scapular push-up isolates the serratus anterior muscle, vital for proper scapular tracking during overhead arm movements. You can do this simple exercise from a straight-arm push-up position (see photos) or from a plank position with your elbows and forearms flat on the floor. I suggest using the plank position for learning the feel of this exercise then advance to doing it with straight arms.

1. Assume the classic plank position with elbows under your shoulders, a neutral spine, and tight abs and spinal erectors.

2. Keeping your torso stiff and straight, allow your chest to sag downward between your arms.

3. Now drive your elbows and forearms into the floor to return to the top position—feel your scapula slide around your rib cage as the serratus anterior contract. The range of motion is only a few inches.

4. This is a surprisingly rigorous isolation exercise; try to do fifteen to twenty repetitions. This movement is not meant to be heavily loaded, so there's no need to use additional weight. Do one or two sets.

1. Top position.

2. Bottom position.

Scapular Pull-Ups

The scapular pull-up is a training essential in the Hörst gym! Keeping your shoulders healthy and developing proper movement patterns in pulling motions demands the ability to forcefully depress and retract the scapula. Regular use of this isolation exercise will develop better kinesthetic awareness of your scapular position and enable you to climb harder and longer with good form, despite growing fatigue. Furthermore, being able to quickly and forcibly engage the lower trapezius and latissimus muscles will empower you to keep your scapula in proper position when campus training and lunging.

1. Begin in a normal pull-up position with a palms-away grip and hands shoulder width apart.

2. From a full hang with somewhat shrugged shoulders, you want to draw the scapula down and together, thus raising your body slightly but without bending your arms and pulling as in a regular pull-up. The best learning cues are to try to "bend the bar" and think about doing a reverse shrug (i.e., shoulders drawn downward). Do this and you'll feel your head shift backward and your chest raise upward as your scapula pinch together.

3. Hold the top position for 1 second, then return to the starting position. The range of motion is only a few inches to a foot or two (when you get really strong!).

4. Do six to twelve reps, keeping straight arms and tight spinal erectors and glutes throughout. At first you may find this to be a difficult exercise (a sign that you've found a critical weakness to correct!), but resist the urge to overdo it.

5. Add a second set to your workout only after you've mastered the exercise.

Training tip: Strong climbers can do this exercise with full body weight, but I suggest learning with less resistance by keeping your feet on the floor and flexing your knees enough to hang with straight arms from a pull-up bar. Advanced climbers can increase difficulty by making the scaption more powerful, thus raising the body higher and higher (large range of motion) without bending the arms. Do not add weight for this exercise.

1. Begin from an ordinary pull-up starting position.
2. Maintaining nearly straight arms, depress and downwardly rotate your scapula by pressing down on the bar—think about trying to bend the bar (supinating your forearms) and press your chest out.

Shrugs

This exercise strengthens the upper trapezius muscle, which runs from the back of your neck across toward the top of your shoulders and back.

1. Stand erect with your arms by your sides and head facing forward. Hold equal-weight dumbbells in each hand with your palms facing inward.

2. Now shrug your shoulders upward as if trying to lift your shoulders to your ears. Do not bend your arms.

3. Pause at the top position for 1 second, then pull your shoulders backward slightly before returning to the starting position.

4. Continue shrugging at a slow, steady pace for twenty to twenty-five repetitions. Be sure to always pause for 1 second at the top of each shrug.

5. Rest for 3 minutes before performing a second set.

Safety notes: Bend at the knees and hips when lifting the weights off the floor. Maintain a slight bend in your knees and good back posture (brace your core and contract your glutes) while engaging in this exercise. *Training tip:* Initially train with just 10- or 15-pound dumbbells until you feel comfortable with proper execution. Gradually build up to using 20- to 40-pound dumbbells.

1. Starting position.

2. Ending position.

Primary Push-Muscle Exercises

Arm flexion and the hand-to-chest lock-off position are fundamental to almost every climbing movement. These pulling movements are powered by the large muscles of the arms and back—in fact, over time these toned and bulging pull muscles become the physical hallmark of the advanced climber. Unfortunately, beneficial gains in pull-muscle strength often lead to a functional imbalance with the opposing push muscles. Let's delve deeper into this important relationship.

The major push muscles of the upper torso and arms are the pectoralis muscles of the chest, the deltoids and upper trapezius of the shoulders and upper back, and the triceps of the back side of the upper arm. Each of these muscles plays an important role in climbing by helping to stabilize the shoulder joint and in some cases directly contributing to locomotion. Maintaining a high level of conditioning in these push muscles is therefore vital for avoiding injury and supporting climbing performance.

In training the push muscles for climbing, the goal is to increase strength, endurance, and mobility, but without an excessive addition of muscle mass. Consequently, the common bodybuilding strategy of training several sets of ten repetitions per push-muscle group, with the heaviest weight possible, is the wrong program for climbers. Instead you want to train with moderate weights and higher repetitions. Following are five essential push-muscle exercises that target the pectorals, deltoids, and triceps from several different angles that are beneficial to climbers.

Tricep Pushdown

This simple exercise isolates the triceps muscles while engaging the rotator cuff, in a posture and motion similar to pressing down on a locked-off handhold—an important capability on hard routes with large, powerful moves. Many health clubs have a pushdown machine that you can use; otherwise, you can easily kludge a one-arm pushdown rig with a couple of pulleys and a short piece of old rope.

1. Stand with good posture with one hand gripping the pushdown bar (or similar) at shoulder height and with your elbow at your side.

2. Maintaining a stationary elbow (at your side), perform the pushdown motion until your arm is straight. Keep your torso still throughout and resist the urge to raise your elbow in order to execute a dip-like motion.

3. Continue for ten to twelve reps. The training goal is to build strength, so increase the weight if you can do more than twelve reps.

4. Now train the other arm in the same way. Rest for 3 minutes and perform a second set on each side.

1. Starting position.　　*2. Ending position.*

Sling Trainer Pec Flys

This is another exercise that trains the push-muscles in a very climbing-specific way. As you'll soon discover, the Pec Fly motion engages the chest, shoulder, and core muscles in a very similar way to a wide-armed compression climbing move. As described below, the exercise motion is similar to the common dumbbell flys and cable crossover exercises, except that you'll be facing downward and using a portion of your body weight as resistance.

1. Adjust TRX sling trainer (or similar apparatus) so that the handles are about waist height. Grasp the handles with straight arms extended to the front.

2. Now take one step back (farther back makes the exercise harder) and lean forward until your arms are weighted. You want to do this exercise with a slight bend in the elbows (about a 150-degree elbow angle).

Adam Ondra training TRX pec fly at home. CLAUDIA ZEIGLER

3. Begin to spread your arms to the side so that your torso descends in between. Keep your arms slightly bent throughout, but maintain the same elbow angle.

4. Stop the descent as your arms approach the widest possible position (arms nearly parallel with the floor), and immediately push the handles back toward the floor to raise your torso back to the starting position. You should feel your pectoral muscles doing the brunt of the work.

5. Do not stand straight up to unweight your arms—as you near the starting position, immediately reverse direction and begin the next repetition.

6. Continue for a total of ten to twelve reps.

7. Rest for 3 minutes and perform a second set. Increase resistance by moving your feet back and lowering the TRX handles a bit.

Alternate exercise: Dumbbell pec flys offer another effective way to train arm compression strength. Using an incline bench adjusted about 30 degrees above horizontal, begin with straight arms extended toward the ceiling and then lower the dumbbells out to the side. Bend your arms slightly during the descent, and stop short of the dumbbells dropping below chest level. Immediately raise dumbbells back to the starting position, straightening your arms quickly during the ascent. Do two sets, the first with lighter weights for twenty repetitions and the second with heavier dumbbells that make doing ten reps difficult.

1. Alternate start.

2. Alternate finish.

Shoulder Press

The shoulder-press motion is almost exactly opposite that of pulling up while climbing—therefore, no exercise is more central to antagonist-muscle training. Although you can execute this exercise with a common health club overhead-press machine, performing dumbbell shoulder presses provides a more complete workout, including some extra work for the rotator cuff and scapular stabilizers.

1. Sit on a bench with good upright posture and feet flat on the floor.

2. Begin with bent arms, palms facing forward, and the dumbbells positioned just outside your shoulders.

3. Press straight upward with your palms maintaining a forward-facing position. As your arms become straight, squeeze your hands slightly inward until the dumbbells touch end-to-end.

4. Lower the dumbbells to the starting position. The complete repetition should take about 2 seconds.

5. Continue this motion for fifteen to twenty repetitions. Strive for smooth, consistent motion throughout the entire set.

6. Rest for 3 minutes and perform a second set.

Training tips: Women should start with 5-pound dumbbells and advance to 10- or 15-pounders when they can do twenty reps. Most men can begin training with 15- or 20-pound dumbbells and then progress to 25 and 30 pounds as they are able to achieve twenty repetitions. Over the long term it's best not to progress beyond about 40 percent of your body weight (total weight lifted), since frequent use of heavier weights may build undesirable muscle bulk.

Shoulder Press:
1. Begin with dumbbells just outside shoulders.
2. Press straight up; touch dumbbell ends.

Bench Press

The bench press is a staple exercise of power lifters and bodybuilders, but it's also useful to climbers striving to maintain stable, healthy shoulders. The key is to use only moderate resistance—begin with a weight equal to about 30 percent of your body weight and progress up to about 75 percent (no need to go higher). For example, a 160-pound climber would begin training with two 25-pound dumbbells (50 pounds total) and progress up to training with, at most, 50-pound dumbbells or 120 pounds with an Olympic bar.

1. Lie flat on a bench with bent legs and feet flat on the floor.

2. Using an Olympic bar or two dumbbells, begin the exercise with your hands just above chest level and palms facing your feet. If you're using a bar, your hands should be a few inches wider than your shoulders.

3. Press straight up with a slow, steady motion. If using dumbbells, squeeze your hands together to touch the ends of the dumbbells together upon reaching the top position.

4. Return to the starting position, pause for a moment, and then begin the next repetition. With a bar, be careful not to bounce the bar off your chest. The goal is slow, controlled movement that takes about 2 seconds per repetition.

5. Continue for fifteen to twenty repetitions.

6. Rest for 3 minutes before performing a second set.

Alternate exercise: If weights are unavailable, you can use push-ups to provide a similar workout. Begin with your hands shoulder width apart and build up to doing two sets of twenty-five repetitions. If necessary, move your hands closer together to increase training resistance. Conversely, beginners should do push-ups with their knees on the floor until they are able to progress to the normal feet-on-floor position.

1. Starting position. 2. Ending position.

Dips

Dips are an excellent exercise for strengthening the many muscles of the upper arms, shoulders, chest, and back. What's more, the dip motion is quite similar to the mantle move in climbing and thus provides a very sport-specific benefit! Some health clubs and gyms possess a parallel-bar setup ideal for performing dips. Alternatively, you can use the incut 90-degree corner of a kitchen counter, or set two heavy chairs in a parallel position. A set of gymnastics rings are my personal favorite, as they provide a more dynamic (and difficult) workout.

1. Position yourself between the parallel bars, rings, or similar apparatus.

2. Jump up into the straight-arm starting position with your hands drawn in near your hips.

3. Slowly lower until your arms are bent 90 degrees—do not lower beyond this point!

4. Immediately press back up to the starting position.

5. Continue this up-and-down motion, with each repetition taking about 2 seconds. Strive to complete eight to twenty (hard) repetitions.

6. Perform two or three sets with a 3-minute rest between each set.

Safety notes: Don't rush or bounce through this exercise. Never lower yourself beyond a 90-degree arm bend. Stop immediately if you experience any shoulder pain.

Training tip: If you are unable to do at least eight dips, enlist a spotter to reduce the resistance as needed so that you can reach this goal. The spotter should stand behind you and lift around your waist or, more easily, pull up on your ankles (bend your legs and cross them at the ankles to facilitate this).

1. Dips: Jump up into straight-arm position.

2. Lower into a 90-degree arm bend, then push back up.

Aicacia Young climbing Pay at the Pump (5.12d/5.13a), Reimer's Ranch North Shore, Texas. MERRICK ALES

Core-Training Exercises

In rock climbing, the core muscles play a key role in enabling your arms and legs to maximize leverage and transfer torque from hand to foot and vice versa. Every full-body climbing movement calls the core muscles into action and, on overhanging climbs, being able to generate a high level of core stiffness is the linchpin of your climbing machine.

Talk of core conditioning is in vogue these days, and the six-pack-abs look is indeed highly coveted by climbers and nonclimbers alike. But there's more to the core than meets the eye. Think of your core as the area between your shoulders and hips, a region that serves as the foundation for all physical movement. Given this understanding, we realize that while stunning abs may be the hallmark of the core, they are but one of many different muscle groups that contribute to a strong, stable core.

In rock climbing, the core muscles play a key role in enabling your arms and legs to maximize leverage and transfer torque from hand to foot and vice versa. Furthermore, the core muscles are what provide body tension when you're trying to make a long reach or twisting body movement. In fact, every full-body climbing movement calls the core muscles into action. Consequently, a lack of core strength makes executing climbing moves harder—a performance overcharge—especially when venturing onto steep terrain. So if you frequently struggle on vertical to overhanging routes, it's a safe conclusion that your difficulties are due to a combination of poor technique and insufficient upper-body and core strength.

So what's the best method of training these muscles? Sit-ups or abdominal crunches are the obvious choices; however, these exercises target only a small portion of your core muscles. Other popular options are yoga and Pilates, which bring all the muscles of the torso into play. Despite the rigors of these classes—which are excellent for developing body awareness, flexibility, and general conditioning—they will fail to develop a high level of climbing-specific core strength. So while participating in yoga or Pilates classes is a worthwhile endeavor, there remains a need to engage in supplemental core training that activates the core muscles in more strenuous and climbing-specific ways.

Frequently climbing on steep terrain is an excellent way to strengthen core muscles, though some climbers may be in a catch-22 situation of not having enough strength to adequately train on steep terrain. If this sounds familiar or if you are new to climbing, then a commitment to regular core training will be time well invested. More advanced climbers can similarly benefit from supplemental core conditioning—in particular, the posterior chain and total core exercises described late in this chapter may prove challenging and advantageous.

This chapter provides four categories of core exercises to select from in planning your workouts. While there's no need to perform all eighteen exercises in a given workout, you should pick one or two from each group. Make a commitment to engage in core training at least three days per week, and you will build a solid foundation from which to improve your climbing for years to come!

	Exercise	Page	Beginner	Intermediate	Advanced
Anterior Core	Feet-Up Crunches	97	X	X	X
	Hanging Knee Lifts	98	X	X	X
	Mountain Climber Plank	99	X	X	X
	One-Arm Elbow and Side Plank	100	X	X	X
	Sling Trainer "Marine Core"	101		X	X
	Windshield Wipers	102		X	X
Posterior Core	Superman	103	X	X	X
	Reverse Plank	104	X	X	X
	Reverse Mountain Climber Plank	105		X	X
	Side Hip Raises	106		X	X
Total Core and Posterior Chain	Dumbbell Snatch	108		X	X
	Sumo Deadlift with Dumbbell or Kettlebell	109	X	X	X
	Barbell Deadlift	110		X	X
	Barbell Squat	112		X	X
Climbing-Specific Core	Roof Lever-Ups	113		X	X
	Steep Wall Cut & Catch	114		X	X
	Steep Wall Traversing	115	X	X	X
	Front Lever	116			X

Anterior Core Exercises

The anterior core comprises all the muscles you see between your shoulders and hips when you look in the mirror—this may explain why anterior core exercises are what most people spend most of their time training. Got to have those six-pack abs, right?

While the abdominals are indeed the hallmark of the anterior core, there's much more to effectively training this zone than simply cranking out a hundred crunches. Each of the following six exercises trains the anterior core in a somewhat different way. Select three of these exercises for each workout—be sure to include Windshield Wipers, as I consider them the one must-do core exercise for climbers.

Feet-Up Crunches

This feet-up version of the abdominal crunch excels in isolating the upper abdominals while eliminating the lower back strain caused by active hip flexor muscles (when doing old-school sit-ups).

1. Lie on the floor with your legs bent at about 90 degrees and your feet hovering in the air about knee height above the floor.

2. Cross your arms over your chest or place your hands behind your head (harder), but do not interlace your fingers behind your neck.

3. Now lift your shoulder blades off the floor and exhale as you "crunch" upward. The range of motion is small—the goal is to lift your upper back off the floor, but not to ascend all the way to your knees as you would in old-school sit-ups.

4. Continue up and down at a brisk pace that takes just over 1 second per repetition—but don't go so fast that you are bouncing off the floor!

5. Perform as many crunches as possible. Your long-term goal should be fifty to one hundred repetitions. As your conditioning improves, you can perform a second set after a 3-minute rest.

Safety note: When performing crunches with hands behind your head, it's important to never pull on your neck or head.

1. Starting position.

2. Ending position.

Hanging Knee Lifts

This strenuous exercise targets the lower abdominal muscles in a somewhat climbing-specific way—much like lifting your legs on an overhanging route or raising your center of mass under a bulge or overhang.

1. Mount a pull-up bar, the bucket holds of a fingerboard, or a set of Pump Rocks with your palms facing away.

2. Briskly lift your knees upward and contract your abdominals tightly in order to bring your knees up to your chest.

3. Pause for a moment, and then lower your legs slowly until they return to a near dead hang.

4. Immediately begin the next upward repetition, and continue this curl-up motion at a steady pace until you can no longer perform the full range of motion. Your goal is to do fifteen to twenty repetitions, but this may take some time to build up to.

5. Rest for 3 minutes before performing a second set or moving on to the next abdominal exercise.

1. Starting position.

2. Ending position.

Mountain Climber Plank

This exercise takes a standard plank and makes it more dynamic, difficult, and climbing specific by adding a knee-to-elbow motion. I'm not a fan of the long-duration static planks now in vogue (when in climbing do you hold a sustained core contraction for minutes at a time?), but I do like this dynamic plank because it turns on and off different aspects of the core with each repetition (just like climbing movements do).

1. Set up in the top position of a standard push-up, with hands directly beneath your shoulders and your head, hips, and feet in a straight line.

2. Bring one knee to the same side elbow, pausing for a moment before straightening the leg back behind you.

3. Next, bring the other knee to the same side elbow; pause and return to the starting position. This makes for one repetition, but keep going!

4. Perform twenty to fifty (hard) repetitions. At a pace of about 3 seconds per repetition, doing one set will take a full minute or two—a great core endurance exercise!

Training tips: Don't lift your hips, nor let them sag. Try to maintain a nearly straight line, from head to toes, throughout the exercise.

1. Starting position.

2. Bring knee to elbow.

One-Arm Elbow and Side Plank

This is another dynamic plank variation that targets the obliques and hips, as well as the anti-extension capabilities of the abdominals. Like the previous exercise, do high-repetition sets to train core endurance capabilities in a dynamic situation in which different aspects of the core contract and relax with each side-to-side repetition.

1. Begin in the standard elbow plank position with only your toes, elbows, and forearms touching the floor.

2. Now lift one arm, rotate your torso, and open up fully to raise the free hand to a vertical position. Contract your inner and outer core muscles as needed to remain stable and hold this top position for 2 seconds.

3. Return to the starting position and immediately lift the other arm, opening up to face the other side, and extend the hand to the ceiling. Again, hold the top position for 2 seconds. This makes one repetition.

4. Continue for ten to twenty-five (hard) repetitions; at a pace of about 6 seconds per repetition, doing one set will take 1 to 2.5 minutes.

1. Starting position.

2. Alternate raising each arm.

Sling Trainer "Marine Core"

When it comes to strengthening the anterior core's anti-extension capabilities, nothing beats the Marine Core! This is a difficult, non–entry-level exercise.

1. Adjust your sling trainer (or ring set) to hip height when you are in a kneeling position. Kneel about one foot away from the handles, and straighten your arms to grip the handles (or rings) with a palms-down grip.

2. Now stiffen up from knees to shoulders and push your hands forward until your arms and torso form a nearly straight line. Hold this position for 2 seconds, and then return to the starting position.

3. Repeat this same exercise motion for a total of five to twelve (hard) repetitions.

4. Do two or three sets with at least a 3-minute rest in between.

Training tips: Don't let your hips sag, or raise upward—maintain a stiff, nearly neutral spine throughout. Cease execution mid-set if you can't maintain proper form.

1. Starting position.

2. Ending position.

Windshield Wipers

This is a fantastic—and relatively difficult—exercise that targets the abdominals, obliques, and all the muscles of the upper torso and shoulders. Initially, it may take a few workouts to get the hang of this exercise, but motor learning and strength gains will come quickly!

1. Begin hanging palms away from a pull-up bar, and then lift your legs upward until your back is nearly parallel to the ground and your shins are near the level of the bar.

2. Now lower your legs to one side, then immediately return to the top position and lower to the other side. This side-to-side motion is like windshield wipers tracking from 9 o'clock to 3 o'clock and back again.

3. Continue for six to twelve (hard) repetitions, trying to maintain a flat back position that's roughly parallel to the ground throughout.

4. Do two or three sets with 3 minutes rest in between.

Training tips: It helps to bend your arms slightly and think about "bending the bar" with your hands throughout the entire exercise—this will better activate your rotator cuff and scapular stabilizers, making the exercise a bit easier and less stressful on the shoulders.

1. Begin with feet pulled up and shins near bar. 2. Drop both legs to 9 o'clock position. 3. "Wipe" back past the starting position and down to a 3 o'clock position.

Posterior Core Exercises

Exercises that target the posterior core are missing from many climbers' training programs. Taking a few minutes to do a couple of the following exercises would be a wise thing, as would doing some of the total core and posterior chain exercises described in the next section. Do these two or three days per week for a few months, and you'll improve posterior chain proprioception, gain core stiffness for improved center-of-mass positioning on super-steep routes, and discover a new ability to extend powerfully on dynamic moves.

Superman

The Superman is an entry-level posterior core exercise, ideal for your initial forays into this kind of training. Specifically, this is a quasi-isolation exercise that targets the commonly weak muscles of the lower back.

1. Lie facedown on the floor with your arms extended overhead, your legs straight with pointed toes, and your head in a neutral position.

2. Begin by simultaneously raising one arm and the opposite leg as high as comfortably possible.

3. Hold the top position for 1 second, then return to the starting position.

4. Repeat by raising the opposite arm and leg off the floor simultaneously. Again hold for a second in the top position before returning to the floor.

5. Continue this alternating exercise motion for a total of twenty repetitions or until you can no longer perform a slow, controlled movement.

6. Rest for 3 minutes before performing another set, or move on to the next exercise.

1. Facedown, raise left arm and right leg. 2. Then right arm and left leg.

Reverse Plank

As the name implies, this is pretty much the reverse of the standard plank described earlier—it strengthens anti-flexion muscles rather than anti-extension as in the downward-facing plank. You can do this exercise with either your elbows or hands as support—either way, you'll work many of the muscles of the shoulders, upper and low back, hips, and hamstrings.

1. Begin in a sitting position with legs extended, then lean back and support your upper body with your elbows and forearms on the floor or, alternatively, with straight arms and your hands carrying the weight.

2. Now lift your hips off the floor by driving your elbows and heels into the floor. Attain a position with your shoulders, hips, and knees all in line. Think about squeezing your glutes and lower back muscles to prevent your hips from sagging downward.

3. Hold the reverse plank for 20 to 60 seconds (hard). Do one or two more sets with 3 minutes rest in between.

Reverse plank.

Reverse Mountain Climber Plank

This difficult exercise is the flipped-over version of the mountain climber plank (described in the anterior core section).

1. Set up as in a reverse plank with straight arms, hands and feet carrying the weight, and your shoulders, hips, and feet aligned.
2. Now lift your right foot off the floor and imagine that you are high-stepping onto a foothold. Bring your right knee out to the side for a moment (see photo), then return to the starting position. Though your hips may sag slightly, strive to maintain straight arms and a stiff, nearly straight body line throughout.
3. Next lift your left foot and raise the knee out to the side as if you were high-stepping onto a foothold. Immediately return it to the starting position (both legs straight).
4. Continue alternating knees out to the side at a steady, brisk pace.
5. Do eight to fifteen (hard) repetitions, stopping the exercise early if you can't maintain straight arms and a stiff, nearly straight body line.

Training tip: Concentrate on sustaining a strong contraction of the hamstring, gluteal, and low back muscles.

Reverse mountain climber.

Side Hip Raises

This difficult exercise targets the obliques along the side of your torso, although both the posterior and anterior core contract as well.

1. Lie on your side on the floor. Press up with your floor-side arm, keeping it straight and supporting your weight so that your body forms a triangle with the floor. Rest your free arm along the other side of your body.

2. Keeping your supporting arm straight, lower your hip until it touches the floor, then immediately raise it back up to the starting position.

3. Repeat this lowering and raising of the hip in a slow, controlled manner for ten to twenty (hard) repetitions.

4. Rest for 1 minute and then switch sides to perform another set.

5. Rest for 3 minutes before performing one more set on each side (if you are able).

1. Beginning position.

2. Maintaining a straight arm, lower hips toward floor and then press back up.

Total Core and Posterior Chain Exercises

While not widely recognized by climbers, the muscles of the posterior chain—the spinal erectors, quadratus lumborum, glutes, and hamstrings, among others—are extremely important in providing the core stiffness and explosiveness necessary for steep, powerful moves. Consider that it's by way of rapid rate of force development throughout the posterior chain that you create explosive power in making burly deadpoint and lunge moves. Given that the lower back and hip extension muscles are commonly weak among climbers, you will likely benefit greatly by doing a few sets of posterior chain exercises on a twice-per-week schedule.

Detailed below are four exercises that will fortify your core from shoulders to hips, strengthen the posterior chain, and, in fact, also train your rotator cuff and scapular stabilizers to turn on quickly. Doing these exercises, therefore, is a win, win, win proposition. Furthermore, if you follow the exercise guidelines exactly, you'll acquire strength gains mainly via neurological adaptations rather than hypertrophy (i.e., little or no gain in muscle mass).

Efficient movement over steep terrain and roofs demands a strong core and posterior chain.

Dumbbell Snatch

An important physical capability in sports is being able to quickly turn on (and off) the core muscles. In climbing, sticking a difficult deadpoint or lunge move demands lightning fast recruitment of your core, from shoulders to hips, at the instant you hit the destination handhold. While far from a climbing-specific exercise, the dumbbell snatch is beneficial in two ways: (1) It trains explosive triple extension of ankles, knees, and hips (as in a climbing jump move), and (2) it demands a rapid, near-maximal firing of the entire core as you initiate the lift and again when you stick the finish position with the dumbbell straight-arm locked overhead.

1. Stand with feet just over shoulder width apart and toes pointed about 20 degrees outward. With the dumbbell positioned between your feet, bend equally at your knees and hips to grab onto the dumbbell. At the starting position your lower back should be flat and the working arm hanging straight down from the shoulder; extend the free arm out and backward for balance as needed.

2. The snatch is then executed in one coordinated, continuous, and explosive motion. It begins with knee extension, then hip, knee, and ankle extension simultaneously (the triple extension); the arm remains straight initially, and you want to keep the elbow over the dumbbell as long as possible as you jump off the floor.

3. As your shoulders shrug at the end of the jump, allow the dumbbell to launch upward and then drop your body underneath the dumbbell to attain a partial squat position with the dumbbell locked out overhead.

4. Stand up into the finish position with the dumbbell, shoulders, hips, and feet all in line. Contract your core completely to stick the finish position and hold for 1 second.

5. Lower the dumbbell and push your hips backward to return to the starting position.

6. Pause for a few seconds between each snatch—let go of the dumbbell, stand tall, and relax for a couple seconds before repeating the lift. Do five to eight repetitions. Repeat with the other hand.

Training tip: This is a technical lift, so begin with a moderate weight (15 to 25 pounds) and increase the weight when you can do eight explosive repetitions with good form and control.

1. Starting position. 2. Ending position.

Sumo Deadlift with Dumbbell or Kettlebell

The dumbbell sumo deadlift is an excellent gateway exercise for the more difficult barbell deadlift described next. Both forms of deadlift are excellent for training the posterior chain, core stiffness, the trapezius, and rotator cuff. I believe that every serious climber should do either this exercise or the barbell deadlift twice per week. The training time investment is small, but the benefits are multiple.

1. Begin in a straddling position over a dumbbell so your feet are one and one-half shoulder widths apart and toes angled out about 20 degrees. Flexing at both the knees and hips, lower down to grasp the ends of the dumbbell with two hands (or matching hands if using a kettlebell).

2. With flexed knees and hips, a straight back and upward slanting torso, and arms hanging straight down from the shoulders, tighten your abs and begin the lift by extending the knees. The hips should quickly begin to extend too; however, the knees should extend fully before the hips reach full extension. During the final third of the lift, think about driving your hips forward and then pulling your shoulders back (and scapula together).

3. Finish standing tall, like a soldier at attention, at the top position, but do not hyperextend your back and do not shrug your shoulders.

4. Lower the dumbbell by pushing your rear end back and bending at the hips (maintain a straight back) and then at the knees.

5. Face more or less forward throughout the lift, but with a slight downward gaze near the bottom position.

6. Continue for a total of ten to fifteen repetitions. Rest for 3 minutes before doing an optional second set.

Training tip: Train this lift twice per week, favoring a lighter weight and good technique over going super heavy. Many people begin with a 15- to 30-pound dumbbell or kettlebell and build to twice this weight over a year or so. Advanced lifters can do one set of dumbbell sumo deadlift as a warm-up before doing the barbell deadlift described next.

1. Starting position.
2. Ending position.

Barbell Deadlift

Deadlift is an exercise I really didn't "get" until recent years—it's now one of my favorite exercises, as I've come to appreciate its many benefits. Not only does the deadlift turn on the nervous system like no other exercise, but it also lights up all the core muscles and strengthens the typically weak posterior chain of a climber.

Regardless of your age and ability, I strongly recommend some deadlifting if you have access to the weight equipment. No, you shouldn't be deadlifting like power lifters (i.e., many heavy sets), nor like the CrossFitters who commonly do many high-rep sets with a more moderate load. The protocol I recommend, after a light warm-up set of six reps, is three sets of deadlifts with reps of five, four, and three per set. Take a 3- to 5-minute rest between sets, and add 10 to 20 pounds with each successive set. The weight used should be heavy enough to make each set difficult, but not so heavy that your technique is compromised. Do this twice per week, and you'll be amazed at how strong you get while gaining little or no muscle mass. Furthermore, I believe you'll be pleasantly surprised to discover that deadlifting makes you feel very good, and you'll likely climb better!

The starting position is somewhat similar to the dumbbell sumo deadlift except that your feet should be a bit less than shoulder width apart (10 to 12 inches apart for most people) and parallel.

1. Set up with the bar over the middle of your feet and about one and a half inches from your shin, and then push your rear end back and flex at the hips and knees in order to grab onto the bar with an overhand grip. At the starting position check that your arms are just outside of your legs, your scapula are above the bar and your knees are over the bar.

2. Now think about squeezing your chest up by engaging the muscles in the mid-back and then letting the contraction continue down into the lower back until it is tightened into contraction too. Fix your eyes on the floor at a point 12 to 15 feet in front of you to maintain a neutral neck position. Before you begin the pull, get the weight back off your toes and onto your mid-foot.

3. Take a deep breath, tighten your abs, and drive your feet into the floor, and think about dragging the bar up your legs. Focus on driving your hips forward and then pulling your shoulders back (and scapula together) as you approach the top position—your lower back must be kept in extension throughout the lift (not over-extended nor rounded).

Table 6.1—Deadlifting Protocol for Rock Climbers

Set	Weight (% of 1RM)	Reps/Set	Rest
Warm-Up	50–60%	6	3–5 minutes
1	70%	5	3–5 minutes
2	80%	4	3–5 minutes
3	85–90%	2–3	3–5 minutes

This deadlift protocol will maximize neurological strength gains without triggering significant hypertrophy. 1RM is your estimate of the heaviest weight you could deadlift for one repetition.

4. Finish standing tall, like a soldier at attention, but do not hyperextend your back and do not shrug your shoulders.

5. Lower the barbell by pushing your rear end back and bending at the hips (maintain a straight back) and then at the knees. Face more or less forward throughout the lift, but with a slight downward gaze near the bottom position.

6. Pause at the bottom for 1 second before beginning the next repetition—it's not a deadlift if you bounce the bar off the platform!

Warning: This is a technical lift, and I recommend consulting a coach on your initial forays into the wonderful world of deadlifting. Furthermore, do not deadlift if you have an active back problem, do not deadlift more than twice per week, and do not increase your weights so fast that your form is compromised. But do stretch and foam roll your hamstrings, glutes, and lower back muscles at the end of your workout and before bed on the eve after your deadlifting.

1. Starting position.
2. Ending position.

Barbell Squat

The squat is another excellent full-body exercise that, like the deadlift, lights up the core muscles in addition to working leg and hip extension. Doing two brief sets (five to eight reps, never more) with moderately heavy weight is a great workout, and it's unlikely to lead to any gain in muscle mass. Learning to squat with proper technique is important—if possible, enlist a coach to help you get started. The lift requires a free weight set and squat rack, so it may not be an option unless you belong to a gym with the necessary equipment; as an alternative, buy a few dumbbells and train with the sumo deadlift described earlier.

1. Set up under the racked bar, then position it across your mid- to upper trapezius and take a grip wider than shoulder width. Take a deep breath and unrack the bar—carefully back up a step or so to clear the hooks (that were holding the bar).

2. Set your feet about shoulder width apart and with an outward flair of around 20 degrees. Take another deep breath and contract your inner core, then begin the descent—think about sitting in a chair behind you rather than a sense of going straight down. Knees should track over your toes and not collapse inward. Your chest will naturally tilt down as you descend, but strive to keep your weight back on your feet as if sitting down.

3. For a full squat, descend until your thighs are parallel to the floor; beginners may want to stop short of this (three-quarter squat). At the bottom, immediately reverse direction by driving your feet into the floor and extending simultaneously at the knees and hips—think of pushing your head toward the ceiling to quickly regain the top position. Breathe out as you near the top of the lift.

4. Pause for a moment in the top position before taking another deep breath and beginning the next repetition. To maximize the core workout, try to bend the bar over your shoulders throughout the lift—this action will maximally recruit your outer core including the latissimus dorsi, pecs, rotator cuff, and trapezius.

5. Continue for a total of five to eight reps (never more), being sure to maintain a flat lower back throughout the lift.

6. Rest for 3 minutes before doing a second set.

Training tips: Begin squatting with a modest weight, say, around 40 percent of your body weight. Over the course of a year or two, you can work toward squatting your body weight—in my opinion, there's no reason for a climber to train with weights any heavier.

1. Starting position. 2. Ending position.

Climbing-Specific Core

These last four core exercises are both climbing-specific and quite difficult. If you are a novice climber, you should aspire to graduate to these exercises over the course of a year or two, depending on your initial level of physical fitness. Well-trained climbers, however, should make these exercises a mainstay of their exercise program and supplement with a variety of other exercises from earlier in the chapter.

Roof Lever-Ups

This strenuous exercise is half curl-up and half front lever, and it effectively trains both the anterior and posterior core.

1. Climb up (or jump or get boosted) to a large jug hold on the roof of a bouldering cave, and begin from a straight-arm hang.
2. Pull up halfway (elbows around 90 degrees), then forcefully drop your head and shoulder back and lift your feet upward to latch one foot onto a roof hold as far away as possible. Focus on powerfully firing your entire core musculature at the instant your foot contacts the hold.
3. Match feet on the hold, and then relax your core as much as you can without losing the foothold—note the submaximal amount of stiffness needed to maintain the hand-foot connection.
4. Now release your feet and return to the straight-arm starting position.
5. Do three to eight (hard) repetitions. Rest for 3 minutes before doing a second and third set.

Training tip: Make this exercise harder by doing less of a pull-up before each lever-up (super-strong climbers can do this exercise with nearly straight arms throughout).

Engage more distant footholds to make the exercise more difficult.

Steep Wall Cut & Catch

This is another great core exercise that is very specific in developing core strength for hard, steep wall climbs. Perform this exercise on a very steep bouldering wall with lots of large, positive holds. A 65-degree wall is ideal.

1. Pick an easy- to moderate-difficulty boulder problem, and ascend it in the unconventional way of letting your feet cut off after every hand move and then immediately drawing them back up to the wall to catch onto a foothold.

2. Continue in this way up the entire problem, if possible. While certainly not the most efficient way to ascend the route, this exercise trains the core muscles to fire and relax in quick succession— an extremely important attribute for hard climbing.

3. Do three to five laps with 1 to 3 minutes rest in between.

Steep Wall Cut & Catch.

Steep Wall Traversing

Climbing overhanging walls is the ultimate core-training exercise, and it's obviously the most specific. The best training strategy is to traverse sideways across a long overhanging wall, or back and forth across a shorter one. The only drawback to this exercise is that lack of finger strength and climbing ability will prevent some climbers from traversing long enough to adequately work the core muscles.

1. Select a section of wall that overhangs 30 to 50 degrees past vertical.

2. Using medium-size handholds and small footholds, traverse across the wall at a steady pace. Avoid extremely technical or strenuous moves.

3. Lead with your feet—reaching or swinging your lead foot as far as possible—and fish for a foothold that you can stick by quickly stiffening your core. The longer the horizontal move, the more your core muscles will need to work to maintain balance and stability. Allow your body to twist and turn as needed to execute the moves, and concentrate on contracting your core muscles to prevent body sag, sway, or swing.

4. Continue traversing for about 60 seconds—or continue for 2 minutes to make for a real core endurance exercise!

5. Rest for 3 minutes before performing a second set traversing in the opposite direction.

The longer the horizontal reach or step, the more effective the core workout.

Front Lever

Introduced to climbing by the legendary boulderer John Gill, the front lever is the gold standard of core-muscle strength. It is a very difficult gymnastics move, so expect this exercise to feel hard—or even impossible!—at first. Fortunately, you can make it a bit easier by simply bending one leg or by having a spotter hold your feet.

1. Begin by hanging straight-armed from a bar or a set of Pump Rocks or rings (harder).

2. Pull up halfway, then push your hands forward, drop your head backward, and lift your legs. Do all this in a single quick motion while attempting to position your entire body—head to toe—parallel to the ground. Squeeze tightly throughout your shoulders, torso, buttocks, and legs to hold this position. It helps to think about bending the bar and pushing your hands toward your hips, even though you'll be in a stationary position.

3. The goal is to hold the lever for 2 seconds before lowering yourself slowly to the starting position.

4. Rest for a second or two in the dead hang position, then power back up into a front lever again. Hold for 2 seconds.

5. Continue for a total of two to five (hard) repetitions.

6. Do two or three sets with a 3- to 5-minute rest between sets.

Safety note: The front lever places a great deal of stress on your shoulders and elbows (just like steep climbing), so it is inappropriate for novice or out-of-shape climbers or anyone with ongoing elbow or shoulder problems.

1. Front lever with bent leg. 2. Front lever with straight legs—harder!

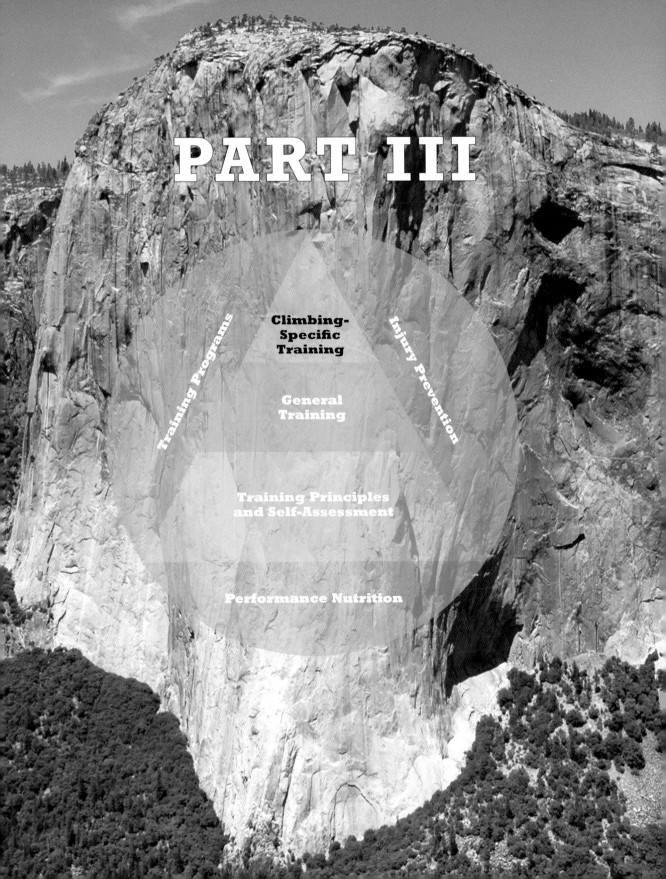

PART III

Climbing-
Specific
Training

Injury Prevention

Training Programs

General
Training

Training Principles
and Self-Assessment

Performance Nutrition

Anna Davey hanging onto Choad Warrior (27/5.12d), Mountain Quarry, Perth, Australia. DANE EHM

Limit-Strength Training Exercises

What other sport could possibly ask you to pull your body weight on just a few fingertips or on just one arm? As a result, targeted finger and arm-strength training is uniquely important for climbers.

Perhaps more than any other sport, climbing places extreme demands on your fingers and arms. Depending on the angle of the rock and size of footholds, your fingers and arms may need to support anywhere from less than 1 percent up to 100 percent of your body weight. Compounding these demands is the infinite variety and size of handholds, which can range from a handlebar jug down to a tiny edge or one-finger pocket. What other sport could possibly ask you to pull your body weight on one or two fingertips? This is, of course, an extreme scenario that only elite climbers will encounter; still, the dwindling size of handholds on climbs rated 5.10 and harder does require a level of finger and arm strength not common among flat-landers or novice climbers.

The focus of this chapter is then obvious: to help you strengthen your fingers and arms. In your formative days, simply going climbing a few days per week is the only training you'll need to improve in this area. As you improve and adapt to the demands of midlevel climbs, however, you'll discover that gains in strength plateau and become a limiting constraint on performance. It's at this point that engaging in a smart, targeted training program of the finger flexor and pulling muscles becomes important to future improvement.

Developing strength—that can be exploited explosively as needed—requires use of exercises that train both *limit strength* and *power*. Limit strength is the absolute strength you can summon in gripping a marginal hold or making a difficult pulling move, whereas power relates to a muscle's rate of force development—how quickly you can summon peak force to make a dynamic move or quickly latch onto a hold (contact strength). The focus of this chapter is developing limit strength; the next chapter will present a dozen excellent power-training exercises.

This chapter is broken into two parts: The first part details nine exercises for training important limit strength in the finger flexor muscles, while the second part details eight great exercises for building more pulling and lock-off strength.

Finger-Strength-Training Exercises

According to the principle of specificity, effective finger training must necessarily target the neuromuscular system in ways that are specific to climbing. Therefore, fingerboard hangs, campusing, and bouldering are all valid ways to train finger strength for climbing, whereas a hand-held squeeze device is a waste of time as anything other than a warm-up or rehab exercise. The degree to which a given exercise will produce gains in functional grip strength for climbing can be estimated by considering the following requirements—the more of these requirements that are met, the more effective the exercise will be at producing usable gains in climbing grip strength.

Muscles Targeted	Limit-Strength Training Exercise	Page	Beginner	Intermediate	Advanced
Finger Flexors	Bouldering	121	X	X	X
	Hypergravity Bouldering	122		X	X
	Fingerboard "Minimum Edge" Hangs	124		X	X
	Fingerboard Maximum-Weight Hangs "10-Second" Protocol	125		X	X
	Fingerboard Maximum-Weight Hangs "7-53" Protocol	127			X
	Hypergravity Isolation Training— Maximum-Strength Protocol	128		X	X
	Heavy Finger Rolls	130		X	X
	Pinch Ball Hangs	132		X	X
	Wide Pinch with Wrist Extension	133	X	X	X
Arms & Torso	Weighted Pull-Ups	134	X	X	X
	Lat Pull-Down	135	X	X	X
	Square Pull-Ups	136		X	X
	Typewriters	137		X	X
	Scapular Pull-Ups	138		X	X
	Uneven-Grip Pull-Ups	139		X	X
	One-Arm Lock-Offs	140			X
	System Wall "Isolation"	142	X	X	X
	Steep Wall "Lock-Offs" (aka "Touches")	143		X	X

- The exercise must be performed at near-maximum intensity throughout the entire set. In climbing-specific finger training, you can increase intensity by decreasing hold size or adding weight. Of course, there's a definite limit to how small a hold you can train on comfortably—holds smaller than about 10mm (⅜ inch) deep are often painful to train on. While it's good to practice hanging on small holds, extensive training sessions are best performed on a somewhat larger hold (many people find 14 to 25mm or ⅝ to 1 inch is ideal) with weight added to your body to increase intensity.

- The exercise must produce muscular failure in less than 12 seconds. As detailed in chapter 1 (page 9), brief, maximal exercise is powered by the anaerobic alactic energy system, so this energy system must be the training focus. Exercising any longer than 12 seconds per set trains strength-endurance (the anaerobic lactic energy system), not maximum strength—this is a critical distinction!

- The exercise must be specific to climbing grip positions and movements. Obviously exercises such as fingerboard and campus training will carry over to climbing better than nonspecific exercises such as finger rolls, squeeze devices, and the like.

- The exercise must focus on a specific grip position for an entire set. In climbing, the rock dictates a random use of varying grip positions. Since strength is grip-specific, such cycling of grip positions allows you to climb longer than if you used the same grip repeatedly. That's great if you are climbing for performance, but it's ineffective for building maximum grip strength. Effective grip-strength training must target a specific grip position to near failure—I recommend training the half crimp, open crimp, open hand, wide pinch, and the three two-finger pocket grips.

Keep these four requirements in mind as you execute the limit-strength finger exercises detailed below and, most important of all, be sure to scale the exercise resistance to be near maximal (so that a high level of fatigue is generated in under 12 seconds). Let's examine nine highly effective exercises for developing functional finger strength for climbers. Select two or three of these exercises for use in a given workout session. Do climbing activities and on-the-rock exercises before advancing to isolation exercises such as hangboard training.

Bouldering

Bouldering is the most straightforward way to train grip strength. Without the constraints of a rope and gear, bouldering allows you to focus on climbing the hardest moves possible. Inherent to hard bouldering, however, are some limiting factors that diminish the potential to build maximum grip strength. Consider that technical difficulties may prevent you from climbing to near the point of muscular failure. Furthermore, the rock or plastic dictates the use of many different grip positions, thus making it difficult to isolate a single grip position and work it to failure.

Despite these limitations, bouldering should be a staple of your training program. It will build some functional strength and, at the same time, develop your mental and technical skills. Consequently it's a good training strategy to couple bouldering with one of the other finger-strength-training exercises described in this section. Use the following training strategy to best stimulate gains in finger strength via bouldering.

1. Select a short boulder problem that appears to be strenuous, but not technically difficult. Favor overhanging problems, which will place more weight on your hands and maximize the training effect. The ideal boulder will be climbable in under 15 seconds, since the goal is to target the anaerobic alactic energy system—if you're getting seriously pumped, then the problem is training strength/power-endurance more than limit strength.

2. Attempt to climb the problem three times with sufficient rest (at least 2 to 3 minutes) between each ascent to allow for a good effort. Doing a problem three times makes one "set."

3. Move on to another strenuous-looking problem that appears to target a different grip position, such as wide pinch, two-finger pockets, open hand, and such. Ascend this problem three times (one set), with adequate rest (2 to 3 minutes) between attempts. Continue bouldering in this way for 30 to 60 minutes (three to ten total sets), and then finish your finger training with one of the isolation exercises described later.

Bouldering for limit strength.

Training tip: Consider setting "theme problems" that isolate a specific grip position; for example, set a crimp-only problem, a pocket-only problem, a pinch-only problem, and so forth.

Hypergravity Bouldering

Advanced climbers with several years of bouldering under their belt eventually reach a point where they no longer achieve meaningful gains in finger strength despite regular, hard bouldering. Fortunately, hypergravity bouldering, weighted fingerboard hangs, and the HIT System workout (all detailed below) are potent training methods that will yield further gains in high-end finger strength. To do this, you'll need to invest in a 5- or 10-pound weight belt (up to 20 pounds for an advanced climber) or fill a fanny pack with 5 or 10 pounds of scuba divers' weights. Here is the best protocol for engaging in hypergravity bouldering—this is an indoor training strategy only!

1. Complete a general and a specific warm-up—that is, work through various warm-up and mobility exercises, and then move on to some moderate climbing and bouldering lasting at least 30 minutes.

2. Clip on your weight belt and predetermine a target number of hypergravity bouldering sets (repeating a problem three times makes one "set") that you will perform. As a guideline, limit yourself to two sets on your initial session, then build to five to seven sets as you gain confidence and strength.

3. Select short, overhanging boulder problems that possess small- to medium-size holds, but no tiny and tweaky features, nor highly dynamic technical moves. Since you are climbing with a weight belt, favor problems that are a couple of grades or more below your limit—you should be able to ascend the route in less than 15 seconds (anaerobic alactic energy system).

4. Climb the problem three times with a rest of at least 3 minutes between ascents—these three ascents (or attempts) make one set.

5. Move on to another strenuous-looking problem that appears to target a different grip position. Consider taking the time to set "theme problems" that possess only holds of a certain shape and size—this is the best way to target and train a weak grip position. Do one set of three ascents of each problem, always resting for at least 3 minutes between each ascent.

Training tip: Use a weight belt, not a weight vest, so that the weight added is near your center of mass—this way the added weight is least likely to mess with your climbing technique. Keep added weight at or below 20 pounds, since excessive weight will certainly compromise technique.

Safety notes: Hypergravity bouldering is stressful on your fingers, elbows, and shoulders, and so it's essential that you avoid using tweaky holds, tiny pockets, or arm positions (Gastons) that place your shoulders at risk. Also, eschew problems with awkward body positions and dynamic moves that might result in an out-of-control fall. When climbing with added weight, always jump off a problem (in control) rather than risk an uncontrolled fall.

Hypergravity bouldering with weight belt.

Grip Positions

Although rock dictates a wide range of gripping positions, we can best train maximum grip strength by addressing the six primary grip types. Let's take a quick look at each grip position and the training considerations.

Full Crimp

The full crimp is favored by many climbers because it provides what feels like the most secure lock onto small handholds thanks to its hallmark thumb lock over the top of the tip of the index finger. Unfortunately, the full-crimp grip is the most stressful on the tendons and joints. It's best not to specifically train in this grip position.

Half Crimp

The half-crimp grip is a slight variation of the full crimp in which you do not thumb-lock over the index finger. This reduces tendon stress and softens the aggressive angles on the fingers' first and second joints. Fortunately, targeted training of the half-crimp grip will yield large increases in strength that will make a huge difference on the rock, especially when crimping on small edges, incut pockets, and narrow pinches.

Open Crimp

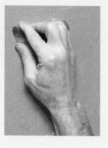

The open crimp is a hybrid grip characterized by the two middle fingers clinging in a half-crimp fashion, while the shorter index and pinky fingers assume the extended open-hand grip. The open crimp is commonly used in fingerboard training.

Open Hand

The open-hand grip is least stressful on the finger joints and tendons—and it can be trained to become your strongest grip position on all but the smallest crimp and incut holds (which require a crimp grip).

Pocket Grip

This is not really a unique grip, but it's worth including here since the pocket grip deserves some dedicated training. While shallow or incut pockets will require a half-crimp-like grip, most pockets (deeper and rounded) are best engaged with fingers extended in the open-hand position. Train the open-hand pocket grip with all three pairs (or "teams") of fingers. Advanced climbers can ease into training one-finger pockets with the middle finger.

Pinch Grip

The pinch grip is vital for latching on to protruding holds. Fortunately, our hands are designed to excel at pinching thanks to strong thumb muscles that help anchor this grip. Pinches of less than about 3 inches in width place the fingertips in a half-crimp-like position (hyperextended DIP joint), whereas wider pinches extend the fingers into an open-hand position with an over-extended wrist. While it would be smart to train both narrow and wide pinches, it's the wide pinch grip that should be your primary focus.

Fingerboard "Minimum Edge" Hangs

The following training protocol, loosely based on research by Eva Lopez-Rivera, is what I recommend as an entry-level fingerboard program. A few multiweek cycles will bring noticeable gains in finger strength for intermediate climbers, as well as serve as preparation for delving into weighted fingerboard hangs (described next).

You'll need a fingerboard with many different-size edges and pockets, and then you'll need to experiment a little to identify what features you can hang on for just 15 seconds or so. Actual training hangs should terminate a few seconds before failure of the grip, so I recommend making each hang exactly 12 seconds in length. By design, this training protocol will produce little or no muscle pump as it primarily targets the anaerobic alactic energy system.

Fingerboard train only with the half-crimp, open-crimp, and open-hand grips (see page 123). Eva Lopez's Transgression board is shown here.

1. Do a 12-second hang using a feature that you can barely hold for 15 seconds with maximum effort.

2. Rest for exactly 3 minutes. You can do other training (e.g. core, antagonist, posterior chain, and such) during the rest intervals.

3. Do four more hangs following the above protocol. Each hang should be near maximal (rating of perceived exertion of 9 to 9.5 out of 10), but not quite take you to failure.

4. After doing the first set of five hangs, rest for 5 minutes before doing a second set of five hangs. Initially focus on training the half-crimp and open-crimp grip—one set each.

Advanced climbers can do additional sets that target two-finger pockets (open-hand grip) and pinch grip. Be sure to rest at least 5 minutes between sets (see table 7.1).

Training tips: Always use good hangboard technique: Maintain tension throughout your shoulders and upper torso by engaging your scapular stabilizers; take a deep breath upon beginning each hang; do not relax your shoulders and allow them to elevate into an exaggerated shrugged position as you fatigue; and relax from the hips down through your legs (do not lift knees excessively). Never fingerboard train with the full-crimp (with thumb lock) grip!

Table 7.1 "Minimum Edge" Fingerboard Protocol

Duration of Each Hang	Hangs per Set	Rest Between Hangs	Intensity (scale of 1 to 10)	Number of Sets	Rest Between Sets
12 secs.	5	3 mins.	9–9.5	2–5	5+ mins.

Note: Select hangboard features (size and shape) that you can barely hold for 15 seconds, although all hangs must terminate at 12 seconds.

Fingerboard Maximum-Weight Hangs "10-Second" Protocol

A period of dedicated "minimum edge" fingerboard training will eventually lead you to the point of needing to train on tiny, painful edges to keep with the protocol detailed above. Enter the "maximum weight" protocol, which involves using larger, more comfortable holds, but with added weight to create sufficiently high intensity for maximum-strength adaptations. The ideal size edge for weighted fingerboard hangs is between 14mm and 20mm (⅝ to ⅞ inch), or a little less than one finger-pad depth—this moderate size lessens skin pain, reduces strain on the distal finger joint, and has been proven effective to develop maximum-strength gains that will carry over to different-size edges on the rock.

Weight plates hanging from the belay loop of an old harness (with leg loops removed for simplicity).

This and the next exercise present two maximum-weight hangboard protocols that really work. Do two to five sets of one or the other—not both!—focusing mainly on the half-crimp or open-crimp grips, although advanced climbers may want to dedicate one or two sets to pocket or wide pinch grips. The amount of weight added will be significant (generally between 25 and 100 pounds), so you'll need to invest in a large weight vest, several weight belts, or hang a combination of free weight plates from the belay loop of your harness. The latter is the best solution since you can easily unclip the weights to de-load your body between hangs and sets.

1. Do a 10-second hang using a feature that you can barely hold for 13 seconds with maximum effort.

2. Rest for exactly 3 minutes.

3. Do four more hangs following the above protocol. Each hang should be near maximal (rating of perceived exertion of 9 to 9.5 out of 10), but not quite take you to failure.

4. After doing the first set of five hangs, rest at least 5 minutes before doing a second set of five hangs. Initially focus on training the half-crimp and open-crimp grip—one set each.

Advanced climbers can do additional sets that target two-finger pockets (open-hand grip) and pinch grip. Be sure to rest at least 5 minutes between sets (see table 7.2).

Table 7.2 Maximum-Weight "10-Second" Protocol

Duration of Each Hang	Rest Between Hangs	Hangs per Set	Intensity (scale of 1 to 10)	Number of Sets (aggregate of all grips trained)	Rest Between Sets
10 secs.	3 mins.	5	9–9.5	2–5	5+ mins.

Note: Your training weight should be heavy enough to cause failure in 13 seconds, although all hangs must terminate at 10 seconds.

Overview of Fingerboard Training

Since its advent in the mid-1980s, the fingerboard has become the most used type of training equipment among climbers—and for good reason: The weighted fingerboard hang is the single most effective isolation exercise a climber can do. What's more, the fingerboard is economical, and it can be mounted in just about any apartment or home.

The obvious strengths of fingerboard training are its ease of access and the ability to isolate a wide variety of grip positions. While not appropriate for beginners, experienced climbers can progressively add weight to their body (hypergravity) to train maximum grip strength with a series of brief, high-intensity hangs. The strategy for training strength-endurance is to use lighter loads and a higher number of hangs, but with less rest in between (see chapter 8).

Being able to vary the training load is an important aspect of effective fingerboard training. While you can indeed adjust intensity up and down by using smaller and bigger holds, respectively, it's also important to be able to adjust resistance while training on a specific hold such as the common 20mm (3/4-inch) edge. To increase resistance, simply wear a weight vest or hang free weights from the belay loop of your climbing harness. For resistances less than body weight, you can employ a pulley system with counterweights—especially useful for training one-arm hangs and learning one-arm pull-ups.

Always train with good hangboard technique: Maintain moderate tension throughout your shoulders and upper torso by engaging your scapular stabilizers; relax from the hips downward and avoid lifting your knees excessively; and most important, do not relax your shoulders and allow them to elevate into an extreme shrug position near your ears. Also, it's vital to do preparatory and concurrent training of the scapular stabilizers and rotator cuff muscles—select from exercises detailed in chapter 5, pages 80–87).

The author maximum-weight training two-finger pockets with 60 pounds hanging from the belay loop of his harness. Nicros Nexgen hangboard shown here.

A word of caution: Misuse of the fingerboard has contributed to tendon injuries in countless climbers. Fingerboard training should be limited to just two days per week and, ideally, as a supplement to climbing rather than a replacement for actual climbing. A gradual warm-up is essential beforehand, including a general activity to elevate heart rate, followed by various mobility exercises and some self-massage as outlined in chapter 3. Complete your warm-up with some pull-ups on large holds. It's also a good idea to conclude your fingerboard training with a few sets of antagonist training of the wrist stabilizers.

Fingerboard Maximum-Weight Hangs "7-53" Protocol

This is a more advanced maximum-weight protocol that I created to train maximum strength and foster more aerobic power, since it stresses the muscles to increase rate of CP resynthesis between hangs. It's also a very time efficient protocol if you are doing multiple sets.

1. Do a 7-second hang using a feature that you can barely hold for 10 seconds with maximum effort.

2. Rest for exactly 53 seconds. This way each hang-rest couplet takes exactly 1 minute.

3. Do two more hangs following the above protocol. Each hang should be near maximal (rating of perceived exertion of 9 to 9.5 out of 10), but not quite take you to failure.

4. After doing the first set of three hangs, rest at least 5 minutes before doing a second set of three hangs. Initially focus on training the half-crimp and open-crimp grip—one set each.

Advanced climbers can do a second set for each half- and open-crimp grips, or do additional sets that target two-finger pockets (open-hand grip) and pinch grip. Be sure to rest at least 5 minutes between sets (see table 7.3). Limit yourself to a maximum of five sets.

Training tip: Record the details of your hangs, including hold size, weight used, and the number of hangs and sets, in a training notebook, Excel spreadsheet, or training app. In the months and years to come, you'll undoubtedly document some significant gains in finger strength!

Sloper training with weight vest on Jason Kehl's Iron Palm hangboard by So iLL.

Table 7.3 Maximum-Weight "7-53" Protocol

Duration of Each Hang	Rest Between Hangs	Hangs per Set	Intensity (scale of 1 to 10)	Number of Sets (aggregate of all grips trained)	Rest Between Sets
7 secs.	53 secs.	3	9–9.5	2–5	5 mins.

Note: Your training weight should be heavy enough to cause failure in 10 seconds, although all hangs must terminate at 7 seconds.

Hypergravity Isolation Training—Maximum-Strength Protocol

Hypergravity Isolation Training (HIT) is a cross between hypergravity bouldering and weighted fingerboard hangs. The unique HIT Strip System provides a platform on which you can target a specific grip position for a single set of wall climbing. Since HIT Strip training involves actual climbing (unlike fingerboard training), it calls into action the entire chain of climbing muscles, from the finger flexors to the arms, to the many core muscles of the torso. This novel exercise is unquestionably one of the best pathways to becoming a stronger climber.

It's ideal to use the HIT workout as part of a training cycle or an off-season program; however, you can also use HIT once weekly during your climbing on-season. As part of an off-season (winter) program, you might do four to six HIT workouts over the course of a two- or three-week maximum-strength mesocycle, and then switch to another training modality (aerobic or anaerobic endurance) for a few

weeks. Given its stressful nature, it's best to cycle on and off this exercise every couple of weeks. Learn more about the HIT System in the "HIT System Training Tips" sidebar on page 169.

The maximum-strength HIT System protocol trains six basic grip positions in sets lasting a maximum of 15 seconds—no set should go longer, otherwise the training focus becomes anaerobic lactic. The grips trained are half crimp, pinch, open hand, and the three "teams" of two-finger grips. There will be enough near transfer from these fundamental positions to make your fingers stronger in any configuration on the rock. Perform one to three sets for each grip position—those new to the HIT workout should begin with one set—beginning with the most difficult grip position for you. Most people work through the grips in this order: pinch, two-finger "third team" or outside pair (pinky and ring finger), two-finger "second team" or inside pair (index and middle finger), two-finger "first team" or middle pair (middle and ring finger), half crimp, and open hand. The entire HIT workout is done "open feet," meaning that you can place your feet on any holds on the wall. Here's how you would perform a HIT set on the pinch holds—all the other grips are trained with exactly the same protocol.

HIT Strip training two-finger pocket "third team" with weight belt.

1. Sitting below the first HIT Strip, begin by gripping the first set of right- and left-hand pinch holds, then pull up and grab the next higher left-hand pinch hold. Place your feet on any holds you like.

2. Continue climbing with the next higher right-hand pinch hold and the next higher left-hand pinch hold until both hands are on the top two pinch holds.

3. Begin descending immediately, alternating left and right pinch holds back down until you are holding the bottom two pinch holds—this will take you nearly 15 seconds, so end the set now.

4. Upon stepping off the wall, use a stopwatch or phone app to time a rest of exactly 3 minutes before beginning the next set. Meanwhile, record the total number of "reps" (hand movements) and weight used in your training notebook.

5. After your 3-minute rest, proceed immediately with a second set of pinch grip (advanced) or begin training the next grip position (two-finger "third team") by utilizing the identical two-finger pocket holds on each HIT Strip. Once again climb up and down the HIT Strips one time using only this grip position.

6. Continue on to train all six grip positions, following as close as possible the protocol detailed in table 7.4.

Training tip: Use weight belts to add weight, since having the extra weight near your center of mass will have the least impact on your climbing technique; above about 30 pounds you'll need to use a weight vest. The commonly weak two-finger third team and pinch grips may require little or no additional weight, but if doing one full up-and-down lap is easy, then you will need to add weight next time. Ideally, you want to add enough weight to make ten consecutive hand moves difficult (effort of 9 out of 10). Advanced climbers can reduce the rest interval to just 2 minutes—this will make successive sets more difficult and reduce the amount of added weight.

Table 7.4 HIT System—Maximum-Strength Protocol

Grip Position	Weight Used HIT "Novice"	Weight Used HIT "Advanced"	Set Duration (reps/set)	Sets	Rest Between Sets
Pinch	None	20 lb.	<15 secs. (8–15 reps)	1–2	3 mins.
2-Finger "3rd Team"	None	20 lb.	<15 secs. (8–15 reps)	1–2	3 mins.
2-Finger "2nd Team"	6 lb.	30 lb.	<15 secs. (8–15 reps)	1–2	3 mins.
2-Finger "1st Team"	8 lb.	40 lb.	<15 secs. (8–15 reps)	1–2	3 mins.
Half Crimp	10 lb.	40 lb.	<15 secs. (8–15 reps)	1–2	3 mins.
Open Hand	10 lb.	40 lb.	<15 secs. (8–15 reps)	1–2	3 mins.

* Weights are approximations for a 160-pound climber. Use similar percentages of your body weight.

Heavy Finger Rolls

What this exercise lacks in specificity to climbing, it makes up for in high-intensity neuromuscular stimulation. Perhaps more than any other exercise, heavy finger rolls produce noticeable hypertrophy (an increase in the size of muscle cells). Therefore, tremendous training synergy can result from coupling heavy finger rolls with a climbing-specific exercise such as fingerboard repeaters and campus training.

One barrier to engaging in heavy finger roll training is finding the necessary weight-training equipment. You will need access to a 200-pound free-weight set, a bench-press bar with ball-bearing sleeves, and a squat rack. If you belong to a traditional health club or well-equipped climbing gym, then you are in luck. Otherwise, you'll need to determine whether training with this exercise is worth the significant investment in equipment (around $500)—although it will also come in handy for antagonist muscle training.

1. First, you need to set up the equipment to facilitate training with heavy weights. Set the squat rack so that the bench-press bar rests at about knee height. Load weight plates onto the bar to a warm-up weight of roughly one-half your body weight.

2. Stand in the middle of the squat rack and grip the bar with your hands shoulder width apart and thumbs pointing outward. Now lift the bar to gain the exercise stance with the bar lightly touching your thighs. Body position is critical to reduce strain on your lower back, elbows, and wrists—bend slightly at your knees, center your hips and shoulders over your feet, and maintain good posture with your lower back straight and your head up. It helps to perform this exercise standing in front of a mirror, so you can monitor your technique while looking straight ahead.

3. Begin rolling the bar up and down in your fingers. The range of motion is only the few inches from the open-hand position to the closed-hand position. Ideally you want to lower the bar as far as possible without it falling from your hand. The squat rack is your spotter just in case the bar does slip from your fingers. Maintain a still, stable body position throughout the exercise—do not jerk the weight with your arms in an attempt to perform extra reps.

4. Continue rolling the bar up and down for a total of ten to fifteen warm-up reps, and then replace the bar on the rack.

5. Rest for 3 to 5 minutes, then move on to the first of four training sets. (See table 7.5.)

6. Your training weight must be heavy to be effective. Use body weight as a starting value, but increase the weight as needed to make training to eight repetitions difficult. Well-trained individuals may need to use as much as 150 percent of body weight. Rest for 3 to 5 minutes between sets.

Table 7.5 Heavy Finger Rolls

Sample Program for a 160-Pound Climber			
Set	Weight	Reps	Rest Between Sets
Warm-Up	95 lb.	10–15	3–5 mins.
1	155 lb.	5–8	3–5 mins.
2	185 lb.	5–8	3–5 mins.
3	195 lb.	5–8	3–5 mins.
4	205 lb.	3–5	3–5 mins.

Safety notes: Maintaining proper form is critical— cease this exercise if you experience pain in your knees, lower back, shoulders, elbows, wrists, or fingers.

Training tips: Heavy finger rolls are best used as an off-season exercise to trigger hypertrophy during an intensive maximum-strength training program.

1. Stand with hips and shoulders over your feet, with a slight bend in arms and knees. Maintain a tight core and neutral back position.

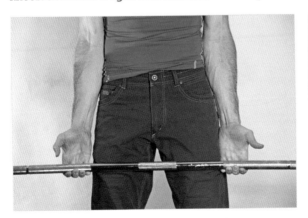

2. Roll the bar from an open-hand position to. . .

3. a closed-hand position.

Pinch Ball Hangs

While you may only infrequently encounter pinch moves on the rock (they are much more common on indoor walls), training for greater pinch strength will save the day when you are faced with a strenuous pinch move. While your normal cling grip is controlled by the finger flexors of the forearm, the pinch grip also calls into action the intrinsic muscles of the hand—specifically the lumbricals (palm) and, most important, the pollicis brevis and pollicis longus, which flex the distal and proximal phalanx of the thumb, respectively. Twice-per-week training will produce significant gains in these commonly undertrained muscles. It's best to train these muscles with isometric contractions via stable pinching of different-size holds. The two common training methods are (1) to pinch and hold a heavy object at your side while in a standing position, and (2) to hang from a pair of pinch holds with arms extended overhead. The former method is my preference, as it reduces the total volume of hanging on the shoulders (already a vastly used position in fingerboard training and climbing); however, this exercise presents a popular way to pinch train by hanging on to a pair of pinch balls.

Pinch training on Synrock Wrecking Balls.

1. Pinch balls are commonly manufactured with diameters of 3, 4, and 5 inches. Begin training with 3-inch-diameter balls (easier), but introduce a few sets of wider pinch-ball hangs as your strength improves.

2. Since your goal is to develop pinch strength (specifically, to strengthen the thumb muscles), you should use one of the fingerboard strength-training protocols detailed in tables 7.1 to 7.3.

3. I suggest using the 7-53 protocol—hang for 7 seconds, then rest for 53 seconds.

4. Do three consecutive hangs, then rest for 3 to 5 minutes before performing a second set.

5. Begin with just two sets (three hangs per set), using a 3- or 4-inch pinch ball for your initial workouts.

6. Build up to a total of five sets, including a set or two with the more difficult 5-inch pinch balls.

Safety note: Be sure to use proper hangboard training form—that is, supinate your forearms and maintain some tension through the shoulders to avoid descending into the stressful, potentially injurious shrugged-shoulder position.

Wide Pinch with Wrist Extension

This is a must-do exercise, as it trains two critical aspects of your grip strength. First, this pinch exercise obviously trains the small muscles that control the thumb (in pinch gripping). Just as important, however, the wide pinch grip strengthens the finger extensor muscles with the fingers fully extended—critical for improved wrist stability and injury prevention. While you may be able to find some kind of a pinch block on the Internet, you can easily kludge a rig by screwing together three short pieces of a 2x4. Another option is pinching a thick bumper weight plate. Anyway, the exercise is straightforward.

1. Stand upright with good posture and level shoulders.
2. Pinch the wood block or bumper plate with a straight arm and extended wrist; hold this position for 10 to 30 seconds.
3. Repeat the exercise on the other side.
4. Do two to five sets with at least 2 minutes rest in between.

Training tip: Initially, I suggest training for strength-endurance, which will require a light weight that allows a full 30-second hold. Longer term, consider using a heavier weight that allows only a 10-second hold.

Wide pinch with wrist extension. 1. Using a bumper plate. 2. Wood blocks.

Pull-Muscle Strength-Training Exercises

This section details nine excellent exercises for developing limit strength in the muscles that enable you to pull hard and lock off on steep climbing terrain. Just as in building limit strength in the finger flexors, however, you must perform each exercise in a way that produces rapid fatigue. As explained earlier, exercises that last much longer than 12 seconds train the anaerobic lactic energy system and, consequently, train endurance rather than limit strength. Effective strength training via these exercises, then, may require adding weight to your body (by way of a weight vest, weight belt, or free weights hung from the belay loop of a harness) so as to limit each training set to just three to six repetitions. Select two or three of these exercises for use in any given workout.

Weighted Pull-Ups

Upon being able to do about eight solid body-weight pull-ups, you will need to add resistance to continue training maximum strength in the pulling muscles. Weighted pull-ups should be a staple exercise of every intermediate, advanced, and elite climber.

1. After doing a thorough warm-up, including some basic mobility and stability exercises, add an amount of weight to your body that would allow you to do a maximum of eight repetitions. Your goal with this first set is to do just six reps, thus stopping before total muscle failure.

2. Carefully mount the pull-up bar or hangboard with a palms-away grip and hands about shoulder width apart.

3. Explode upward as fast as possible to reach the top position with the bar near (or touching) your upper chest.

4. Lower with a slower, more controlled motion and stop just short of a straight-arm hang position (which must be avoided when training with added weight).

5. Begin the next repetition, and then continue for a total of six reps.

6. Rest for 3 minutes before doing another set.

7. Do at least two more sets, increasing the weight by 5 pounds for each successive set. Advanced climbers can do up to six total sets.

Pull-ups with a 60-pound weight vest.

Training tip: If you are new to weighted pull-ups, you will discover that adding just 10 or 20 pounds makes for a much more difficult pull-up—you will also discover remarkable gains in pull-up strength in just a few weeks of training! Long term, the amount of weight you need to add may be upward of 50 percent of body weight (or more) in order to make doing three to six pull-ups a near-maximal exercise. I suggest using a training weight that would allow just eight repetitions if you were doing a single maximal set.

Lat Pull-Down

If you belong to a health club such as Golds Gym, Lifetime Fitness, or similar, the lat pull-down is likely the only machine that offers a climbing-specific movement. The lat pull-down is so sport-specific that many climbing gyms now include a lat pull-down machine in their training area. If you have access to one, use it!

While body weight and hypergravity pull-ups are fully sufficient for effectively training strength-endurance and limit strength, respectively, the lat pull-down can be employed occasionally as a change-up to your training (principle of variation). Not only does this machine enable you to quickly adjust the resistance (much faster than, say, adjusting the amount of weight hanging from your harness for hypergravity pull-ups), it also allows you to easily vary the width of your grip as well as the angle of your torso while pulling down. This latter variation enables you to simulate pulling down on overhanging rock by simply leaning backwards (away from the machine) and pulling the bar toward your mid-chest rather than the top of your chest (as in a regular pull-up).

Vary each set of lat pull-downs by changing hang spacing and by pulling the bar to your chin, chest, and behind your head to touch the neck.

Another novel exercise for strong climbers is the one-arm lat pull-down—an excellent gateway exercise for developing the strength to do a one-arm pull-up. Grip the middle of the bar with one hand and pull in a slow, but powerful motion toward the center of your chest. Initially, train with your palm facing you, but graduate to training with a palm-away grip as your strength improves.

Regardless of the exercise you choose to do on the lat pull-down machine, effective limit strength training demands use of a weight so heavy that doing five to eight reps is difficult. Begin with three sets and build to as many as six sets, if this is the only limit-strength pulling exercise you are doing for a given workout. Rest for 3 minutes between sets.

Square Pull-Ups

This pull-up variation is a bit more climbing specific since it emphasizes lock-off positions and uneven arm force application.

1. Grip a pull-up bar with hands about 50 percent wider than shoulder width, and begin by doing a pull-up to reach the top position.

2. While maintaining the top position, shift to the left by pulling your left hand in against your chest as you push your right hand out to the side as if trying to straighten your arm.

3. Now lower slowly until your left elbow reaches an angle of about 120 degrees.

4. Immediately shift your torso rightward to a position under the right hand so that the right elbow is now flexed at an angle of about 120 degrees.

5. Pull-up to the top position with your right hand locked off against the right side of your chest and your left arm extended in a nearly straight position.

6. Hold the top position, with chin over the bar, and shift left until your left hand is once again touching your chest—this completes the square pull-up, but keep going!

7. Do two sets of three to six square pull-ups with a 3-minute rest between sets. Do the second set in the opposite direction, and add weight when you find doing two sets of six repetitions to be easy.

Square pull-up progression.

Typewriters

This exercise is similar to the square pull-up except that you slide side-to-side, like an old-fashioned typewriter, while maintaining the top position of the pull-up.

1. Grip a pull-up bar with hands at least 50 percent wider than shoulder width, and begin by doing a pull-up to reach the top position.

2. While maintaining the top position, shift to the right by pulling your right hand in against your chest as you push your left hand out to the side as if trying to straighten your arm.

3. Hold the lock-off position with the right arm for 1 second, then slide left to attain a left arm lock-off with the left hand touching the side of your chest. Hold this position for 1 second. This makes one repetition.

4. Continue sliding right and left for a total of three to six repetitions.

5. Do two sets of three to six Typewriters with a 3-minute rest between sets.

Training tip: To increase difficulty, you can add a 5- or 10-pound weight belt or simply release your grip with the extended arm so that each 1-second lock-off is being held mainly by the locked-off arm. I suggest resting the palm of the released hand on the bar for balance, stability, and ease of re-gripping the bar to begin the next Typewriter movement.

 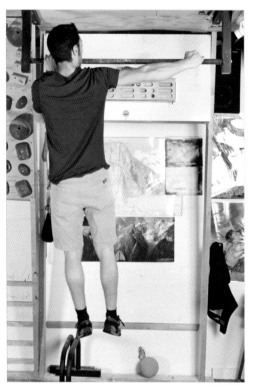

1. Slide right to lock-off position.   *2. Slide left to lock-off position.*

Scapular Pull-Ups

The scapular pull-up is a training essential in the Hörst gym! Keeping your shoulders healthy and developing proper movement patterns in pulling motions demands the ability to forcefully depress and retract the scapula. Regular use of this isolation exercise will develop better kinesthetic awareness of your scapular position and enable you to climb harder and longer with good form, despite growing fatigue. Furthermore, being able to quickly and forcibly engage the lower trapezius and latissimus muscles will empower you to keep your scapula in proper position when campus training and lunging.

1. Begin in a normal pull-up position with a palms-away grip and hands shoulder width apart.

2. From a full hang with somewhat shrugged shoulders, you want to draw the scapula down and together, thus raising your body slightly but without bending your arms and pulling as in a regular pull-up. The best learning cues are to try to "bend the bar" and think about doing a reverse shrug (i.e., shoulders drawn downward). Do this and you'll feel your head shift backward and your chest raise upward as your scapula pinch together.

3. Hold the top position for 1 second, then return to the starting position. The range of motion is only a few inches to a foot or two (when you get really strong!).

4. Do six to twelve reps, keeping straight arms and tight spinal erectors and glutes throughout. At first you may find this to be a difficult exercise (a sign that you've found a critical weakness to correct!), but resist the urge to overdo it.

5. Add a second and third set to your workout only after you've mastered the exercise.

Training tip: Strong climbers can do this exercise with full body weight, but I suggest learning with less resistance by keeping your feet on the floor and flexing your knees enough to hang with straight arms from a pull-up bar. Advanced climbers can increase difficulty by making the scaption more powerful, thus raising the body higher and higher (larger range of motion) without bending the arms. Do not add weight for this exercise.

1. Begin from an ordinary pull-up starting position. 2. Maintaining nearly straight arms, depress and downwardly rotate your scapula by pressing down on the bar—think about trying to bend the bar (supinating your forearms) and press your chest out.

Uneven-Grip Pull-Ups

This is an excellent exercise for developing one-arm and lock-off strength. As the name implies, doing uneven-grip pull-ups requires a setup that offsets one hand 12 to 24 inches lower than the other. You can do this by simply looping a sling over a pull-up bar or extending one of a pair of free-floating rings or similar.

1. It's best to learn the exercise with an opposing grip—do this by standing under the pull-up bar facing longways with the high hand gripping the bar palm inward (thumb pointing backward) and the low hand gripping the sling with a two-finger-pocket or pinch grip.

2. From this bottom position initiate upward movement by pulling with both hands; however, focus on pulling hardest with the higher hand. As you ascend past mid-height, begin pushing downward with the low hand to aid the pulling of the high hand.

3. Finish by pulling the bar down along the side of your head to achieve a tight lock-off position.

4. Hold the top position for 1 second before beginning a controlled descent. Stop short of reaching a straight-arm position and immediately begin the next repetition.

5. Do three to five reps, then dismount and rest for 2 minutes before doing three to five reps with the other hand gripping the bar. Perform two or three sets on each side.

Training tip: Begin uneven-grip pull-up training with your hands offset by just 12 inches; increase the displacement when you can do more than five reps. Advanced climbers can do this exercise with both hands in a palms-away grip position.

1. Start positon.
2. Pull up until your chin reaches the bar.

One-Arm Lock-Offs

The ability to hold a steady one-arm lock-off is vital for hard bouldering and roped climbing. This exercise is obviously very specific to this need, but it does demand a high level of base strength for proper execution. If you cannot hold a solid one-arm lock-off, it would be best to train with weighted pull-ups or uneven-grip pull-ups rather than attempt this exercise. Twice-a-week training with one-arm lock-offs is a perfect gateway exercise to eventually being able to do a one-arm pull-up. You can do one-arm lock-offs using a pull-up bar or a single free-floating ring.

One-arm lock-off variation.

1. Begin with hands side-by-side and in opposing grips (palms facing each other). The beginning position for each repetition is with hands extended overhead, but not completely straight.

2. Let's train the right arm first: Pull up with both arms to reach a high lock-off position with the bar or ring pulled in tightly near your right cheek.

3. Immediately let go with the left hand and hold the static lock-off position as long as possible—when you begin to lose the lock-off, lower as slowly as possible, but *do* grab back on with the other hand before your elbow reaches an angle of 120 degrees.

4. Immediately commence with another pull-up, this time locking-off in the top position with the other arm.

5. Do two or three repetitions with each arm.

6. Rest at least 3 minutes before doing another set or two on each side.

Safety note: Be sure to lower in a slow, controlled manner and never drop forcefully into the fully straight-arm position.

Variation: Hold the top lock-off position for 3 to 5 seconds, then lower to a 90-degree arm angle and pause here for 3 to 5 seconds (per photo).

Training to Do a One-Arm Pull-Up

The one-arm pull-up is a benchmark exercise for elite climbers. Amazingly, some of the world's top climbers can do more than five consecutive one-arm pulls (really hard), and a few ridiculously strong individuals can do a one-arm pull-up while holding 20 pounds (or more) in their free hand! This is obviously not an exercise to rush into training—doing so tempts injury and may be demoralizing—but it is worth playing around with if you've been climbing at a high level for a few years and already possess a high level of base pull-muscle and stabilizer strength. If you can do a few hypergravity pull-ups with more than 25 percent of body weight added and a solid one-arm lock-off, then you are likely ready.

First, you'll want to learn a one-arm pull-up using a palms-inward grip and by pulling in a neutral position with the bar finishing in a lock-off near the cheek of the pulling arm side. Over time you'll learn to do a one-arm pull-up with the palm facing away and the bar finishing below your chin. The best transition into one-arm pull-up training is by way of a counterweight pulley system; this way you can gradually reduce the amount of counterweight help over the course of many weeks of training. (Alternatively, you can stand in a Thera-band looped over the pull-up bar—stand with the leg opposite the pulling hand.) Either way, do three to five one-repetition sets of aided one-arm pull-ups, using the least amount of counterweight support as possible. Rest for 2 to 3 minutes between each one-rep set.

When you sense you are ready to attempt your first body-weight one-arm pull-up, I suggest you stand on a box that allows you to begin with just the slightest bend in your pulling arm. Before initiating the one-arm pull-up, it's vital that you tighten your shoulder muscles (engage the rotator cuff and scapular stabilizers) and then think about screwing your forearm inward (supination) as you perform the pull-up motion. Concentrate on pulling the bar down past your cheek (working arm side) and finish in a tight lock-off position—hold a solid finish like a champ, and then take pride in having done your first one-arm pull-up!

Train one-arm pull-ups twice per week by doing three sets of one repetition with each arm. Long term you may be able to do multiple one-arm pull-ups, at which time you can begin one-arm pull-up training by holding a 5- or 10-pound dumbbell in your free hand.

System Wall "Isolation"

The utility of a System Wall is in being able to isolate and fatigue a specific combination of grip and arm positions while performing actual climbing movements and body positions. While the fingerboard and campus board are better tools for training finger strength and contact strength, the System Wall excels at building pull-muscle strength across a wide range of arm positions. With a well-equipped System Wall, you can isolate a variety of undercling and side-pull positions, pulling and twisting Gaston moves, and compression moves between widely spaced holds. Ultimately, your imagination is the only limitation when it comes to training unique arm and body positions. You can even create a System Wall "Isolation" that mimics a crux move on some outdoor project you're working—that's functional training of the highest degree!

Given access to a good System Wall, you may want to reduce time spent bouldering (by 10 to 20 minutes) in order to dedicate a little time to isolation training. While you can certainly use small (difficult) handholds to train finger strength on a System Wall, it is my belief that it's best to use a fingerboard to train the finger strength and a System Wall to train arm positions, body positions, compression, and other specific movements. Each System Wall session should have a focus—what arm and body positions seem to be your weakness on the rock? For many climbers huge functional gains are possible via System Wall training that isolates long reaches from undercling and side-pull positions, extending reach off a lock-off hold (by pressing it down), twist-locking acutely and deeply for maximum reach, and compressing and slapping up a series of distant holds.

1. Pick two to four different System Wall "Isolations" to train over the course of several training sets.

2. Suppose your first isolation is a long reach off a crimp side-pull hold—mount the System Wall with both hands gripping identical crimp side-pulls. Place feet on identical footholds or a wood strip.

3. Engage your hips and core, twist, and pull off one side-pull hold in order to reach up with the other hand to engage a high hold (of any type).

4. Bring your other hand up to a similar hold high on the board, then immediately return to the starting position. You can either reverse the moves or simply step off the wall and immediately regain the starting holds.

5. Now do the same side-pull move but with the opposite hand side-pulling. Again, match hands high on the wall and then return to the starting holds.

6. Do three to five consecutive repetitions on each side, being sure to use the same holds and body position each time.

7. Rest for 3 minutes, and then perform the next System Wall "Isolation."

Training tips: Strive for tight body positions and full extension with each repetition—there's little benefit to doing incomplete movements with sloppy technique and poor body position. Increase resistance by doing longer moves or by adding weight (via weight belt) rather than using holds so small and poor that you can't bear down and fully recruit the core and pulling muscles that you intend to train.

A System Wall doesn't need to be large to be effective at strengthening specific arm and body positions.

Steep Wall "Lock-Offs" (aka "Touches")

This is an excellent exercise for developing lock-off strength and climbing-specific core stiffness. You can do Steep Wall Lock-Offs on an overhanging bouldering wall, a HIT Strip or System Wall, or a campus board with foot strips.

1. Begin with matched hands on a pair of good holds (or large campus rung) and both feet on a toe board or footholds.

2. Pull into a tight lock-off position with one hand and reach as high as possible with the other hand. Touch the wall for 2 seconds with the free hand while maintaining a solid lock-off with the other. Twist and stiffen your body as needed to maximize your reach. Resist grabbing on with the reaching hand—the goal is to stress the lock-off position for a full 2 seconds.

3. Return to the starting position and immediately pull into a tight lock-off with the other arm. Again, reach as high as possible with the free hand and touch the wall for 2 seconds.

4. Continue for a total of three to six lock-offs on each side, then take a 3-minute rest.

5. Do two to five sets.

Training tip: Increase difficulty by using a steeper wall or adding a weight belt, but not by using smaller handholds—the focus here is training lock-off strength, not finger flexor strength.

1. Beginning position.

2. Lock-off position.

James Simmons flying up The Actual Parchments (5.13a), Turtle Wall, St. George, Utah.
GEORGE BRUCE WILSON

CHAPTER 8

Power-Training Exercises

When it comes to power training, it's exercise quality, not quantity, that matters most. Done right, a pure power workout mostly involves resting, with only brief intermittent bursts of high-power, high-intensity exercise.

When climbers talk about power, they are typically referring to the need to make quick, strenuous reaches or lunges on steep terrain. This type of movement is the stuff of steep sport climbs and V-hard boulder problems.

Physiologically, your ability to move powerfully is a function of how fast your muscular motor units can be called into play and how well they are trained to fire in unison. Effective power training, then, must target the nervous system with fast, dynamic motions that are far different from the strength- and endurance-training exercises covered in chapter 7 and chapter 9, respectively.

Inherent to power training are high dynamic-force loads, which provide beneficial training stimuli but also threaten the joints and tendons of the fingers, arms, and shoulders. For this reason, many of the power-training exercises covered in this chapter are inappropriate for beginner or recently injured climbers, as well as anyone lacking the maturity and discipline to follow the training and rest guidelines. Furthermore, it's important to develop sufficient strength in the muscles that stabilize the shoulders and wrists (per chapter 5) before engaging in the most intense power-training exercises in this chapter.

One of the most basic and fundamental rules of effective power training is that each bout of exercise must be brief, so as to not cause breathlessness or even a minor pump. Power training is all about targeting the anaerobic alactic energy system, which fatigues within 6 to 12 seconds of near-maximum-intensity exercise. Therefore, any exercise lasting more than about 12 seconds per set will fail to train high-end power and instead target the anaerobic lactic energy system, which facilitates power-endurance (the subject of the next chapter).

Adequate rest between power exercises and workouts is another critical factor in determining the quality of your training and the results gained. To make a near-maximal effort with every power-training set, it's essential to rest at least 3 minutes between each bout of exercise—the exception is when training aerobic power, which demands shorter between-set rests of just 30 seconds to 1 minute. Similarly, adequate rest between workout days is important for recovery of the nervous system—as a rule, limit yourself to two pure power-training sessions per week. Chapter 11 will provide a framework for scheduling your workouts, and in most cases you'll want to train pure power and limit strength together.

One final point of emphasis from Coach Hörst before we cast off into a sea of power-training exercises: Constantly remind yourself that it's exercise quality, not quantity, that matters most in power training. Strive for maximum intensity and movement speed with each exercise, and then rest more than you think you need to between sets and exercises. Done right, a pure power (or limit strength, per chapter 7) workout is mostly about resting, not actual training, as you'll be resting at least 180 seconds for every 10 seconds of training time (a

Muscles Targeted	Power-Training Exercise	Page	Beginner	Intermediate	Advanced
Finger Flexors	One-Arm Traversing	147	X	X	X
	One-Arm Lunging	148		X	X
	Campus "Bumps"	149		X	X
	Campus Laddering (No Skips)	150		X	X
	Campus "Switch Hands"	152			X
	Campus Double Dynos on Small Rungs	153			X
	HIT System Pinch Hold Double Dynos	154			X
Arms & Torso	Power Pull-Ups (aka Chest-Bump Pull-Ups)	155		X	X
	Big-Move Boulder Problems	156	X	X	X
	Gym Rope Climbing	157		X	X
	Clap Pull-Ups	158			X
	Boulder Campusing (aka Monkey Business)	159			X
	Campus Board "Laddering" (with Skips)	160		X	X
	Campus Board Double Dynos on Large Rungs (with Skips)	161			X

rest-to-work ratio of at least 18:1)! So if you are getting pumped or extremely fatigued, you can be sure that you are not engaging in an effective high-end power-training routine.

This chapter is divided into two parts: (1) exercises for developing contact strength (aka "finger power") and (2) exercises for increasing power in the pulling muscles of the arms and back.

Contact Strength Exercises (aka "finger power")

Contact strength is your ability to quickly grab a hold and stick it—some people call this finger power, although the contraction is nearly isometric, unlike traditional expressions of muscular power. This trait is directly related to the speed at which you can recruit the forearm muscle's motor units and summon peak force, a capacity called "rate of force development" (see chapter 1, page 4).

While the maximum-strength exercises described in chapter 7 will yield some improvement in contact strength, the power-developing reactive-training exercises in this chapter emphasize rate of force production and movement speed, rather than absolute force production. Since fast, dynamic movements are fundamental to effective reactive training, the resistance used (training load) must be significantly less than in the maximum-strength exercises. For some climbers the resistance will need to be less than body weight (achieve by training "feet on") to allow for the rapid movement and turnover (change in direction) that's essential for effective reactive training. More advanced climbers with no recent history of finger, elbow, or shoulder injury can partake in the more difficult feet-off exercises that are generally classified as "campus training." If in doubt as to your readiness to engage in campus training exercises, err on the side of excessive prudence and begin with the tamer feet-on exercises (less than body weight).

Following are seven reactive-training exercises listed in order from least stressful (lowest force load and injury risk) to most severe (highest force and injury risk). Controlled one-arm traversing and one-arm lunging are the ideal icebreaker exercises for climbers wishing to add some reactive training to their routines, as each one-arm catch involves a mild shock loading of the forearm muscles. Contact strength gains achieved through this form of feet-on "reactive light" training are limited, however—beyond a certain point you will need to graduate to feet-off campus training, which produces a much higher shock load, to stimulate further gains. This progression into fully dynamic campus training must be gradual, over the course of months and years, and in low doses. Constantly remind yourself that it takes just a few sets of reactive training to impart the necessary stimuli for gains in contact strength. Resist the urge to do an excessive number of sets (more than five to ten), which, while fun and perhaps gratifying, provides little added training stimuli and increases injury risk.

One-Arm Traversing

One-arm traversing is a simple yet effective gateway exercise into reactive training. All you need is a vertical wall with lots of medium to large holds that will enable easy foot movement and quick hopscotching of your hand from hold to hold as you traverse the wall. Doing one-arm traverses isn't about doing hard moves or getting pumped—it should feel more like an interesting game than a workout.

1. Select a vertical section of an indoor wall with enough room to traverse 10 to 20 feet on closely spaced medium- to large-size handholds and solid foot placements.

2. Climb up onto the wall so that your feet are just a foot or two off the floor. Now remove one hand from the wall and hold it behind your back. Begin traversing with small, quick hops from one handhold to the next. Always advance your leading foot before moving your hand, in order to keep your center of gravity over your feet and maintain balance throughout.

3. Continue traversing for eight to twelve total hand moves, and then step off the wall.

4. After a brief rest, step back up onto the wall and traverse the opposite direction using your other hand.

5. Perform two or three one-arm traverses with each hand.

Safety note: It's important to perform small, controlled "hand hops" that allow you to catch the next hold with a slight bend in your elbow—this way your rotator cuff and scapular stabilizers will be engaged.

Leading with your feet, traverse with controlled single-hand lunges.

One-Arm Lunging

Once you are proficient at one-arm traversing on vertical walls, you can proceed to one-arm lunging at the base of a slightly overhanging wall. This exercise is also done "feet on," but the slightly steeper angle creates a more forceful catch. This extra stress will trigger higher rates of force production than one-arm traversing, thus making one-arm lunging a good transition into the feet-off campus training exercises that follow. You can do this exercise using the bottom two large holds on a campus board or two juggy holds at the base of a slightly overhanging section of climbing wall. Ideally you can set a few modular holds specifically for performing this exercise. Set two footholds about a foot off the ground, and then set two large, rounded holds that fit your hand nicely (open-hand grip), one in front of your face and the other about 10 to 15 inches above that. If training on a campus board, you'll need to lunge between the two lowest large holds on the board with your feet on the floor below the board (see photo).

1. Assume a balanced starting position with your weight evenly on both feet and your hands gripping the higher of the two holds you'll be lunging between.

2. Now let go with one hand and hold it by your side or behind your back. Begin with an inward pull with the engaged arm, and at the deadpoint (moment of quasi-weightlessness on that hand) let go and drop the hand down to catch the lower hold with a partially bent arm (important). The best cue for maintaining a properly engaged shoulder is to keep your chest pushed out throughout the exercise.

3. Absorb the downward energy of the "catch" and immediately recoil upward to quickly grab back onto the starting handhold. This makes one repetition.

4. Continue with brisk up-and-down lunging for six to ten total hand movements—total duration of exercise is 10 seconds or less.

5. After a brief rest, perform an identical set of one-arm lunging with the other hand.

6. Do two or three total sets with each arm, resting at least 3 minutes between sets.

Safety note: This exercise dynamically loads all components of the fingers and arms. Proceed with caution, and cease the exercise if you experience any sense of joint or tendon discomfort. Most important, never catch the rung or hold with a straight arm or hollowed chest.

1. Start from the higher handhold.
2. Drop down to catch the lower hold.
3. Lunge back to regain the starting hold.

Campus "Bumps"

As the name implies, this exercise involves bumping one hand up successive rungs while the other hand remains fixed on a low rung. Like most campus board exercises, you'll be using momentum to assist with the upward hand bumps—still, each rung "catch" will elicit a high rate of force development in the finger flexors, which is of course the training goal here.

1. Begin by hanging from a low rung with shoulders engaged (not shrugging) and arms just slightly bent.
2. Pull with both arms to begin the upward motion, then advance one hand up successive rungs— "bump, bump, bump"—as fast as possible.
3. As the active hand advances up the board, keep the opposite arm engaged and pulling down into a lower and lower lock-off position. This way you are training a one-arm lock-off with the lower arm, while the other hand is training contact strength—an exercise two-for!
4. Given a campus board with normal rung spacing, you'll likely be bumping the active hand just three or four times before you jump off and call it a set.
5. Do one set on each side and then rest 3 minutes before doing another pair of sets.
6. Initially, do just two or three sets on each side. Long term, you can progress to doing five to ten sets, if you are doing no additional campus training.
7. Increase difficulty by using smaller holds or adding a small amount of weight (ankle weights or belt) rather than skipping rungs or stretching for an out-of-reach rung (potentially injurious).

Safety note: Your highest bump hold must not be with a straight arm and shrugged shoulder—this is a critical distinction, as many shoulder injuries occur when individuals repeatedly campus with fully extended arms.

Bump one hand up successive rungs as you increasingly lock off with the low arm.

Campus Laddering

As the name implies, this exercise involves climbing in a hand-over-hand, ladderlike motion up the campus board with no aid from the feet. Unlike double dynos (described later), this laddering exercise uses controlled dynamic movements that are less likely to get you injured. Consequently, this is a better staple exercise for regular use by most climbers. An important distinction when ladder training: Using smaller holds and shorter reaches trains contact strength, whereas using larger holds and longer reaches trains pulling power and lock-off strength (covered later in this chapter). The focus here is on contact strength, so you should use the smallest-size holds that you can ladder (no rung skips) without slipping off partway through the exercise.

1. Hang with nearly straight arms from the bottom rung of the campus board. Your hands should be about shoulder width or slightly less apart.

2. Striving for fluid motion, briskly climb hand-over-hand up the campus board using alternating rungs for your left and right hands. Maintain engaged shoulders throughout the ascent—think about keeping your chest pressed outward.

3. Ascend the board's first eight to ten rungs as fast as possible and, upon reaching the top, jump off. End your ascent before reaching the top if you stall out or need to pause midway up the board.

4. Rest for 3 minutes before doing another set.

5. Begin by doing just three sets, but build toward a maximum of ten sets.

6. Increase difficulty by using smaller rungs or adding 5 to 10 pounds around your waist rather than skipping rungs.

Training tip: Think of this exercise as an alactic sprint—laddering eight to ten rungs should take just 4 to 8 seconds. Assuming a padded floor, you should jump off from atop the board rather than descending hand-over-hand—this extra time spent descending the board will turn this into a power-endurance exercise, which is not the goal here.

Campus laddering on small rungs. Avoid grabbing rungs with straight arms and/or lax shoulders.

Tips for Safe and Effective Campusing Training

Developed in the late 1980s by Wolfgang Güllich at the Campus Center in Nuremberg, Germany, campus training is the gold standard for training upper-body power and contact strength for climbing. The campus board is a unique training platform that allows for various reactive-training and quasi-plyometric exercises that train recruitment and rate of force development in the finger and arm flexors. This type of dynamic training is a real boon for high-end sport climbers and boulderers.

While feet-off "campusing" is the most common method of training among elite climbers, feet-on campus training with the toes resting on small holds or wooden strips is the preferred method for more intermediate climbers wanting to dabble on the campus board. An ideal campus board rig will include at least three different-size strips (roughly 20mm, 40mm, and 60mm "jug" or open-hand sloper) and foot strips at a few different heights under the board.

Unfortunately, the campus board is widely misused, both by individuals not strong or experienced enough for the high dynamic loads and by some elites who overutilize this training platform. No one with less than two years climbing experience should use a campus board without use of footholds—their tendon strength is unlikely to be ready to carry the load. Even elite climbers should limit campus training to less than 10 percent of total training time. Finally, anyone wanting to campus train should first engage in several months of scapular stabilizer and rotator cuff training (see chapter 5) and continue with this training indefinitely. Here are several more guidelines for safe and effective use of the campus board.

- Engage in campus training only if you are an advanced-intermediate (leading 5.11 or bouldering V5) to elite climber with no recent history of finger or arm injury. Favor feet-on exercises and feet-off laddering and bumps. The highly stressful double-dyno exercise must be reserved for only highly trained and advanced (5.13/V8) climbers.

- Warm up thoroughly. Spend at least one-half hour performing various warm-up activities and bouldering to fully warm the finger, arm, shoulder, and back muscles.

- Use only the open-hand and open-crimp grips when doing feet-off campusing.

- Never engage a rung with a completely straight arm and shrugged shoulder—this will wreck your shoulders in short order! Upward grabs should always be done with a slight elbow bend and properly positioned scapula (keep your chest pressed out and you're likely doing it right).

- Emphasize quality over quantity—it's better to do a few perfectly executed explosive sets rather than many reckless sets with poor technique.

- Do not campus train while in a state of high fatigue or if you have any doubts about the health of your fingers, arms, or shoulders.

- Immediately terminate your campus training at the first sensation of pain in your fingers, elbows, or shoulders (common among people who campus with poor technique and weak scapular stabilizers).

- Campus no more than twice per week, and cycle on and off campusing every couple of weeks.

- Youth climbers should abstain from campus training, especially during peak growth velocity (ages thirteen to sixteen) when growth plates are most easily injured.

Campus "Switch Hands"

Whereas the previous campus training exercises all involved advancing one hand while the other hand remained engaged on a rung for support, the "switch hands" exercise escalates to moving both hands simultaneously, albeit for just a small distance of about 10 inches. Still, this dynamic movement demands an even higher rapid rate of force development in the finger flexors to successfully re-grasp the rungs after the double release move. The switch hands exercise, therefore, is a good segue toward eventually performing the most difficult double-dynos exercise (page 153). Do this exercise using medium- to large-size rungs (not slopers) and an open-hand grip.

1. Begin with your hands on successive rungs, then tighten down your scapula (cue: *chest out!*) and bend your arms slightly to gain a good starting position before lifting your feet off the floor.

2. Initiate the exercise with a short but sharp pull—only a few inches—to create upward momentum, and then, at the deadpoint, quickly switch hands to the opposite rungs. You'll latch back onto the rungs as your center of mass begins to descend, so you'll need to momentarily absorb this energy with your pulling muscles before initiating the next upward pull and hand switch.

3. Continue switching hands as fast as possible, for up to ten or twelve total hand switches.

4. Rest for 3 minutes before doing another set.

5. Begin by doing just two sets per workout; advanced climbers can do up to five sets.

Training tip: There's a little bit of timing involved in doing this correctly, but if you're strong enough to rightfully employ this exercise you'll quickly acquire the skill and be able to do about ten to twelve successive switches in only about 5 seconds. This is a bang-bang exercise that, if done correctly, involves very little upward and downward movement of the torso. The exercise itself is pure anaerobic (alactic) power.

Simultaneously switch hands between adjacent rungs.

Campus Double Dynos on Small Rungs

The double-dyno exercise is the pinnacle of campus training with its double-handed, fully airborne flight between rungs. Done on smaller rungs and without skipping (rungs), this exercise focuses more on finger flexor recruitment, whereas using large rungs and greater flight distance (skipping rungs) equally trains finger and pull-muscle power. The focus now is on developing finger contact strength via more synchronous motor unit recruitment and neural disinhibition, so the protocol here is smaller rungs and little or no rung skipping.

Every climber must acknowledge, however, the extremely stressful and potentially injurious nature of this exercise. Are your fingers tendons, rotator cuff, and scapular stabilizers ready for this level of stress? It's my belief that the answer is "no" for over 95 percent of climbers. I discourage use of this exercise if you've been climbing less than four years, don't climb 5.13 or V8, can't do at least five hypergravity pull-ups with one-third of your body weight added, and can't easily ladder up and down the campus board in a 1-3-5-7-7-5-3-1 sequence.

1. Begin by hanging from one of the middle rungs, with slightly flexed arms and engaged shoulders.

2. Simultaneously let go with both hands and drop to catch the next lower rung with flexed arms, engaged shoulders, and chest out.

3. After a brief amortization phase of energy absorption in the pull muscles, explode upward with both hands to catch the starting rung. This is one full repetition, but don't stop!

4. Without hesitation, drop down to again catch the next lower rung, and again explode back up to the starting rung.

5. Continue for three to five repetitions (six to ten total hand moves), and then dismount. The turnaround time must be as fast as possible—ideally less than one-half second—and the total exercise time is less than 10 seconds.

6. Do two to five sets with at least 3 minutes rest in between.

7. Use this exercise no more than twice per week.

Safety notes: End the exercise prematurely rather than risk a failed downward catch (but have a bouldering pad in place just in case). Terminate your campus training at the first sign of pain in your fingers, arms, or shoulders. Better safe than sorry!

Training tip: You can make this exercise slightly easier by beginning on a low rung and double dynoing up four to eight successive rungs without any drop-downs.

No-skip double dynos on small rungs.

HIT System Pinch Hold Double Dynos

If you have access to a HIT Strip System, you can use the large juggy pinch holds to train pinch-grip contact strength. This novel exercise will really amp your pinch strength!

1. Begin with your hands pinching the lowest pair of HIT Pinches.

2. Pull hard with both arms and simultaneously advance both hands to grip the next pair of HIT Pinch holds.

3. Immediately pull hard again to advance both hands to the next and then the next set of HIT Pinches. Strive to maintain upward momentum from one movement to the next.

4. Upon reaching the top pair of pinch holds (usually the fourth), jump down and immediately return to the first pair of HIT Pinches.

5. Without taking any rest, do a second double-dyno ascent of the HIT Pinch holds. Completing two laps consists of six total double-hand movements—this makes for one set.

6. Do two or three sets with at least 3 minutes rest in between.

*Use the **HIT System Pinch** holds to train rate of force development in the pinch-grip muscles.*

Pull-Muscle Power-Training Exercises

The previous chapter presented several exercises for developing limit strength in the pulling muscles, and now in this chapter you're learning how to recruit those muscles more powerfully. While essential for long-term progress into the higher grades, power training is not something you should rush into or do in high volume. Sadly, it's not uncommon for a highly enthusiastic and motivated climber to get injured due to inappropriate use of power-oriented exercises. As explained earlier, it's essential to develop stability before strength, and strength before power—so if you aren't already training to strengthen your rotator cuff, scapular stabilizers,

and antagonist muscles, please hold off on using the following power-training exercises. Dedicate at least two months to this crucial preparatory training before moving on to intensive training of limit strength (chapter 7) and power.

When you are physically ready to add some pull-muscle power training to your program, begin with a few sets of power pull-ups, big-move bouldering, and gym rope climbing—these are the first three exercises presented below, because they are good icebreaker exercises. While at first you will want to add just a few sets of power training to your routine, long-term gains in high-end power (for higher-end climbing!) will demand a greater commitment to training limit strength and power. As you progress into the realm of an advanced climber (breaking into 5.13s and V8s), you will want to occasionally couple your strength- and power-training exercises into a "complex." A few examples of effective training complexes are (1) a set of weighted pull-ups followed by a set of power pull-ups, (2) a set of hypergravity bouldering followed by a set of campus laddering, and (3) a set of weighted fingerboard hangs followed by a set of campus double dynos. Always perform your training complex in the order of strength exercise first and power exercise second—do one right after the other with little rest in between (less than 1 minute).

Power Pull-Ups (aka Chest-Bump Pull-Ups)

One of my favorite exercises! While not too different from a regular pull-up, the power pull-up—if done correctly—is actually much harder. What makes the power pull-up unique (and difficult) is the power needed to accelerate your body upward so that there's enough momentum to carry your upper chest into the bar. In doing a regular pull-up, your body is typically decelerating as you near the top position, but with the power pull-up your goal is to accelerate into the bar. Therefore, each power pull-up ends with a forceful chest bump into the bar—no chest bump, no power pull-up!

1. Grip the pull-up bar palms-away and hands about shoulder width apart.

2. Begin each repetition with a slight bend in your arms, and the thought of trying to bend the bar—this will fully recruit your rotator cuff and scapular stabilizers.

3. Now pull up explosively and with the intention of bringing the bar down to meet the pectoral muscles of your chest. Really strong climbers (see photo) will pull the bar down to touch their upper abs!

4. As you near the top of the pull-up, squeeze your shoulder blades together and lean your head back slightly—this will help push your chest up into the bar.

5. Lower back to the starting position at a more moderate speed and stop short of going into a dead hang. Immediately begin the next repetition.

6. Continue for a total of five to ten (hard) repetitions. Again, a rep does not count if your chest doesn't forcefully contact the bar.

7. Do one to three sets, always resting for at least 3 minutes between sets.

Training tip: While you may initially only be able to pull the bar down to touch your upper chest, make it your long-term goal to pull the bar lower—to touch your lower pectoral muscles and, ultimately, your upper abs. This training progression will develop awesome pulling power!

Pull up as fast as possible in order to touch your chest or upper abs to the bar.

Big-Move Boulder Problems

If you are an avid boulderer, then you are likely already using this training strategy. The goal is to climb several four- to eight-move boulder problems that involve numerous powerful movements between relatively good holds. The ideal boulder will feature mainly positive medium- to large-size holds that will not challenge your grip strength, and lengthy reaches that demand tight lock-offs, powerful arm movements, and an occasional all-out dynamic move or lunge. When you find the right route, try to send it five times with about a 3-minute rest between ascents. Strive to refine your movement and improve climbing economy with each successive ascent—this way, you'll learn to climb more accurately and effectively through strenuous movements, despite growing fatigue. If you own a home wall, consider setting a few moderately difficult, big-move boulder problems that you can climb a few times each and every workout.

Ascend nontechnical problems that involve several large powerful movements. These do not have to be "official" (taped) problems—create your own!

Gym Rope Climbing

Gym rope climbing is one of the very best ways to develop awesome upper-body power, and so any serious climber would be wise to incorporate some arm-only gym rope climbing into their power-training program. Think of this exercise as campusing up a 1.5-inch-thick gym rope! Since gripping a thick gym rope is a rather simple task, this exercise singles out the large pulling muscles even better than most campus board exercises. Furthermore, many climbers can generate a higher rate of ascent in climbing a gym rope (versus climbing a campus board), and, therefore, the power output is greater—just what you want for taking your power to the next level!

"Sprinting" up the gym rope at the Hörst home!

1. After a lengthy warm-up of pull-ups and mild upper-body stretching, begin from either a standing or sit-down (harder) position and grip the rope with both arms near full extension, but not completely straight.

2. Begin with an explosive two-arm pull, and then continue upward as fast as possible using quick, crisp hand-over-hand movements. The goal is to maintain smooth, steady upward movement for the duration of the ascent, although it may take some time to develop the necessary arm strength and power.

3. Upon reaching the top, slowly lower down with controlled arm-over-arm movements—do not drop down in a fast, jerky manner that will shock-load the elbows and shoulders.

4. Perform three to eight (an elite alactic-power workout) total laps on the rope, always taking at least a 3-minute rest between ascents. Optimal adaptations (and gains) to power training come from high-quality, full-speed efforts—think of each ascent as a sprint! Therefore, it's better to do four full-speed sprint ascents, rather than eight low-powered "jogs" up the rope.

Training tips: Think about pulling the engaged hand down to meet your upper chest and, when reaching up, grab the rope with your arm less than fully extended (an elbow angle of between 120 and 150 degrees). *Safety note:* Always have a bouldering pad beneath the gym rope. If you sense a loss of control, in ascending or descending, immediately clamp down on the rope with your feet rather than risk falling.

Clap Pull-Ups

Similar to the power pull-up (described previously), the clap pull-up requires you to accelerate into the top position of a pull-up, but in this case you must pull so fast as to create enough elevation to clap your hands together above the bar. This is a very difficult exercise, so expect it to take time to develop the power and timing to release the bar and clap near the deadpoint. Here's a good learning progression.

1. Grip the bar palms-away with hands a bit less than shoulder width apart.

2. Begin just like the power pull-up by accelerating into the bar, but rather than touching your chest to the bar, instead release the bar for an instant as you approach the deadpoint. Immediately re-grab the bar without moving your hands at the top of each pull-up.

3. Next, try to release the bar and touch index fingers together before re-grabbing the bar. It helps to lean your head and shoulders back slightly.

4. With practice you'll eventually develop the strength and timing (and confidence!) to clap your hands at the top of each pull-up.

5. Strive for sets of three to six repetitions.

6. Do two or three sets with a rest of at least 3 minutes in between.

Accelerate into the top of a pull-up so that you can clap hands at the deadpoint.

Boulder Campusing (aka Monkey Business)

Boulder campusing is a popular indoor training exercise among advanced climbers—it's also a heck of a lot of fun if you're strong enough to do it right! The goal is to ascend a section of overhanging wall by simply climbing hand-over-hand with no aid from the feet. This exercise is similar to campus board laddering, and the same injury warnings apply: Boulder campusing with straight arms and shrugged shoulders will get you injured, likely sooner than later.

1. Select three- to eight-move routes with medium- to large-size holds that you can engage with an open-hand grip. The perfect route would be void of small or tweaky holds, awkward arm positions, and reaches that are so long you can't help but use (dangerous) straight-arm positions.

2. When you find a boulder with the perfect hold combination, do it three to five times with about a 3-minute rest between ascents.

3. After doing the first boulder campusing route a few times, rest for 5 minutes while you search for another good route to monkey around on.

4. Build up to doing a maximum of ten sets (aggregate of all ascents and routes).

Safety notes: Use of good campusing technique is essential—your reaching arm must engage each hold with some observable bend in the elbow. Have a friend shoot a short video of your boulder campusing to self-assess the quality of your technique. Favor boulders with fewer moves and short reaches to ensure use of good campusing technique.

Campus laddering up juggy holds on a bouldering wall is an excellent pull-muscle power-training exercise.

Campus Board "Laddering"

As presented earlier in this chapter, campus laddering up small holds and without rung skips is an effective method of training contact strength. In the context of training pulling power, however, the best approach is to use larger rungs and longer, more powerful pulls. Most campus boards have at least three different-size rungs (you want to use the largest), with each stack numbered from 1 to 8, and perhaps higher. The most basic ladder sequence is 1–3–5–7, beginning with both hands on rung #1 and ending with both hands on rung #7. A more advanced ladder sequence is 1-4-7, although this isn't something you should be in a rush to train. If you regularly fail in attempting the 1-4-7 sequence—or if you engage the #4 or #7 rungs with fully extended arms—then you simply aren't strong enough to do this exercise. Here are a few tips to proper campus laddering.

- Always engage the rungs with open-hand or open-crimp grips. No full crimping!

- Practice gripping the rungs with a slight inward hand rotation (supination)—this helps get a bit more of your pinky finger onto the rung.

- With each hand-pulling movement, think about screwing your arm (supination) into the shoulder socket—this better engages the rotator cuff.

- To protect your shoulders, be sure that the reaching hand always engages the rung with a slight bend in the elbow and strive to keep your chest pressed out throughout the laddering process.

- As with all power-training exercises, it's essential to move as fast as possible. In the case of a 1-3-5-7 ladder sequence, it should take but a few seconds to make the ascent. Think of this exercise as a sprint—if you need to pause or break sequence, then you're either too tired or too weak to be doing this exercise.

- Begin by doing just three sets per workout, but build toward a maximum of ten sets over months and years.

- Rest at least 3 minutes between sets, so that you can make a quality effort with each alactic sprint up the board.

Training tip: Elite climbers can train aerobic power (for enhanced recovery ability) by decreasing the rest interval to just 30 to 60 seconds between sets.

Safety note: Regularly engaging campus rungs with a fully extended arm and an elevated (shrugged) shoulder will quickly lead to shoulder pain and, perhaps, injury. Please heed my advice on this—I can name more than a few climbers who have wrecked their shoulders due to overuse and misuse of a campus board. There's no way that the bragging rights of having done a 1-4-7 sequence is worth going under the knife and losing a year of climbing!

Using large rungs, ladder up the board skipping as many rungs as possible.

Campus Board Double Dynos on Large Rungs

The double-dyno exercise, performed on small rungs, was described earlier in this chapter as an advanced finger-training method for developing contact strength. When done using larger rungs and greater flight distance (skipping rungs) the double dyno trains pull-muscle power in addition to contact strength. These are the two most popular versions of this difficult exercise.

Double-Dyno Ascent: Beginning from the bottom rung, pull hard with both hands and simultaneously advance them up to grab the next higher rung. Upon engaging the rung, immediately pull again to advance both hands simultaneously to the next rung. Continue ascending the stack, striving to maintain upward momentum from one movement to the next—this is hard, but it will come with practice. Dismount the board when you reach the top or hit a stall point partway up the board. Do three to five sets with 3 minutes rest in between. Make the exercise harder by skipping rungs (1-3-5-7).

Double-Dyno Up-Downs: This is the paramount of campus training, both in terms of the potential for neural adaptations and the potential for injuring a finger tendon or pulley. Proceed with caution! Begin hanging from one of the middle rungs (say #3), with slightly flexed arms and engaged shoulders. Simultaneously let go with both hands and drop to catch the next lower rung with flexed arms and engaged shoulders. After a brief amortization phase of energy absorption in the pull muscles, explode upward with both hands to

Double dyno between large rungs, skipping one or two rungs if possible.

catch one rung above the starting rung. This is one full repetition, but don't stop! Without hesitation, drop down again to catch the next lower rung, and again explode back upward to catch two rungs higher. Continue for three or four repetitions. The sequence of rungs engaged, as described above, is: 3-2-4-3-5-4-6-5-7. An easier double-dyno sequence is 3-2-3-2-3-2-3, whereas a more advanced sequence is 3-2-4-2-4-2-4-2-4. Do one to five (elite) sets with at least a 3-minute rest between each set.

Training tip: As with all power-training exercises, high-speed and high-quality movements are paramount to getting the most out of your double-dyno training. The turnaround time in "rebounding" off the low rung must be less than one-half second—if you have trouble catching the low rung or need to pause to gather yourself between movements, then you're either using too small of a rung or you're too tired (or weak) to be doing the exercise.

Cameron Hörst crushing The Madness
(5.13c), Red River Gorge, Kentucky.
ERIC HÖRST

CHAPTER 9

Strength/Power-Endurance Training Exercises

The anaerobic lactic energy system—the primary energy system for 20-second to 2-minute bursts of strength/power-endurance—is the least trainable of the three energy systems. Still, this vital energy system must be trained specifically, especially in the final weeks before a competition or period of performance climbing.

The two previous chapters revealed dozens of exercises for developing the limit strength and bursts of high-end power needed to pull through a single maximum climbing move or short crux sequence. In this chapter you'll learn to train for the grip-strength endurance and power-endurance needed to prevail through a longer, sustained, near-maximal sequence on a hard boulder problem or roped climb.

The ability to sustain high power output for 30 seconds to 2 minutes is largely a function of your anaerobic capacity. More physiologically complex, however, is the capability to prevail through many intermittent bursts of high power output, which depends on the aggregate development of anaerobic capacity and aerobic power (which facilitates micro recovery between brief bursts of power). Most climbers refer to the above-mentioned traits as "power-endurance"—an acceptable term for the ability to sustain powerful locomotion with the arms, although strength-endurance is a better term in reference to the fatigue resistance of the finger flexors. Anyway, the burning muscle pump is the hallmark of the anaerobic lactic (glycolytic) energy system being pushed to near its limit, and, of course,

many boulder and redpoint attempts fail when the forearm muscles "pump out" and fail.

Consequently, many climbers focus the bulk of their training efforts on increasing strength-endurance (of the fingers) and power-endurance (of the pulling muscles). While a few weeks of such anaerobic-capacity training will often bring favorable adaptations and some noticeable gains on the rock, many climbers train this energy system too frequently and too long without variation. It's interesting to note that climbing (or training) to the point of a maximal pump more than about two or three days per week over the long term often leads to decreasing endurance, likely due to the damage that chronic acidosis does to mitochondria function and related enzymes. If you have ever engaged in high-volume strength/power-endurance training for weeks on end, only to discover that you're pumping out even faster on the rock, you now know why. So what's the best strategy for training anaerobic capacity?

In chapter 1 I presented a primer on the three energy systems that together power all climbing movements. Interestingly, the anaerobic lactic energy system—the primary energy system for 20-second to 2-minute bursts of strength/power-endurance—is the least trainable of the three energy systems. Making significant year-over-year gains in anaerobic capacity, then, requires dedicated limit strength and pure power training as well as regular exercise and climbing to increase aerobic power and capacity. (As explained in chapter 1, increasing anaerobic and aerobic power will have a strong

Muscles Targeted		Power/Strength-Endurance Exercise	Page	Beginner	Intermediate	Advanced
Fingers (strength-endurance)		Short-Duration Fingerboard Repeaters	165	X	X	X
		Long-Duration Fingerboard Repeaters	166		X	X
		Bouldering 4x4s	167	X	X	X
		Hypergravity Isolation Training—Strength-Endurance Protocol	168		X	X
		System Wall Repeaters	170		X	X
		Small-Rung Ladder Laps (No Skips)	170		X	X
Arms & Torso (power-endurance)		Pull-Up Intervals	172	X	X	X
		Power Pull-Up Intervals (Chest-Bump Pull-Ups)	173		X	X
		Frenchies	174		X	X
		Square Dance	175		X	X
		Big-Holds, Big-Move 4x4s	176	X	X	X
		Campus Ladder Laps on Big Holds	177		X	X
		Gym Rope Intervals	179			X
		Route Intervals	179	X	X	X

positive influence on your anaerobic capacity.) The best training approach, then, is to partake frequently in anaerobic alactic exercise (see chapters 7 and 8) and local aerobic energy system exercise (per chapter 10), and then to perform a two- to four-week mesocycle of pumpy anaerobic lactic strength/power-endurance training prior to a climbing road trip or competition. This approach will boost all three energy systems, prevent overtraining, and provide you with the important anaerobic lactic system adaptations (cellular buffering and increased anaerobic enzymes) in the final weeks before your event.

All the exercises in this chapter are designed to target the anaerobic lactic energy system, so get ready to become highly pumped and fatigued. The first section presents exercises for developing strength-endurance in the finger flexor muscles, while the second section details exercises to train power-endurance in the large pulling muscles.

Strength-Endurance Finger Training Exercises

Endurance local to the forearm muscles is what enables you to hang on through many hard moves in a row. Your ability to persevere through a long sequence of strenuous moves, despite a growing forearm pump, is a function of the mind and body's tolerance to the fatiguing effects of cellular acidosis (intracellular buffer capacity), intercellular transport of metabolic by-products such as lactate and H+ ions, and the rate at which the working muscles can reoxygenate during brief rest intervals. The six upcoming exercises will all compel the above-mentioned adaptations—noticeable improvements will come in just two to four weeks of dedicated strength-endurance training.

Short-Duration Fingerboard Repeaters

Repeaters are the standard fingerboard exercise for developing strength-endurance and the ability to climb onward despite a building pump. There are many different repeater protocols in the public domain, but below I will outline what I feel are the three most effective approaches. First, I'll present two short-duration repeater protocols as detailed in tables 9.1 and 9.2.

5-Second Protocol: The beauty of this repeater protocol is that it closely simulates how we climb on the rock with brief, intermittent periods of forearm muscle contraction and relaxation. The brief rest intervals allow blood flow to reoxygenate the working muscles and remove metabolic by-products, so that you can endure for a minute or two (or longer). Begin with the Level 1 protocol, which alternates between 5-second hangs and 10-second rest. One set is composed of twelve consecutive intervals (this will take exactly 3 minutes), after which you'll take a 1-minute rest. Do three to five total sets. In future workouts, increase difficulty by using smaller holds or by advancing to the Level 2 protocol.

10-Second Protocol: This protocol has four levels of difficulty, with each successive level providing short rest intervals between the six hangs that comprise each set. Each series of six hangs is followed by a 1-minute rest, after which you commence with the next set of six repeaters. Do up to five sets of six hangs. If doing these five sets at the Level 1 protocol isn't difficult, then use smaller holds or advance to the Level 2 protocol for the next workout. If you eventually come to find Level 4 training less than difficult, then you can add a 10-pound (or more) weight belt.

Training tip: An important distinction with regard to the grips you will train here: Research has determined that two primary muscles used in gripping the rock, the flexor digitorum profundus (FDP) and the flexor digitorum superficialis (FDS), contribute to force generation in crimp gripping at a ratio of 3:1, respectively. When open-hand gripping, however, force generation from these two muscle groups comes at nearly a 1:1 ratio. Given this knowledge, you can understand the importance of training both the half-crimp and open-hand grips—a good way to do this is to simply alternate between half-crimp and open-hand grips with each successive set.

Table 9.1 Short-Duration Repeaters—"5-Second" Protocol

Difficulty Level	Duration Hang/Rest (secs.)	Number of Hangs per Set	Number of Sets	Rest Between Sets
Level 1	5/10	12	3–5	1 min.
Level 2	5/5	18	3–5	1 min.

Table 9.2 Short-Duration Repeaters—"10-Second" Protocol

Difficulty Level	Duration Hang/Rest (secs.)	Number of Hangs per Set	Number of Sets	Rest Between Sets
Level 1	10/30	6	3–5	1 min.
Level 2	10/20	6	3–5	1 min.
Level 3	10/10	6	3–5	1 min.
Level 4	10/5	6	3–5	1 min.

Long-Duration Fingerboard Repeaters

Long-duration repeaters are a bit less specific to how we generally climb, although they may roughly simulate the longer-duration forearm contractions common to shaking out at a mid-climb rest position. This point aside, the extraordinary benefits of long-duration repeaters are first, that longer-sustained contractions occlude blood flow—this ischemia results in an increasingly hypoxic and acidic cellular environment. Then, during the rest periods, forceful reperfusion (restoration of blood flow) develops throughout the forearm flexor muscles, as you recognize the "pump" feeling develop. This cycle of ischemia and reperfusion is an apparent stimulus for beneficial adaptations, although the mechanisms responsible are not fully understood.

The Zlagboard and its training app directing a repeater workout. W W W . Z L A G B O A R D U S A . C O M

1. Using a medium- to large-size four-finger edge hold (about 20–50 mm, or ¾ to 2 inches in depth), begin training with the Level 1 protocol.

2. The first set of four hang-rest intervals will take exactly 4 minutes, after which you'll rest for 1 minute (see figure 9.3).

3. If you find that Level 1 is not difficult, advance to Level 2 for the remainder of the sets.

4. For future workouts increase difficulty by advancing to Levels 3 and 4 (really hard!) rather than using smaller holds.

Safety note: Good fingerboard technique is essential for repeater training—maintain engaged shoulders throughout each set, and end a hang early if you sense your shoulders beginning to loosen and shrug significantly upward.

Table 9.3 Long-Duration Repeaters

Difficulty Level	Duration Hang/Rest (secs.)	Number of Hangs per Set	Number of Sets	Rest Between Sets
Level 1	30/30	4	3–5	1 min.
Level 2	30/15	4	3–5	1 min.
Level 3	60/30	4	3–5	1 min.
Level 4	60/15	4	3–5	1 min.

Bouldering 4x4s

The bouldering 4x4 is a common indoor climbing method of training strength-endurance in the finger flexors and power-endurance in the larger pulling muscles of the arms and torso. Physiologically, 4x4s are kind of a climber's equivalent of "gassers" sprint training performed by speed-endurance athletes, such as soccer, hockey, and football players. This increasingly difficult workout trains both anaerobic capacity and aerobic power, if you follow the protocol outlined below. The short recovery periods are just as important as the brief spells of bouldering—so use a timing app or stopwatch to get it right.

There are many different ways of doing 4x4s, but here is the most straightforward and my personal favorite—and it's a great protocol to do with a training partner. The 4x4 involves doing four ascents (each) of four different boulder problems. Selecting the right problems is a bit tricky, as you want each to be hard enough to push you but not so hard you'll fail (except, perhaps, on the fourth pass). Obviously, you'll need to choose problems a few grades below your maximum level—for example, if your current (this season) hardest boulder ascent is a V9, then you should select problems in the V4 to V6 range for your 4x4s. For the purpose of finger strength-endurance training, select boulders with smallish holds, but avoid any big stopper reaches. Each ascent should take 30 seconds or less, so don't pick long and involved problems or any that require stopping to rest.

1. Climb the first boulder problem—this should take no more than 30 seconds. Now rest for the remainder of the first minute. Have a training partner time your climbs and rests per table 9.4.

2. Do a second, third, and fourth lap on the first boulder problem using the exact same climb-rest scheme.

3. Upon completing the fourth ascent (actually, at the end of the fourth full minute), take 4 minutes of complete rest—if you're training with a partner, you can now time her set of four climbs.

4. Next, repeat this process on the second of your four chosen boulder problems. Again, you have one full minute of climb-rest time per lap, after which you get 4 minutes of rest (while your partner does her second set of four ascents).

5. Repeat with the third and fourth boulder problems. All totaled this 4x4 protocol takes about 30 minutes.

Table 9.4 Bouldering 4x4 Protocol

4x4 training is best done with a partner. Spot and encourage each other to push harder and stay with protocol!

	Boulder 1		Boulder 2		Boulder 3		Boulder 4	
	Climb	Rest	Climb	Rest	Climb	Rest	Climb	Rest
Ascent 1	~30 secs.	~30 secs.	~30 secs.	~30 secs.	~30 secs.	~30 secs.	~30 secs.	~30 secs.
Ascent 2	~30 secs.	~30 secs.	~30 secs.	~30 secs.	~30 secs.	~30 secs.	~30 secs.	~30 secs.
Ascent 3	~30 secs.	~30 secs.	~30 secs.	~30 secs.	~30 secs.	~30 secs.	~30 secs.	~30 secs.
Ascent 4	~30 secs.	~30 secs.	~30 secs.	~30 secs.	~30 secs.	~30 secs.	~30 secs.	~30 secs.
Rest	4 mins.		4 mins.		4 mins.		4 mins.	

Hypergravity Isolation Training—Strength-Endurance Protocol

While the movement is the same as described in the HIT System Maximum-Strength Protocol (chapter 7, page 128), here you will be using lighter weights (or just body weight) and climbing for a much longer duration to train strength/power-endurance (anaerobic capacity). The acceptable extremes for duration of each set are 20 seconds and 2 minutes, although I believe that 30 to 90 seconds is ideal (see table 9.5). Consider taping your fingers (Figure-8 method) for skin protection so that you can push hard throughout each set, rather than needing to terminate early due to skin pain. See the "HIT System Training Tips" sidebar for additional guidelines.

Strength/power-endurance training of half-crimp grip pulls on the HIT System.

Table 9.5 HIT System—Strength-Endurance Protocol

Grip Position	Weight Used HIT "Novice"	Weight Used HIT "Advanced"	Set Duration (reps/set)	Sets	Rest Between Sets
Pinch	None	5 lb.	20–40 secs.	1–3	3 mins.
2-Finger "3rd Team"	None	5 lb.	20–40 secs.	1–3	3 mins.
2-Finger "2nd Team"	None	10 lb.	30–60 secs.	1–3	3 mins.
2-Finger "1st Team"	None	10 lb.	30–60 secs.	1–3	3 mins.
Half Crimp	None	20 lb.	45–90 secs.	1–3	3 mins.
Open Hand	None	20 lb.	45–90 secs.	1–3	3 mins.

*Weights are approximations for a 160-pound climber. Use similar percentages of your body weight.

HIT System Training Tips

In the mid-1990s I set out to develop a climbing-specific method for training functional strength in the important finger and arm flexor muscles, as well as the vital muscles of the shoulders and core. Much experimentation with equipment designs and training protocols led to what I call Hyper-gravity Isolation Training (HIT). While similar to the more variable System Wall training (page 142 in chapter 7), HIT workouts are highly focused on training specific grip positions while pulling and twisting up a severely overhanging wall. Since I first promoted this exciting training method in my book *How to Climb 5.12* in 1997, HIT Strip workouts have been utilized by thousands of climbers around the world. The effectiveness of HIT (not to be confused with the popular weight lifters' "HIT workout") is a result of its fulfillment of the four fundamental requisites for training grip strength detailed on pages 120–121 in chapter 7.

The adjacent photo depicts me training on the third-generation HIT Strips and HIT Pinches (available at www.Nicros.com), a unique platform I developed for optimal HIT workouts. Each HIT Strip possesses identical crimp edges and two-finger pockets that are ideal for laddering up and down until failure, although in lieu of the HIT Strips you can also arrange pairs of identical crimp, pocket, and pinch holds to train on. The ideal wall angle for HIT is 45 to 55 degrees past vertical. Weight added around the waist is increased or decreased to produce near failure of the finger flexors in the required amount of time—12 seconds if using the HIT maximum-strength protocol (see chapter 7) and 30 to 90 seconds when using the HIT strength/power-endurance protocol described in this chapter. Here are a few more tips for effective HIT Strip training.

Two-finger pocket training on the HIT Strip System by Nicros, Inc.

- Use a snug-fitting weight belt(s) or a weight vest, and adjust the weight for each grip position. Record weights used in a training notebook.

- Climb briskly and without hesitation—no stopping or chalking mid-set. Always step off the wall as opposed to risking an uncontrolled fall while climbing with added weight.

- Climb with normal foot movements and body turns. Small- to medium-size footholds are best, because too much thought on footwork will slow you down.

- Rest breaks between sets must be exactly 2 or 3 minutes; more advanced climbers should use the former. Use a stopwatch and stick to the planned order and schedule of exercises.

- Keep a training notebook in which you log each set, weight added, the number of reps (hand moves) performed, and the length of rest intervals. This way you'll always know what weight you need for a given set, and you can quantify and track your gains in finger strength!

- Tape your fingers using the Figure-8 method (page 171) to reduce skin pain, especially when training with high weight loads.

- Visit www.TrainingForClimbing.com for more information on building a dedicated HIT System Wall.

System Wall Repeaters

A System Wall is a specialized training platform with a large assortment of differing holds organized so that each half of the wall is a mirror image of the other. System Walls typically overhang anywhere from 20 to 45 degrees past vertical, and they are often only 6 to 8 feet wide and 9 to, at most, 15 feet high. Common uses of a System Wall include working undercling arm strength and reaches, one-arm lock-offs and hand bumping, deadpoint moves, compression moves, and twist-lock moves, among many other possibilities. A well-outfitted System Wall with dozens of different holds can offer a really good targeted workout of the forearm (gripping) muscles, the larger pulling muscles of the arms and torso, and the many core muscles of the torso.

In terms of training strength-endurance of the forearm flexors (and power-endurance of the pulling muscles), you'll want to use a protocol very similar to the HIT System strength-endurance protocol outlined in table 9.5. Initially it will take a little experimentation, but the goal is to develop four to six different "theme repeaters" that you can climb up and down through—using identical left and right hand/arm positions—for between 30 and 60 seconds without stopping. Since System Walls are short, you'll likely need to lap up and down through the sequence a few times to reach the desired training time and level of fatigue. On a less steep System Wall (closer to just 20 degrees past vertical), you may be able to climb for 60 to 90 seconds for each set, whereas a steeper wall may limit your training set to just 20 to 40 seconds. Either way, take a 3-minute rest between each set.

Use System Wall repeaters to isolate and strengthen specific movements. BRIAN FLICK

Do one or two sets of each of four to six different "theme repeaters," for a total of four to twelve sets in aggregate. Long term, you can increase difficulty by using smaller holds, larger arm moves, and more difficult and strenuous body positions, as well as by adding a weight belt.

Small-Rung Ladder Laps (No Skips)

Ladder laps are a popular strength/power-endurance exercise, but there are two distinctly different ways to train with them. Later in this chapter you'll learn about doing ladder laps with rung skips to train power-endurance in the pulling muscles, but in this exercise you'll be laddering on smaller rungs with no skips to target grip strength-endurance. You'll need to experiment a little to determine the smallest-size rung on which you can successfully ladder up and down for at least two consecutive laps.

1. Hang with nearly straight arms from the bottom rung of a campus board. Your hands should be about shoulder width or slightly less apart.

2. Striving for fluid motion, briskly climb hand-over-hand up the campus board using alternating rungs for your left and right hands. Ascend the board as fast as possible.

3. Upon matching hands on the top rung, begin to downclimb the board, again going hand-over-hand without skipping any rungs.

4. When you reach the bottom rung, immediately begin laddering back up the board.

5. Continue with these up-and-down ladder laps for a total of 30 to 60 seconds (hard).

6. Rest for 3 minutes before doing another set.

7. Do two to five sets with at least a 3-minute rest between sets.

Safety note: It's important that you only use the open-hand or open-crimp grips (see chapter 7, page 123). If you find yourself beginning to use a half-crimp or full-crimp grip due to growing fatigue, move to a larger-size rung so that you can continue with the open-hand grip.

Taping to Reinforce Tendons

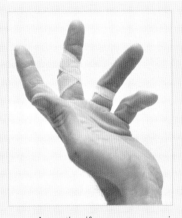

Circumferential taping at the base of the fingers has been shown to slightly reduce the stress placed on the finger tendon pulleys. Although I do not advocate the use of taping all the time, it is a good practice if you are recovering from a tendon injury or engaging in a stressful climb or exercise, such as fingerboard, hypergravity, and campus training. The A2 ring method is more common, but the Figure-8 method is useful for protecting the skin during hypergravity training or on high-volume climbing days. Most people tape only the middle and ring fingers, since these are the most commonly injured fingers. Use the strongest, stickiest tape you can find—German Leukotape is the best (one application may last all day), while many cheaper American tapes quickly stretch, loosen, and lose effectiveness (thus, frequent retaping is necessary).

A2 Ring Method: The A2 ring method (see ring finger in photo) involves firm circumferential taping at the distal end of the proximal phalanx—that is, just above the A2 pulley and immediately below the PIP joint. Use a narrow strip of tape, approximately 0.4 inch (10mm) wide, and wrap as tightly and as close to the PIP joint as possible without restricting blood flow. This may take a bit of experimentation, but remember that loose finger taping serves no function other than protecting the skin. Remove and reapply fresh tape every few hours to maintain the necessary tightness throughout a full day of climbing.

Figure-8 Method: The Figure-8 method (see middle finger in photo) may provide additional tendon support to the A3, A4, and cruciform pulleys, and it's very effective at preventing skin wear (and pain) when you're climbing on sharp pockets or rough indoor holds. Tear a long strip of tape, approximately 16 inches (40cm) in length by 0.75 inch (18mm) wide. With a slight bend in the finger, begin with two turns of tape over the proximal phalanx (on top of the A2 pulley), and then cross under the PIP joint and take two turns around the middle phalanx. Cross back under the PIP joint and conclude with another turn or two around the base of the finger.

Power-Endurance Training of the Pulling Muscles

The focus of this section is training to increase anaerobic capacity in the larger pulling muscles, which will provide what you'll perceive to be better power-endurance in climbing. While actual climbing—be it a bouldering 4x4 or a series of short, pumpy climbs—is obviously the most specific training method, you can also use isolation exercises to target the anaerobic lactic endurance system of the pulling muscles of the arms and torso. Such anaerobic endurance training is hard, grueling work that requires repeated, sustained bursts of relatively high-intensity exercise that yield a growing muscle pump and burning sensation.

Detailed in this section are eight exercises that will really pump you up! Regular use of a few of these exercises—twice weekly is enough for most climbers—will yield significant gains in power-endurance. As pointed out earlier, however, you mustn't train anaerobic power too often or without a break every few weeks, because intensive anaerobic lactic energy system training can lead to over-training and performance declines. Consult chapter 11 for guidance on periodizing your training and the need to occasionally taper and break from extensive training.

Pull-Up Intervals

This is a great exercise that trains the pull muscles to persevere through the fatiguing effects of acidosis (and other by-products of anaerobic glycolysis), as well as strengthens the recuperative influence of the aerobic system (aerobic power). The training goal is to complete twenty pull-up intervals, each exactly 1 minute in length. For example, if you are doing five pull-ups per interval, it may take 10 seconds to complete the five pull-ups, and thus you have the remaining 50 seconds to rest before beginning the next interval (see table 9.6). Use a stopwatch or timing app to stay on a tight schedule for all twenty intervals.

Train using a pull-up bar or the largest holds on a fingerboard. Increase the difficulty by adding one pull-up per interval, rather than using smaller handholds or adding weight. Conversely, reduce the number of pull-ups per set, as needed, to complete the full 20-minute interval workout. This is an excellent home training exercise, requiring only a pull-up bar, for individuals without a home wall or easy access to a climbing gym.

Table 9.6 Sample Pull-Up Interval Protocol

Interval	# of Pull-Ups	Approx. Work/Rest (secs.)	Interval	# of Pull-Ups	Approx. Work/Rest (secs.)
1	5	10/50	11	5	10/50
2	5	10/50	12	5	10/50
3	5	10/50	13	5	10/50
4	5	10/50	14	5	10/50
5	5	10/50	15	5	10/50
6	5	10/50	16	5	10/50
7	5	10/50	17	5	10/50
8	5	10/50	18	5	10/50
9	5	10/50	19	5	10/50
10	5	10/50	20	5	10/50

Power Pull-Up Intervals
(Chest-Bump Pull-Ups)

In chapter 8 I introduced you to the power
pull-up, which involves accelerating your
body upward so that there's enough momentum to carry your chest into the bar (see
page 155 for a refresher on how to do it
properly). This exercise protocol is nearly the
same as the pull-up interval described previously, except that you are only going to do
ten total intervals composed of four power
pull-ups per interval. The 10-minute power
pull-up protocol shown in table 9.7 is quite
difficult to complete—as a rule, if you can't
do a single set of eight power pull-ups, then
you aren't ready for this exercise (train limit
strength and pure power for a few months
and you'll likely be ready). On the other
hand, if you're so strong that doing ten sets of
four power pull-ups feels easy, then increase
to doing five or six reps per set. And finally,
remember that each power pull-up must end
with a forceful chest bump into the bar—no
chest bump, no power pull-up!

Power pull-up intervals.

Table 9.7 Power Pull-Up Interval Protocol

Interval	# of Pull-Ups	Approx. Work/Rest (secs.)	Interval	# of Pull-Ups	Approx. Work/Rest (secs.)
1	4	4/56	6	4	4/56
2	4	4/56	7	4	4/56
3	4	4/56	8	4	4/56
4	4	4/56	9	4	4/56
5	4	4/56	10	4	4/56

Frenchies

While it's been more than twenty years since I first coined the name "Frenchies" and popularized this exercise in my 1994 training book, *Flash Training*, this exercise is no less grueling and effective in developing power-endurance in the large pulling muscles. Make Frenchies a staple of your power-endurance training and you'll undoubtedly climb stronger!

1. Begin with a single pull-up (palms away, hands shoulder width apart) and lock off in the top position for a 4-second count.

2. Now lower to the bottom (starting position) and pull up to the top again, but this time immediately lower yourself halfway down to an arm angle of 90 degrees. Hold a solid lock-off here for a 4-second count, then again return to the bottom position.

3. Immediately crank another complete pull-up, but this time lower to a lock-off with an arm angle of about 120 degrees—hold this lock-off for 4 seconds before returning to the bottom position. This sequence of three lock-offs constitutes a single cycle, and it will take about 15 seconds (assuming it takes 1 second for each pull-up)—but don't stop yet!

4. Continue on with another cycle (or more) until you can no longer pull up or hold a 4-second lock-off. Record the number of cycles (or partial cycles) in your training notebook. Each set of Frenchies should last between 30 seconds (about two cycles) and 90 seconds (six cycles, which is really badass!).

5. Do a total of two or four sets with a rest of at least 5 minutes between sets.

Training tips: If you can't complete two full cycles, stand in a Theraband girth-hitched to the pull-up bar or enlist a spotter to remove some body weight by lifting around your waist. Conversely, you can add a 10- or 20-pound weight belt once you are able to do four or more cycles per set.

1. Lock off at top position.   *2. Lock off at 90 degrees.*   *3. Lock off at 120 degrees.*

Square Dance

This exercise is best performed on a System Wall or campus board with foot strips. Since you'll be training pull-muscle and lock-off endurance, it's important to use large handholds so that your forearms don't pump out. The goal is to "square dance" for between 45 seconds and 90 seconds. The exercise is simple, albeit a bit boring—here's the progression.

1. Beginning with matched hands on a large low hold, pull up with both hands and then reach up to grab a large high hold.
2. Next, match hands at the high spot.
3. Immediately drop the leading hand back to the starting hold.
4. Finish by bringing the trailing hand down to match on the starting hold.
5. Hang here for a few seconds, if you like, before repeating the sequence with the other hand leading the way.
6. Keep your feet fixed on the same holds throughout the "square dance," and modulate exercise intensity by varying the distance you reach with each upward movement.
7. Continue in this way for up to 90 seconds, but step off the wall before reaching complete failure.
8. Do two to four sets with only partial recovery between each set—a work-to-rest ratio of 1:2 or 1:3 is ideal.

System wall "square dance" using large holds and with feet on a modular hold or wood strip.

Big-Holds, Big-Move 4x4s

Earlier in this chapter you learned a bouldering 4x4 protocol (see table 9.4) for training strength-endurance in the finger flexor muscles. The bouldering 4x4 protocol for developing power-endurance in the pulling muscles is identical, except that you must select boulder problems with better handholds but longer, more powerful arm and body movements. The ideal boulder will demand that your large pulling muscles and core work hard, while not fatiguing the finger flexors to the point of failure. If you fail on one or more of your sixteen boulder ascents, it should be due to fatigue in the pulling muscles (a failed big move, lunge, or lock-off) and not due to failure of the finger flexors (inability to maintain your grip). Therefore, it's best to err on the side of doing routes with too large of handholds, rather than too small, for the purpose of training power-endurance in the pulling muscles.

In my opinion it's best to discriminate between strength-endurance training of the finger flexors and power-endurance training of the pulling muscles, instead of training them both at the same time. One effective approach is to do a bouldering 4x4 that targets the pulling muscles (as described here) and then, after a rest break of at least 20 minutes, do another bouldering 4x4 that targets the finger flexors (as described earlier in this chapter). Follow the 4x4 protocol described in table 9.4 for both sets.

Big-holds, big-move 4x4s

Campus Ladder Laps on Big Holds

This exercise is very similar to the small-rung ladder laps described earlier in this chapter (see page 170), except that this variation utilizes the largest rungs and involves doing rung skips so as to target the large pulling muscles of the arms and back. Strong climbers will be able to ladder lap the campus board with a 1-3-5-7-7-5-3-1 sequence. A somewhat easier approach is to ascend via 1-3-5-7 (skipping rungs) and then descend using every rung (7-6-5-4-3-2-1). Each up-and-down lap will take 10 to 15 seconds, so strive to do between two and four laps per set in order to reach the desired exercise duration of 30 to 60 seconds. Do two to five sets with at least a 3-minute rest between sets. Advanced climbers can reduce the rest break to 60 seconds to train aerobic power (recovery ability of CP resynthesis) in addition to anaerobic capacity.

Ladder laps using large holds and skipping rings, when possible. The goal is to fatigue the pulling muscles, not the finger flexors.

Indoor walls provide an ideal platform for interval training, in which you alternate between climbing and resting.

Gym Rope Intervals

As explained in chapter 8 (see page 157) no-feet gym rope climbing is one of the best pure power arm exercises on the planet! In the context of this chapter on power-endurance training, doing a series of gym rope intervals is as effective as they are brutal to perform. Since gripping a thick gym rope is a rather easy matter, this exercise singles out the large pulling muscles in a way similar to doing large-rung ladder laps. However, a strong climber can generate a higher rate of ascent in climbing a gym rope (versus climbing a campus board), and, hence, the power output is greater. The shorter but intense interval protocol detailed below trains alactic power and aerobic power more than anaerobic capacity—still, you will perceive a marked increase in high-end power-endurance after just a few weeks of training.

1. After a lengthy warm-up of pull-ups and mild upper-body stretching, begin from either a standing or sit-down (harder) position and grip the rope with both arms shy of full extension.

2. Climb the rope as fast as possible—strive for quick, crisp arm-over-arm movements all the way to the top.

3. Upon reaching the top, slowly lower down with controlled arm-over-arm movements. The full up-and-down lap should take just 10 to 20 seconds, depending on whether you're climbing a 15-, 18-, or 20-foot rope.

4. Rest for exactly 1 minute, and then begin your next lap on the rope.

5. Do three to ten (hard!) gym rope intervals, being sure to limit rest breaks between ascents to just 1 minute.

Safety note: Always have a bouldering pad beneath the gym rope. If you sense a loss of control, in ascending or descending, immediately clamp down on the rope with your feet rather than risk falling.

Route Intervals

This final exercise involves repeating laps on a moderately difficult gym route, which obviously will train both strength-endurance of your finger flexors and power-endurance of your pulling muscles. The ideal route would be steep, strenuous, and sustained enough to get you pumped, yet not so technically difficult that you're likely to fall off the route. More specifically, select a route that's one or two number grades below your limit and of a length that you can climb in a steady 2- to 3-minute push. Given that you'll need a belayer, it's best to pair up with someone who also wants to do a set of route intervals. You can climb on toprope or lead.

1. Climb your first lap up the route—move at a brisk, steady pace and avoid pausing for longer than a few seconds at a time (to chalk up or look for the next hold). The ascent should take just 2 to 3 minutes and elicit a moderate to major muscle pump (if not, find a harder route).

2. Lower to the ground for a 2-minute rest break, during which you'll pull the rope and tie back in (if lead climbing). This first climb-rest interval should take no more than 4 or 5 minutes.

3. At the end of the 2-minute rest, immediately begin climbing your second lap up the route. Upon reaching the top, lower to the ground and take another 2-minute rest.

4. Continue for three or four intervals, which should take no more than 15 to 20 minutes, respectively.

5. Now take your climbing shoes off and relax for 15 to 20 minutes as you belay your partner on her three to four sets of climbing intervals.

6. Do another set of three or four climbs to make a great anaerobic endurance workout!

*Dan Wachlaczenko
on the classic
Le Teton (5.9+),
Shawangunks,
New York.*
ANDREW CHAO

CHAPTER 10

Local and Generalized Aerobic Training Exercises

The benefits of aerobic training include increased capacity to climb all day while maintaining a high level of performance throughout, resistance to fatigue when faced with an extraordinarily hard or sustained climb, faster recovery between climbs and at brief mid-climb rests.

For many years, rock climbers considered aerobic training to be unimportant and unnecessary. It was a seemingly logical conclusion given the common real-life experience of failing on climbs due to flamed-out forearms or a lack of anaerobic pulling power. But superficial appearances—and apparently obvious conclusions—aren't always correct.

Numerous climbing research studies have determined that the aerobic energy system, in fact, plays a significant role in almost all climbing activities, especially those lasting more than 90 seconds (which have been shown to be powered more by the aerobic pathway than the anaerobic). Consequently, if you are a climber that ever ties into a rope, you can be sure that your level of aerobic conditioning plays a significant role in your performance.

But what about boulderers? Surely doing a short boulder problem doesn't tap into the aerobic energy system. Yes, it's true that the aerobic energy pathway only contributes a small amount toward the total power output in vigorous efforts lasting less than 1

Muscles Targeted	Aerobic-Endurance Training Exercise	Page	Beginner	Intermediate	Advanced
Local & Climbing-Specific Aerobic Training	ARC Traverses ("Recovery Climbing")	183	X	X	X
	Fingerboard Moving Hangs	184		X	X
	Campus Board or System Wall "Hand Play"	185		X	X
	Threshold Intervals on a Treadwall (or Bouldering Wall)	185		X	X
	Route Climbing Intervals	186	X	X	X
	Climb All Day	187	X	X	X
Generalized Aerobic Training	Steady State Aerobic Training	188	X	X	X
	Interval Training	188	X	X	X
	High-Volume Generalized Aerobic Training	190		X	X
	Ultradistance Conditioning	190		X	X

minute. But research has revealed that there's more to this story—recovery between boulder problems and during brief mid-climb rests is a wholly aerobic process! Therefore, a strong aerobic energy system will yield faster recovery, which can make a real difference on long boulders with only brief "micro rests" and in situations with time constraints, such as a bouldering competition or twilight bouldering session.

Make no mistake: I am *not* arguing that you should significantly reduce your strength and power training in order to invest a large amount of time in aerobic training. I've intimated many times throughout this text the importance of deliberate strength, power, and strength/power-endurance training in taking your climbing to the next level. What I'm stressing here is that strengthening your local aerobic power and generalized aerobic capacity is also an important piece of the puzzle, especially considering the critical role of the aerobic system in recovery between exercises and climbs and, in fact, between moves of a climb!

Given this accurate perspective of the aerobic energy system's role in climbing, we can once and for all recognize the value in doing a modest amount of climbing-specific and nonspecific aerobic training. So now let's advance the discussion by examining two types of aerobic training exercises and activities: climbing-specific (those involving climbing movements) and nonspecific (generalized aerobic activities like running).

Climbing-Specific Aerobic Training Exercises

Exercises detailed in this section are designed to train aerobic energy production in the climbing muscles of the forearms, upper arms, shoulders, and upper torso. We often refer to this as climbing-specific or "local" endurance.

Effective local endurance training is only possible if you set aside the desire to climb for performance (near your limit) and instead embrace the potentially boring process of climbing relatively high volumes of only moderately difficult rock (or plastic)—only in using this approach will you specifically target the aerobic energy pathway. No matter if the climbing is done indoors or outside, this training strategy will necessarily involve lots of submaximal climbing at varying intensities. The critical guideline to obey is to never let the climbing intensity ascend significantly into the anaerobic zone, the hallmark of which is a deep muscle pump and shortness of breath. Ultimately, you want to find the threshold of the anaerobic lactic zone and strive to climb mostly just below it (in the aerobic zone), only occasionally crossing into the low end of the anaerobic zone. A light to moderate forearm pump is fine and desirable; however, a flaming pump, heavy breathing, and a growing sense of losing control is a clear sign you've climbed too deep into the anaerobic zone

Figure 10.1—Training Zones for Climbers (RPE)

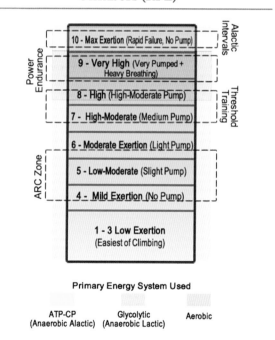

Effective climbing-specific aerobic training must be performed between 5 and 8.5 on the rating of perceived exertion.

(and training power/strength-endurance, not aerobic endurance).

Figure 10.1 presents a subjective scale for determining which energy system you are training. By keeping your perceived exertion and exercise intensity between 5 and 8 (and your forearm muscle pump in the light to moderate range), you can rest assured that you're training at the right intensity to produce favorable adaptations in the aerobic energy system. Self-control and a strong intention to climb mainly between 5 and 8.5 on this scale is essential to properly training this energy pathway. If you push too hard, you'll ascend into the power/strength-endurance training zone (anaerobic lactic energy system), whereas climbing that yields little or no pump is too easy to trigger significant aerobic adaptations (although such ARC climbing is useful as a recovery exercise). Detailed below are six climbing-specific training methods that primarily target the aerobic energy pathway.

ARC Traverses ("Recovery Climbing")

ARC is an acronym for aerobic, recovery, and capillary training. The goal of ARC training is to enhance recuperative blood flow via an extended period of low-intensity climbing. Such a training protocol—if you can stick to it—singularly targets the aerobic energy system and therefore yields little (or no) muscle pump. Done right, this light climbing workout will generate no fatigue to recover from and, in fact, will help accelerate recovery from the previous day's intense workout. The problem, however, is that the typical enthusiastic climber has a tough time visiting a climbing gym and refraining entirely from doing more difficult routes or boulder problems—be aware that even a small sampling of more challenging routes or boulders will sink the ARC.

Rather than calling it ARC training, I prefer the term "recovery climbing," since this unambiguously expresses the actual mission of the activity: Easy climbing that will enhance recovery rather than get in the way of it. The modus operandi we are after is similar to that of a runner going for an easy "recovery run"—the climbing (or running) pace must be so casual that you can hold a conversation throughout. On a perceived exertion/intensity scale of 1 to 10 (see figure 10.1), the ideal recovery-training zone is between a 4 and 6; go any higher and it's no longer an ARC/recovery session. Here's the best way to engage in some ARC climbing.

1. Traverse along the base of a vertical wall, using mainly large holds. While you could climb easy roped routes, traversing untethered will allow you to easily step off the wall at the first sign of a developing pump.

2. If the climbing wall is large enough, you may be able to traverse for 15 to 30 minutes. Do this, and your workout is over—remember, it's a recovery workout!

3. Or do a series of 5-minute traverses with brief rests in between. Aim for a total climbing time of around 30 minutes. Again, don't get pumped!

Training tip: The ARC/recovery climbing protocol is too low intensity to seriously develop the aerobic energy system. Therefore, save this type of recovery training for occasional use the day after a hard maximum-strength or power-endurance workout.

ARC traversing.

Fingerboard Moving Hangs

If you do a lot of your training at home by way of a fingerboard, then the "moving hang" is your ticket to getting a decent local aerobic endurance workout. Moving hangs involve working your hands around the board continuously for several minutes, much like climbing a long, sustained sequence on the rock. Doing this requires somewhere to place your feet while your hands switch holds on the board. The best way to do this is to mount your fingerboard so that it's set out a foot or two from a wall onto which you have mounted a few small footholds or other foot support. Another possibility is to mount the board above a doorway, then position a chair or stool a couple feet behind the board. Either way, you must be able to use your toes for support in order to circulate your hands around the fingerboard.

1. Perform a 10- to 20-minute warm-up comprising some generalized aerobic activity, stretching, and some pull-ups and easy hangs on the fingerboard. You should break a light sweat and feel a slight pump in your arms.

2. Mount the board, then place your feet on footholds or on the edge of a chair.

3. Begin moving your hands around the fingerboard, changing hand positions every 3 to 5 seconds—just as if you were climbing.

4. After a minute or two, you will begin to develop a pump in your forearms. Move both hands onto the largest handholds on the board and shake out each arm for about 30 seconds in an attempt to recover a little.

5. After this brief shakeout, continue moving your hands around the board for another minute or two. Once again, move to the large holds if you need to shake out and rest your muscles a little.

6. Continue in this fashion—being sure to remain in the training zone of 7 to 8.5 out of 10 (see figure 10.1)—with the goal of staying on the board for a total of 5 to 10 minutes.

7. Dismount the board and rest for 5 to 10 minutes before proceeding with a second and third set.

Moving hangs.

Campus Board or System Wall "Hand Play"

This exercise is similar to fingerboard moving hangs except that it's performed on a campus board or System Wall. It's important to note that this is a feet-on campus exercise, so you'll need to place your feet on a chair or on wooden strips or climbing holds bolted onto the wall below. It's important to recognize that this is not a dynamic exercise, so it's in no way like the campus board exercises used to develop contact strength and power. The goal here is aerobic endurance training by way of easy to moderate hand movements around the board and liberal use of shakeouts from the largest holds available. Depending on how much body weight is shifted onto the feet, you should be able to "hand play" around the campus board for at least 3 to 5 minutes. Your goal is to train in the threshold training zone (see figure 10.1), so strive to train at an intensity of 7 to 8.5 on a scale of 1 to 10. Keep the pump under control, and be sure to step off the board before attaining a deep, painful pump—a sign that the anaerobic lactic system has become the predominant energy pathway. Err on the side of too little pump and shorter sets, rather than developing deep fatigue and the need for longer rests. Do three to six (advanced) sets with nearly equal periods of climbing and resting.

Threshold Intervals on a Treadwall (or Bouldering Wall)

A Treadwall is an expensive piece of equipment, but to a climber-for-life type (like me) it's worth every penny. Depending on the size of holds used and the amount of weight added via weight belt (if any), a Treadwall can be effectively used to train anaerobic and aerobic power (via brief, intense intervals lasting less than 20 seconds), anaerobic capacity and the lactic system (hard, pumpy intervals lasting 30 seconds to 2 minutes), or the aerobic energy system by way of longer (3 to 6 minutes) moderate-intensity intervals with equal or shorter rest periods. The focus here, of course, is the latter application of training local aerobic capacity. If you don't have access to a Treadwall, you can also execute the following training protocol on a bouldering wall.

As you can probably surmise by now, the threshold interval protocol is to climb a series of moderate-intensity intervals lasting 3 to 5 minutes. The ideal training intensity is between a 7 and 8.5 out of 10 on the RPE scale (see figure 10.1)—this puts you right at the anaerobic threshold, where the aerobic system is taxed to its limit. A steep Treadwall or bouldering wall (more than 30 degrees past vertical) may make this a challenging endeavor, however, in which case you'll need to use large, juggy holds and frequent shakeouts.

Do four to eight intervals with a 1:1 climb-to-rest ratio. Err on the side of too little pump and only a few sets rather than push it too hard, for too long, and acquire too deep of a pump. End a climbing interval early (say, at 3 minutes) rather than push deeply into the anaerobic zone—if you get a painful pump, experience shortness of breath, and need to fight to stay on the wall, then you're well beyond the target training zone.

Training tip: If there's one liability to owning a Treadwall or home bouldering wall, it's the ease of use (and overuse) and the difficult-to-resist tendency to always climb into the anaerobic zone. Climbers who succumb in this way inevitably end up getting lackluster results (despite all their hard training) and sometimes end up victims of overtraining syndrome.

Threshold interval training on a Brewer's Ledge Treadwall.

Route Climbing Intervals

This is by far the best local aerobic training protocol if you're lucky enough to have a membership at a large climbing gym or a good local crag with some fun, moderate routes. You will need to exert self-control in not getting drawn into climbing for performance—the goal here, as with all the aerobic training exercises, is to engage in sustained climbing that yields just a light to moderate pump. This is an excellent partner exercise, so enlist someone who also understands the value of doing a high volume of moderate climbing. Take equal turns climbing and belaying and you'll have a nice 1:1 climb-to-rest ratio.

To maintain a proper intensity level, choose routes that are two to four number grades below your limit. Accordingly, if you are a 5.12 redpoint climber it's best to train only on routes in the 5.8 to 5.10+ range—yes, these routes will seem really easy, but the training goal is to climb lots of volume and never get more than a moderate pump. Check your hard-climber ego

Pumping laps on a submaximal route at the gym.

at the door and assume a new mind-set and mission—to climb three times as many pitches as anyone else in the gym or at the crag! To do this, you'll likely need to climb ten to twenty (or more) toprope or lead climbs. By keeping the routes easy and the pump relatively "light," both you and your partner should be able to complete between six and twelve routes per hour (on an indoor wall). If you develop a deep muscular pump or labored breathing, immediately move onto easier routes rather than allow your training focus to shift into the anaerobic zone.

Climb All Day

This is the train-as-you-climb strategy. If your climbing goal is to send Grade IV or V routes in a day, then you need to simulate this workload as often as possible to develop the necessary stamina (aerobic capacity). In preparing for a trip to Yosemite, for example, you could train at your local crag by logging ten, fifteen, or twenty submaximal pitches in a long day. Reaching these training goals will take repeated efforts to extend what you are capable of performing not only physically, but also technically and mentally. Climbing a large number of pitches in a day requires both efficient movement and an efficient two-person climbing system. Stamina gains are really an aggregate of enhancements in your ability to perform mentally and physically to a higher level of precision and total volume, and capacity gains in your generalized aerobic system.

It's important to begin this type of stamina training at least three months before the date of your target climb. Plan your training and climbing schedule so that you can engage in climb-all-day stamina training at least once every two weeks and ideally once or twice per week. Clearly, no amount of running or other type of physical stamina conditioning can duplicate or replace this most specific and valuable training method. So get a partner and start climbing!

Nonspecific/Generalized Aerobic Training Exercises

Climbing efforts lasting more than 2 minutes derive energy primarily via the aerobic energy system. If you are a route climber, then, you simply can't skip using some of the climbing-specific and generalized aerobic training exercises described in this chapter. As explained in our earlier discussion of energy systems, brief bouts of high-intensity climbing—as in doing a boulder problem or powering through a crux sequence on a roped route—call the anaerobic energy systems into play, while lower-intensity climbing and recovery of the anaerobic energy systems are facilitated by the aerobic energy pathway. Therefore, a serious route climber must invest time in training all three energy systems, though not in the same workout.

Whereas the first half of this chapter detailed climbing-specific exercises to train local aerobic power production in the climbing muscles (forearms, arms, and pulling muscles of the torso), this section will present several methods of generalized aerobic training that targets the larger cardiovascular system. These activities include conventional aerobic training exercises used by athletes in a wide range of sports to develop what is often referred to as stamina—the ability to resist fatigue while engaging in sustained or intermittent sporting activity for an extended period of time. For a rock climber the long-term benefits of regular nonspecific aerobic training include increased capacity to climb all day while maintaining a high level of performance throughout, resistance to fatigue when faced with an extraordinarily hard or sustained climb, and faster recovery at brief mid-climb rests and between climbs. These benefits are the result of numerous adaptations including increased VO_2 max (cardiorespiratory), increased capillary vascularity, increased central nervous system efficiency, and enhanced glycogen (muscle fuel reserve) storage, which in aggregate results in improved aerobic capacity

A final thought before getting to the details: It would be a mistake for an avid rock climber to engage in an excessive amount of generalized aerobic training; for example, running 20 miles per week (or more) as a competitive runner might do. So while doing two or three 15- to 30-minute, moderate-intensity aerobic training sessions per week is fine for most climbers, doing much more than this may be counterproductive (due to fatigue and catabolic effect to the climbing muscles) for all but big-wall and alpine climbers.

Steady State Aerobic Training

Tempo runs and Concept 2 rowing are the two best steady state activities for climbers. The goal is to run (or row) at a moderately high intensity that not only stresses the slow-twitch muscle fibers, but also begins to recruit some of the fast-twitch oxidative fibers. Running at this "threshold pace" for 20 to 30 minutes not only provides stimulus for favorable cardiovascular adaptations, but it also trains the large exercising muscles (in the legs, hips, back) to better metabolize lactate for energy. The upside, when on a strenuous climb, will be improved processing of lactate and H+ released into the bloodstream from the pulling muscles of the upper body. This is one of the reasons climbers who do generalized aerobic training recover faster—and perhaps can persevere longer—on long, pumpy anaerobic climbs.

These benefits of doing a moderate amount of nonspecific aerobic training haven't been overlooked by some of the best route climbers. Sasha DiGiulian, one of the best endurance sport climbers, and Alex Megos, one of the world's best on-sight climbers, both make running a regular part of their training. Perhaps you should too!

Sussing out the right intensity of running (or rowing) is the key—you don't want to exercise at too low an intensity (as in the runners' popular "long slow distance" pace), or at a high intensity that produces deep fatigue and a great acid load on the body. Aim for a rating of perceived exertion of 8 out of 10, or a heart rate of around 85 percent of maximum (220 minus your age). Two 15- to 30-minute runs per week are enough to gain favorable adaptations. If you desire a third aerobic session each week, I suggest doing an easier "recovery" run with your heart rate between 70 and 80 percent of maximum.

Interval Training

My preferred method of aerobic conditioning is interval training, either by foot or using a Concept 2 rowing machine. Alternating between 30- to 60-second bouts of high-intensity exercise and near-equal periods of low-intensity exercise is not unlike the process of climbing a physical route with multiple cruxes and a few easier sections. While the training movement is vastly different, the cardiovascular system strain and the biochemistry processes involved in regaining homeostasis are the same. This workout will tap significantly into the anaerobic pathway during the fast segments, while the slow segments offer the opportunity to metabolize lactate and buffer H+ (reduce acidosis). One interesting upshot of generalized aerobic training is that the slow-twitch fibers of the large lower-body muscles are trained to utilize blood lactate for energy production—a trait that will enhance your climbing performance on pumpy routes, as the leg muscles help clear lactate spilled into the blood from pumped arms. The result will be a hastened return of homeostasis and faster recovery at a mid-climb rest and between climbs.

Interval training on a track is a highly structured and effective strategy for training anaerobic endurance and stamina.

Aerobic Training for Multipitch and Big-Wall Climbers

If your climbing preference is all-day multipitch climbs or big walls, then performing more frequent and higher volumes of aerobic training is a more important part of your training program than it is for a boulderer or sport climber. The physical trait you are training for is stamina—the ability to resist fatigue while engaging in sustained or intermittent physical activity for an extended period of time (all day or longer). A regular commitment to long-duration aerobic training will yield local and central adaptations that increase your glycogen stores, improve use of fatty acids for fuel, and strengthen your cardiovascular system. Equally important, however, is the gradual recalibration of the central governor that results from long-duration exercise superseding what you've done before. This sort of "brain training," a result of pushing to new limits year after year, is the magic behind the training of world-class endurance climbers such as Alex Honnold, Hans Florine, and, of course, Kevin Jorgenson and Tommy Caldwell.

As in other types of conditioning, there are sport-specific and general ways of stamina training. The most specific—and therefore most effective—approach is to train as you will perform. To develop greater stamina for long days at the crags, then, you would train by frequently climbing all day with the goal of squeezing in as many pitches as possible. Obviously, this approach is not an option for many recreational climbers who only climb outside once per month due to career, school, and family commitments. A more practical training alternative is regular high-volume aerobic activity, such as running and biking, coupled as often as possible with high volumes of climbing at the gym or crag.

Scheduling a sufficient number of climbing-specific and generalized aerobic training workouts per week may require a "two-a-day" approach to your training. The goal here is to engage in two 1-plus-hour workouts in a day. This could include any combination of aerobic activities, such as running, biking, or swimming and a rigorous climbing session at the gym (or half a day at the crags). To maximize the quality of each workout, it's important to have at least a 4- to 6-hour break between the two. For example, you might go for a run in the morning and then climb for a couple of hours in the evening, or vice versa. If climbing is not an option, you would simply perform a morning and late-day aerobic activity of an hour or more each time.

This is, of course, a lot of training and requires a high level of conditioning that might take a few months to build up to. Furthermore, you should begin with just one two-a-day workout per week and gradually advance to as many as three per week. Maintaining proper hydration and eating between the two daily workouts is vital—eating to enhance recovery in preparation for your next workout is central to effective stamina training and performance.

The interval-training protocol is simple: alternate fast and slow bouts of exercise, via running, rowing, swimming, bicycle riding, or some other full-body aerobic activity. When the weather is good, I prefer running intervals on a track (in bad weather I row on a Concept 2) because it gives me a clear, measurable way to segment my training. Two good approaches are to run at a fast pace for a half lap and then walk or jog the remainder of the lap. If you already possess a high level of aerobic conditioning, then you'll probably be able to push hard for a full lap and then jog a full lap. Either way, run (or other) your fast segments at a perceived exertion of 8.5 to 9 out of 10—hard enough to get significantly winded and trigger stopping thoughts. Try to hold the fast pace for the predetermined distance (half lap or full lap), and then pull back to an easy jog or fast walk for the "slow" segment. Continue running fast-slow intervals for a total of six to twelve laps, if using a track, or a total of 15 to 30 minutes if doing some other form of aerobic activity.

High-Volume Generalized Aerobic Training

This (and the next) aerobic training strategy is appropriate only for big-wall and alpine climbers. The goal here is to engage in two to four 45-minute to 2-hour aerobic workouts per week that emphasize mileage over speed. This could be any combination of running, swimming, and cycling. As your conditioning improves, consider doubling up sessions one or two days per week, per the two-a-day training strategy described in the "Aerobic Training for Multipitch and Big-Wall Climbers" box on previous page. This is clearly an advanced aerobic training program, but it might be just the ticket in the months and weeks leading up to a big-wall or alpine climbing adventure.

Ultradistance Conditioning

Ultradistance conditioning—whether climbing, biking, or running—is all about pushing beyond what you are accustomed to in terms of total volume and rigor. This step-by-step one-upmanship of yourself results in a "callusing effect." The benefit of this mind-body callusing is that upon defining a new limit—running your first marathon, climbing your first big wall in a day, or whatever—repeating this feat in the future will not seem as difficult as the first time. While some of this adaptation may be physical, it's believed that the majority of this callusing effect is a result of a recalibration of the brain's central governor (which you can read more about in my books *Maximum Climbing* and *Training for Climbing*).

You can experience and leverage this callusing effect by engaging in stamina workouts and days of climbing that exceed your previous limit. You might do this by adding 0.5 mile to your long-distance run each week or by climbing one more pitch or 100 feet more vertical distance during a day at the crags. The best marathon runners and ultraclimbers typically dedicate one day per week to performing a super volume of physical activity that approaches or exceeds their performance goal or previous limit. Make this your target too.

As your workout volume increases, it's important to maintain an adequate amount of rest in your weekly schedule. Extreme stamina training coupled with too little rest will quickly lead to lethargy and, perhaps, illness or injury. A high-volume training day may require three or more days of rest before you are ready for a repeat workout. In ultra-stamina-performance situations, such as climbing many grueling back-to-back days on a big wall or a high-elevation ascent, the deep level of fatigue that develops may require one to four weeks for complete recovery.

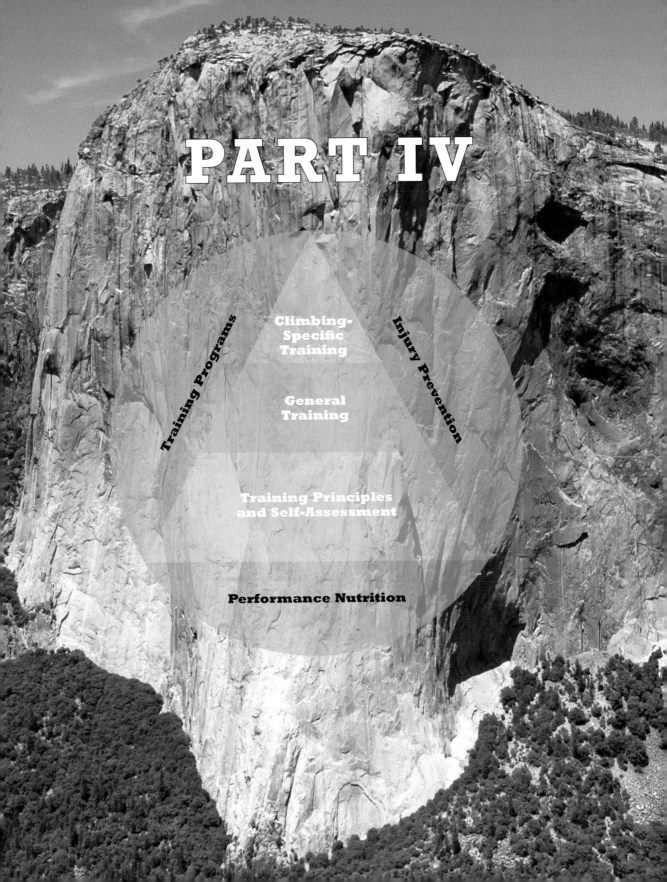

PART IV

Climbing-Specific Training

Injury Prevention

Training Programs

General Training

Training Principles and Self-Assessment

Performance Nutrition

Designing Your Own Training Program

Excellence in climbing requires a commitment to work on all facets of the game—improving technique, refining mental skills, and increasing your physical strength, power, and endurance.

The first ten chapters have provided the many puzzle pieces that make up an effective training program. In this chapter you will learn how to strategically piece together the dozens of exercises to create an optimally effective training program.

Central to designing the best program for you are the results of the self-assessment from chapter 2. Review the graph of your assessment profile on page 24 to see how you scored in each of the eight areas that influence climbing performance. The lowest-scoring areas represent the most immediate constraints to further gains in ability. While some of these areas relate to experience, lifestyle, and mental attributes, several are a direct reflection of your current level of physical conditioning and body composition. On the pages that follow, I will present a training strategy for beginner-, intermediate-, and advanced-level climbers. These strategies will define the breadth and depth of your training program, although you can select the specific exercises you desire for a given workout and vary them as needed to keep the program mentally and physically fresh. You can download additional training programs at my website: www.TrainingForClimbing.com.

As your training feeds back positive results, it's imperative that you modify the focus and makeup of the program to accurately address emerging new constraints. Remember that the limiting constraints on your performance are a moving target—to hit the bull's-eye, you must regularly correct your aim. Retake the self-assessment every season (or year) and use the results to redirect your program. Failing to do this—and executing the exact same climbing workouts—is tantamount to chaining yourself to a set ability level.

Let's take a look at the guidelines for an effective beginner, intermediate, and advanced training program. Consult table 11.1 to determine which program is most appropriate for you.

Beginner Climber's Program

The first step to becoming a better climber—and getting into climbing shape—is simply to climb on a regular basis. Therefore, the most important part of a beginner's training program is to climb two to four days per week. No other training activity will increase your climbing fitness as fast as actually going climbing. That being said, there are several good reasons to engage in supplemental training. First, a modest amount of generalized aerobic training can benefit your climbing by improving stamina and body composition. Similarly, some basic strength and flexibility training will facilitate the learning of climbing moves on increasingly strenuous terrain. Finally, some basic push-muscle training will help mitigate the muscular imbalances—and injury risk—that commonly develop as climbing-specific strength increases.

Table 11.1 Classifications of Ability & Training Program Overview

		Beginner	Intermediate	Advanced
Classification of Ability		• Less than one year climbing experience • Toprope ability 5.10 and under • Little or no lead climbing • Boulder V3 and under • Aggregate self-assessment score <120	• Actively climbing more than one year • Toprope 5.11 to 5.12+ • Lead climbing up to 5.10+ trad or 5.12 sport • Boulder V4 to V8 • Aggregate self-assessment score 121–165	• More than three years' climbing experience • On-sight lead ability of 5.12 sport or 5.11 trad • Redpoint climbing 5.13 and above • Boulder V9 or harder • Aggregate self-assessment score >165
Training Program Overview		• Climb: 2–4x per week • General strength and stability/antagonist training: 2x per week • Generalized aerobic conditioning: 1–4x per week	• Climbing and climbing-specific exercises: 3–4x per week • Stability/antagonist training: 2x per week • Generalized aerobic conditioning: 1–3x per week	• Climbing and climbing-specific exercises: 3–5x per week • Stability/antagonist training: 2x per week • Generalized aerobic conditioning: 1–2x per week

As you progress into the realm of being an intermediate climber—say, breaking into V4/V5 boulders and 5.11 routes—you will need to progress to a more targeted program of climbing-specific exercises. However, the hallmark of a well-designed beginner-level program is precisely that it's *not* highly specific. Many enthusiastic novice climbers make the mistake of advancing to the highly stressful, climbing-specific exercises too soon. Not only does this tempt injury, but it also handicaps your learning of skills and, ultimately, rate of improvement. Follow the program below and you'll safely progress to an intermediate level in a year, perhaps sooner.

Warm-Up and Stretching

Every workout or climbing session should begin with a period of warm-up and stretching activities. Spend 10 to 15 minutes performing a selection of warm-up and mobility activities and stretches from chapter 3. Conclude your warm-up by climbing a few easy, large-hold boulder problems or moderate toprope routes.

Climbing Skills Training

As emphasized above, time spent actually climbing is the best training investment—it will yield improvements in your technical and mental skills as well as physical fitness. Warming up and executing general training exercises are important, but time spent on the wall should make up the majority of your workout. For example, a 2-hour climbing-gym workout might begin and end with 15 minutes of stretching and general training, respectively, while 90 minutes of climbing constitutes the core of the session. Similarly, a day of outdoor climbing should begin with a period of warm-up and stretching before you ever step onto the rock. Often the hike in to the cliff will provide an excellent warm-up, so that you only need to execute a few minutes of stretching before beginning to climb. If you climb half a day or less, consider doing a 30-minute session of general conditioning exercises upon completion of your climbing.

Making the most of your climbing time requires climbing with intention—an intention to refine your climbing skills, challenge yourself on new terrain, and develop the vital mental skills of problem solving, visualization, self-awareness, and thought control. The areas of technique and mental training are gold mines rich in potential for rapid improvement. Here are a few improvement strategies to leverage.

When climbing outdoors, it's important to climb at many different areas so as to expose yourself to a wide range of technical and tactical demands. Each new climbing area visited will build unique skills and therefore grow your technical and cognitive abilities. Another excellent learning strategy is to follow a more accomplished climber up a near-limit (for you) multipitch route—this experience will stretch your mental and physical boundaries and help redefine what you view as possible. Alternatively, you can toprope a difficult single-pitch route a few times with the goal of perfecting your movements and ascent as if it were a gymnastics routine. Incorporating all these strategies into your outdoor-climbing experience will put you on the fast track to the next level of ability.

Inherent to indoor climbing are both limitations and advantages in terms of training skill. The character of artificial walls obviously limits the potential to learn climbing skills, since no indoor wall can mimic what Mother Nature offers in terms of breadth and depth of technical demands and rigor. Fortunately, indoor walls do provide an ideal setting for learning and refining many fundamental skills. A regular schedule of indoor climbing will produce rapid learning of motor skills while also developing a moderate level of physical strength. You can accelerate this process further by incorporating specific technique- and mental-training drills into your session. Detailing the many different climbing drills is beyond the scope of this book, but you'll find dozens of powerful practice drills in my books *Learning to Climb Indoors* and *Training for Climbing*.

Fitness Training

An effective beginner-level training program must also include a modest amount of general fitness training. Depending on the results of your self-assessment in chapter 2, you may need to invest as little as 15 minutes twice per week, or as much as 45 to 60 minutes four days per week, on general conditioning. The most important consideration is your current body composition—excessive body fat or bulky muscles in the wrong places will have a strong negative impact on your climbing performance. In this case regular aerobic exercise is as important as climbing a few days per week. Perform your aerobic activity on nonclimbing days, or in the morning if climbing in the afternoon or evening. Revisit chapter 4 for exercise and diet tips for optimizing your body composition.

General strength training is also worthwhile as long as it doesn't divert your time and focus away from actual climbing. Ideally, you would engage in 15 to 30 minutes of general fitness exercises at the end of your climbing session. Performing a few of the body-weight exercises described in chapter 4 along with a selection of the antagonist and stabilizer muscle exercises in chapter 5 is all that's really needed. The antagonist training can be performed on your climbing or nonclimbing days; however, the pull-muscle and core exercises should be used only on regular climbing days (or in place of climbing days if it's not possible to get to a gym or crag).

Designing Your Program

Designing an effective beginner-level training program is not as complex as you might expect. First, consider that the global goals of this program are pretty straightforward: developing climbing skills, improving general fitness, and avoiding injury. More specifically, you must shape the program so that it addresses the weaknesses identified in your self-assessment. Leverage the appropriate chapters and exercises that best target your limiting constraints. Piecing together a specific routine that you will have time and energy to regularly complete is key. Here are some guidelines for creating a daily workout program and weekly training schedule.

First, you must always distinguish between climbing and nonclimbing workouts. Given the availability of a climbing wall, crag, or boulders, your goal should be to engage in up to four climbing workouts per week. All other training activities—aerobic activity, antagonist exercises, and such—must be fit into your weekly schedule while still allowing at least one or two days of complete rest per week. Table 11.2 depicts two sample microcycles to use as templates in scheduling your weekly training activities.

Once you've penciled in a schedule of workout and climbing days, it's time to plan the body of each workout. While exceedingly long workouts are not necessary (or advisable), you should plan on spending between 1 and 3 hours on a typical workout. For example, a nonclimbing workout of aerobic training and general conditioning exercises might

Table 11.2 Sample Microcycles for Beginners

Four-Day-Per-Week Climbing						
Monday	**Tuesday**	**Wednesday**	**Thursday**	**Friday**	**Saturday**	**Sunday**
R or S/AA*	C/GE/TC	S/AA*	C/GE/TC	R	C/AA*	C/TC
KEY: C=Climbing; GE=General Exercises; S=Stabilizer & Antagonist Training; TC=Total Core & Leg Exercises; AA=Nonspecific Aerobic Activity; R=Rest (*Optional)						

Weekend-Only Climbing						
Monday	**Tuesday**	**Wednesday**	**Thursday**	**Friday**	**Saturday**	**Sunday**
R or AA	GE/S/TC	R or AA	GE/S/TC	R	C/AA*	C/TC
KEY: C=Climbing; GE=General Exercises; S=Stabilizer & Antagonist Training; TC=Total Core & Leg Exercises; AA=Nonspecific Aerobic Activity; R=Rest (*Optional)						

Table 11.3 Beginners' Climbing- and Nonclimbing-Day Workout Templates

Beginner's Workout with Climbing	Beginner's Workout with No Climbing
• 10–15 minutes of general warm-up activity including a few mobility exercises. • 20–40 minutes (or more if climbing outdoors) sub-maximal practice climbing—focus on learning new skills, efficient movement, and mental skills. • 10–30 minutes strenuous bouldering or near-limit roped climbing. • 15–30 minutes of generalized training (core, antagonist, stabilizer, and pull-muscle training). Consult chapters 4, 5 and 6. • 5–15 minutes cool-down—foam rolling and mild stretching.	• 10–15 minutes of general warm-up activity including a few mobility exercises. • 5–8 sets entry-level pull-muscle exercises. • 4–6 total sets of various core exercises. • 2–4 sets of fingerboard repeaters (only if a climber of more than 6 months experience). • 15–30 minutes of antagonist/stabilizer-muscle training. • 5–15 minutes cool-down—foam rolling and mild stretching.

take a little over an hour to complete, whereas a gym-climbing session followed by some general conditioning exercises will take 2 to 3 hours. Either way, your workout should be structured to begin with some warm-up and stretching activities, then progress to climbing activities (if any are planned), and then conclude with general fitness exercises and antagonist/stabilizer training (although this is best done on a nonclimbing day). Table 11.3 outlines two sample workout plans. Consult the relevant chapters to select specific stretches, activities, and exercises to plug into each section of the workout.

Intermediate Climber's Program

Given the steep improvement curve during the formative stage of learning, it's common to reach the intermediate level in a year or two, if not sooner. A hallmark of the intermediate, however, is a much slower rate of improvement—that may even seem imperceptible as you near the advanced ability level. This apparent plateau in performance (which often coincides with breaking into the 5.11 and 5.12 grade and mid-V bouldering grades), on the heels of a year or more of steady gains, can be extremely frustrating. But instead of reacting negatively to such a leveling-off in performance gains, recognize that it is a normal stage of the progression—and one you will rise above given a smart training program. With this realization, you are empowered to begin a new training program that will trigger a new growth phase and soon-to-be success at the lofty grades of 5.12 and 5.13!

Embarking on a new training program must commence with an acute understanding of your true strengths and weaknesses. Take the self-assessment in chapter 2 to obtain fresh insight into the specific areas you need to improve upon and thus target with training. This initiative also demands that you embrace some new training strategies, like hypergravity, interval, and threshold training, as well as increasing your total commitment to climbing. Furthermore, you must make a conscious, sustained

effort to elevate your climbing techniques, tactics, and mental game. Vow to seek out unfamiliar terrain and the types of climbs you have been avoiding up to this point, and then work these routes without ego or a need for success. Willfully exposing yourself to such climbs—and opening yourself up to the possibility of frustration and failure—not only builds character but is in fact the only pathway to becoming a climber of uncommon ability.

One trap to avoid as you progress toward becoming an advanced climber is that of mimicking the training program of other climbers. Doing this goes against the principle of individuality explained in chapter 1—you possess unique strengths and weaknesses, experience, genetics, and goals, so your optimal program will be unlike that of any other climber. Strive to increase self-awareness and to proactively self-direct your training program in a way that is optimal for you. You may also benefit from the objective analysis and input of a climbing coach. Inquire at your local gym to see if they have a trained coach on staff, or visit www.usaclimbing .org for a list of coaches by region.

Let's examine the components of an effective intermediate-level training program.

Warm-Up and Stretching

A period of warm-up and stretching is an important precursor to a successful workout or day of climbing. Although this 10- to 15-minute warm-up may seem so simple that it's expendable, it is in fact essential for individuals of advancing ability, who frequently expose muscles and tendons to a level of stress not before experienced. The bottom line: A brief warm-up primes the muscles and joints for peak performance and injury prevention. Make it a habit.

Climbing as Training

Time spent climbing must always be the central element of your training program, since moving over stone is the only effective pathway to increasing your climbing skills and mental abilities. Many intermediate climbers come to form a climbing preference, such as bouldering, indoor climbing, sport climbing, or crack climbing. While specializing will foster rapid gains in one of these subdisciplines, long-term improvement requires that you continue to gain experience and add skills in a wide range of climbing and rock types. There's a synergistic feedback effect that benefits those who strive for all-around proficiency as rock climbers.

An excellent practice strategy is to vary the type of climbing you engage in every few days or weeks. Regularly alternating among bouldering, steep sport climbing, crack climbing, vertical face climbing, and even slab climbing is like taking skill-building steroids. Not only will you develop an uncommonly broad skill set, but you'll also train your muscles and nervous system in a variety of valuable ways. This leverages the principle of periodization, which rewards those who regularly vary the focus, intensity, and length of their workouts.

While you might simply ad-lib your periodization by switching your climbing focus every week or so, it's best to plan out a more structured schedule. I advocate use of a cyclic workout program that varies climbing and training focus over the course of ten weeks. Such a program is more interesting and motivating, and it will provide superior results compared with training in the same ways week after week. Learn how to leverage the power of a training cycle by reading the "Periodization Training Strategies" sidebar.

Supplemental Pull-Muscle, Finger, and Core Conditioning

It is undeniable that harder, steeper climbs with smaller holds and longer moves demand a higher level of finger and lock-off strength, pulling and lunging power, muscular endurance, and core strength. Therefore, in addition to time spent climbing, an intermediate climber must begin some targeted training of the climbing-specific muscles of the upper body and core. Chapters 7, 8, 9 and 10 provide more than forty different exercises for developing climbing-specific strength, power, and endurance.

Once again, the principle of periodization underscores the importance of varying your training focus every few weeks. In using the 4–3–2–1 Cycle described on page 199, you would select exercises that build general and climbing-specific aerobic endurance for four weeks, maximum strength and power for three weeks, and then strength/power-endurance for two weeks. Selecting the appropriate type of climbing and exercises for use in each phase of the 4–3–2–1 Cycle is the key to maximizing the training effect and providing uncommonly good results!

If you climb three or four days per week, it's important that you perform these supplemental climbing-specific exercises at the end of your climbing session and not on rest days. Depending on the volume and intensity of your climbing, you might execute anywhere from five to ten different supplemental exercises. It would be wise to skip the supplemental exercises at the end of a severe day of climbing that leaves you sore or exhausted.

If you are limited to climbing just once or twice per week, however, it's essential that you engage in 45 to 60 minutes of supplemental training once or twice per week. For example, you might execute eight to fifteen different exercises from chapters 7, 8, 9, 10 on Tuesday and Thursday, and then go climbing on Saturday and Sunday.

Antagonist and Stabilizer Training

If you are serious about climbing your best, then you must also be serious about training the antagonist and stabilizer muscles. A modest investment of 30 minutes, three days per week, is all it takes to adequately train these muscles, thus improving joint stability and reducing risk of common elbow and shoulder injuries. Perform a selection of antagonist/stabilizer exercises (chapter 5) either at the end of your climbing session or on rest days between climbing.

Periodization Training Strategies

In chapter 1 you learned the value of varying your workouts every few days or weeks—a scheduling strategy known as periodization—to maximize the training response and stave off injuries and burnout. Detailed below are two excellent ways to employ periodization, although you should feel free to modify or break from these programs (or jump ahead to the phase 4 "taper") prior to a competition or during your performance season.

The 4-3-2-1 Training Cycle

This is the training cycle that I advocate for the "average climber," and it's best used during off-season training and during multiweek gaps between road trips. The first three phases of this cycle individually target each of the three energy systems and include a lot of actual climbing time to maximize skill development. The one-week fourth phase involves a "training taper," composed of reduced training/climbing volume and active recovery activities. (*Note:* Intermediate and advanced climbers who mainly engage in bouldering can eliminate phase 1, thus making a strength/power-oriented "3-2-1 training cycle.") Let's take a brief look at each phase of this cycle.

Phase 1: The four-week climbing skill and stamina phase involves, well, lots of climbing! This climbing can be done indoors, outdoors, or a combination of both. You must, however, faithfully obey an important distinction of this phase—that is, minimize time spent maximal climbing and "projecting," and instead log lots of mileage on a wide variety of routes that are one to three number grades below your maximum ability. The result of this four-week phase will be improved technique and tactics, acquisition of new motor programs (climbing skills), and the development of local endurance and general stamina. Climbing four days a week is ideal as long as you are not climbing at your limit or to extreme levels of fatigue. You can also engage in general fitness exercises and both climbing-specific and nonspecific aerobic training as described in chapter 10.

Phase 2: Three weeks of maximum-strength and power training is the next step in the cycle, and therefore hard bouldering, weighted exercises (e.g., fingerboard hangs and pull-ups), and reactive training are ideal choices since powerful movements and short, near-maximal effort are hallmarks of this phase. Given the high intensity and physical stress of such training, it's important to take plenty of rest between boulder problems, exercises, and workout days. Moreover, you should avoid training hard on consecutive days, although doing some moderate-intensity aerobic "recovery" climbing and antagonist training is okay on the day after a maximum-strength/power day. Consult chapters 7 and 8 for appropriate exercise selection.

Phase 3: The two-week-long strength/power-endurance phase is the most fatiguing and grueling portion of the cycle. Training at moderately high intensity and with reduced rest between exercises and climbing sets will produce the telltale muscular pump and "burn." Interval training is the cornerstone method of triggering adaptations of the anaerobic lactic energy system. Chapter 9 presents many exercises for improving strength-endurance in the finger flexors and power-endurance in the pulling muscles. I recommend two or three hard anaerobic endurance workouts per week with a fourth aerobic recovery climbing session. This grueling phase is best limited to just two weeks (three at most), since the anaerobic lactic energy system is the least trainable and the most stressful (most likely to lead to overtraining, excessive fatigue, and a drop in performance).

Phase 4: The final phase of the ten-week cycle is a training taper that allows for a peak in strength, power, and endurance to be revealed upon completion of the taper. Climbing and specific training must be limited to just two or three days and with a significant reduction in volume (reduce volume to about one-third of your normal). A small amount of high-intensity exercise is okay (to keep your nervous system primed) through the first five days of the week, but it's essential to keep any bouldering or power-training exercises very brief (just a few sets). The sixth and seventh days must allow for complete rest from climbing—only modest mobility work is advised. Consider taking most of the week off—little or no training—if you feel greatly fatigued and lack motivation after the first three phases of the cycle.

Daily Undulating Periodization (DUP)

This nontraditional form of periodization is a good microcycle strategy for more-advanced individuals engaging in regular outdoor performance climbing. Weekend warriors and pro climbers alike can employ DUP to help maintain all three energy systems during a period of several weeks up to a couple of months, although this approach is unlikely to yield any significant long-term gains (which requires a more focused cycle such as the 4-3-2-1 or 3-2-1).

Here's how to do it: Each one-week DUP cycle must include one or two training or climbing sessions targeting each of the three energy systems. Therefore, if you go bouldering outdoors two days per week, it's these two sessions that serve as your two maximum-strength/power workouts for the week—the remainder of your week's training should include only one aerobic climbing session and one pumpy anaerobic capacity session. Conversely, if you engaged in two days of hard, pumpy route climbing over the weekend (two days of strength/power-endurance training), then your weekday training should involve only a maximum-strength/power (bouldering and anaerobic alactic exercises) session and a threshold or ARC aerobic climbing session. The bottom line: Regardless of your climbing preference, the goal of DUP is to engage in at least one hard workout of each energy system each week. Of course, you must also incorporate two brief sessions per week of supplemental core, antagonist, and stabilizer training—consider the latter to be mandatory.

Designing Your Program

Designing an effective training program must begin with a long-term vision of your goals for the year ahead. These goals may be specific climbs to ascend, a grade to achieve by the end of the season, or just to be in top condition for weekend climbing or a big road trip. Mark target achievement dates on a calendar, along with the dates of possible weekend climbing trips, competitions, or other major events.

Given this framework you can now decide whether you want to begin a 4-3-2-1 Training Cycle or proceed with a self-directed train-as-you-go program. Most climbers get better results given the structure of the 4-3-2-1 Cycle, even if it has to be occasionally broken for a few days due to conflicts or a brief road trip. If you choose the self-directed program, it's important that you still plan out your workouts at least a week in advance. Only

this way will you be sure to schedule enough rest days as well as intelligently premeditate a workout plan for optimal results. Unfortunately, self-directed programs that lack proper planning eventually morph into random or redundant workouts of minimal effectiveness. The key to excellent results is not necessarily training harder, but training smarter—and planning your workouts in advance and acting in accordance with the principles of effective training is the essence of smart training.

Regardless of whether you use the 4-3-2-1 Cycle or a self-directed program, you should use a microcycle to integrate the various types of training into your weekly schedule. Table 11.4 offers several training microcycles that will help you integrate your climbing time, pull-muscle training, antagonist training, and aerobic training into a weekly schedule. The four-day-per-week climbing schedule is optimal; however, if there are no indoor walls or crags near your locale, you can still train to great benefit using one of the weekend-climbing-only microcycles.

As for the particulars of your climbing workouts, consult table 11.5 for an outline of how to best structure your climbing and in-place-of-climbing workouts. Per the microcycles shown in table 11.4, your goal is to engage in a total of four climbing-specific workouts per week. Out of the remaining three days per week, schedule one or two rest days and one or two days of supplemental aerobic training or antagonist training.

Finally, there's the matter of structuring a training schedule over an entire season or the calendar year. Although such macroscale planning can be difficult, there's great benefit to roughing in a tentative schedule of climbing trips, training cycles, and time off from climbing. First, long-term planning is essential for producing the greatest strength gains and climbing improvements over

Table 11.4 Sample Microcycles for Intermediates

Four-Day-Per-Week Climbing—Schedule #1

Monday	Tuesday	Wednesday	Thursday	Friday	Saturday	Sunday
R or S/AA*	C/CE/TC	S/AA*	C/CE/TC	R	C/AA*	C/CE/TC*

KEY: C=Climbing; CE=Climbing-Specific Exercises; S=Stabilizer & Antagonist Training; TC=Total Core & Leg Exercises; AA=Nonspecific Aerobic Activity; R=Rest (*Optional)

Four-Day-Per-Week Climbing—Schedule #2

Monday	Tuesday	Wednesday	Thursday	Friday	Saturday	Sunday
R or S/AA*	C/TC/CE (Str/Power, or S/P-endurance)	C/S/CE (AeEnd)	TC/AA*	R	C/AA*	C/CE/TC*

KEY: C=Climbing; CE (Str/Power)=Strength & Power Climbing Exercises; CE (AeEnd)=Aerobic Endurance Climbing Exercises; S=Stabilizer & Antagonist Training; TC=Total Core & Leg Exercises; AA=Nonspecific Aerobic Activity; R=Rest (*Optional)

Weekend-Only Climbing—Schedule #1

Monday	Tuesday	Wednesday	Thursday	Friday	Saturday	Sunday
R or AA	CE/S/TC	R or AA	CE/S/TC	R	C/AA*	C/CE*/TC*

KEY: C=Climbing; CE=Climbing-Specific Exercises; S=Stabilizer & Antagonist Training; TC=Total Core & Leg Exercises; AA=Nonspecific Aerobic Activity; R=Rest (*Optional)

Weekend-Only Climbing—Schedule #2

Monday	Tuesday	Wednesday	Thursday	Friday	Saturday	Sunday
R or S/AA*	TC, CE (Str/Power or S/P-endurance)	CE (AeEnd)/S	TC/AA*	R	C/AA*	C/CE/TC*

KEY: C=Climbing; CE (Str/Power)=Strength & Power Climbing Exercises; CE (AeEnd)=Aerobic Endurance Climbing Exercises; S=Stabilizer & Antagonist Training; TC=Total Core & Leg Exercises; AA=Nonspecific Aerobic Activity; R=Rest (*Optional)

the course of a season. Furthermore, a training macrocycle enables you to plan out training to produce a peaking effect for an important road trip or competition. Finally, mapping out your climbing and training up to a year in advance empowers you to schedule some time away from climbing each year without adversely affecting your level of conditioning for important events. I strongly advocate a monthlong break from climbing every twelve months to facilitate a recharging of your

motivation and the healing of any of those nagging physical pangs that commonly develop over a season of climbing. Some folks enjoy taking this month off around the Christmas holidays, whereas climbers in southern cities often prefer taking their break during the peak of the summer heat. Table 11.6 shows how one climber filled in her macrocycle over the course of a season. Make copies of the blank macrocycle in appendix B to use in your annual planning.

Table 11.5 Intermediates' Climbing and In-Place-of-Climbing Workout Templates

Sample Skill and Stamina (Aerobic Energy System) Workout (2–4 hours)

- 10–15 minutes of general warm-up activity including a few mobility exercises.
- 75–120 minutes practice climbing and lapping moderate (submaximal, no-fall) routes. Build up to 1,000 feet of climbing; if the gym's routes average 30 feet in length, you'll need to climb 30+ routes (or up and down 15+ times).
- 10–30 minutes strenuous bouldering or near-limit roped climbing.
- 3–5 sets pull-muscle endurance-oriented exercises.
- 15–30 minutes of antagonist/stabilizer-muscle training, doing an aggregate of 8–12 sets—ideally, do this on a rest day from climbing.
- 5–15 minutes cool-down—foam rolling and mild stretching.

Sample Maximum-Strength/Power Workout (1.25–2.5 hours)

- 10–15 minutes of general warm-up activity including a few mobility exercises.
- 30–60 minutes maximal bouldering and hypergravity bouldering.
- 20–40 minutes maximum-strength and power-training exercises. Select appropriate forearm exercises (3–7 total sets) and pull-muscle exercises (3–7 total sets).
- Conclude with 3–6 sets of core exercises.
- 20–40 minutes of posterior chain and antagonist/stabilizer-muscle training, doing an aggregate of 8–12 sets—ideally, do these exercises on a rest day from climbing.
- 5–15 minutes cool-down—foam rolling and mild stretching.

Sample Strength/Power-Endurance Workout (1.5–2.5 hours)

- 10–15 minutes of general warm-up activity including a few mobility exercises.
- 30–60 minutes interval training on rope routes or a Treadwall, or bouldering 4x4s or similar. You should get deeply pumped, yet strive to avoid complete muscle failure until late in the session.
- 20–40 minutes strength/power-endurance exercises. Select appropriate finger flexor exercises (5–10 total sets) and pull-muscle exercises (5–10 total sets).
- Conclude with 3–6 sets of core exercises.
- 20–40 minutes of posterior chain and antagonist/stabilizer-muscle training, doing an aggregate of 8–12 sets—ideally, do these exercises on a rest day from climbing.
- 5–15 minutes cool-down—foam rolling and mild stretching.

Table 11.6 Training and Climbing Macrocycle

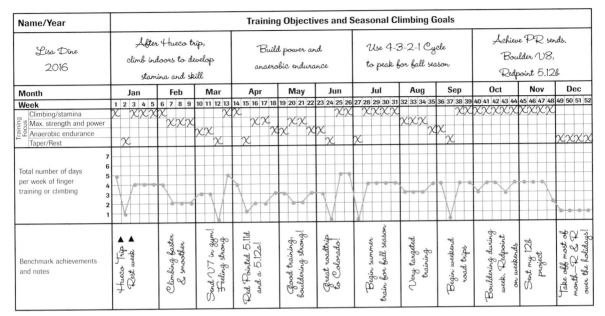

Name/Year	Training Objectives and Seasonal Climbing Goals			
Lisa Dine 2016	After Hueco trip, climb indoors to develop stamina and skill	Build power and anaerobic endurance	Use 4-3-2-1 Cycle to peak for fall season	Achieve PR sends. Boulder V8, Redpoint 5.12b

Training Focus — Climbing/stamina, Max. strength and power, Anaerobic endurance, Taper/Rest (by month Jan–Dec, weeks 1–52)

Total number of days per week of finger training or climbing (scale 1–7)

Benchmark achievements and notes: Hueco Trip! Rest week. / Climbing better & smoother. / Sent V7 in gym! Feeling strong. / Red Pointed 5.11d and a 5.12a! / Good training, bouldering strong! / Great roadtrip to Colorado! / Begin summer train for fall season. / Very targeted training. / Begin weekend road trips. / Bouldering during week. Redpoint on weekends. / Sent my 12b project. / Take off most of month—R & R over the holidays!

Advanced Climber's Programs

If you on-sight 5.12 routes, boulder V9, redpoint 5.13 and above, or frequently climb big walls, then in the context of this book you are an advanced climber in need of an advanced training program. While the potential for further refinement in the areas of technique and the mind must never be overlooked, taking your game to the next level will definitely require greater physical prowess. The physical abilities you need to elevate are highly specific to your area of specialization. This is a critical distinction—to perform at the highest levels as a boulderer, sport climber, or multipitch, big-wall, or alpine climber demands an extremely specific training program that targets the particular limiting constraints of that type of climbing.

Figure 11.1 depicts the limiting physical constraints across the continuum of climbing subdisciplines. Bouldering, sport climbing, and big-wall and alpine climbing place unique demands on the muscles, the cardiovascular system, and the energy systems used to fuel muscle action. Short boulders require brief, powerful movements and

Figure 11.1 Continuum of Climbing Subdisciplines and Primary Physical Constraints

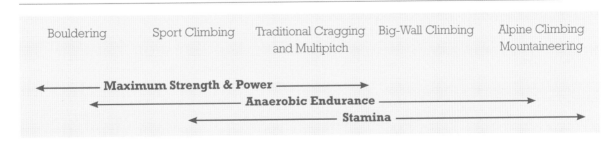

maximum strength, for example, whereas longer boulders and short sport climbs also require a high level of strength/power-endurance in addition to raw power and limit strength. Longer sport climbs and multipitch routes demand strength/power-endurance and aerobic endurance (stamina), but also occasional bursts of strength and power—thus all energy systems are used extensively on half-rope- to multi-rope-length ascents. Meanwhile, most big-wall and alpine routes require high levels of muscular endurance as well as vast stamina, but much less in the way of raw power and limit strength. The bottom line: Advanced climbers must target their training on the specific physical traits and energy systems predominantly used in their preferred type of climbing, in addition to the global constraints identified by the self-assessment.

Another important—and often overlooked—element of an advanced training program is the need to do supplemental exercises to strengthen the stabilizer and antagonist muscles. Many high-level climbers come to suffer elbow, shoulder, and even lower-back injuries due to muscular imbalances resulting from years of climbing-specific training. Extraordinary levels of strength in the finger flexor muscles of the forearms, the pull muscles of the upper arms and back, and the core muscles of the torso can lead to joint instability due to comparatively low levels of strength in the muscles antagonist to these prime movers. Fortunately, regular training of these opposing muscles will improve balance and stability and therefore reduce injury risk. Twenty to 40 minutes of training, two or three days per week, is all you need to reap the benefits of antagonist conditioning.

Now let's examine the key elements for designing a training program for bouldering, sport climbing and multipitch cragging, and big-wall and alpine climbing. Unlike the beginner- and intermediate-level programs described earlier, the strategy here is to narrow the scope of your training and focus primarily on the physical limitations of your current endeavors. In outlining a basic program for each of these three categories, it's assumed that you already possess ideal body composition, exceedingly high technical and mental skill levels, and above-average awareness of personal strengths and weaknesses. While the self-assessment in chapter 2 may uncover an unknown Achilles' heel, advanced climbers typically understand their true limiting constraints and thus recognize what they need to train (or give up) in order to reach the next level of performance.

Training for Bouldering Specialists

As illustrated in figure 11.1, bouldering places a premium on limit strength and power as well as local strength/power-endurance. The muscles of interest are obviously those used to grip the rock, pull up and lock off, and maintain body tension on steep terrain. Consequently, the exercises described in chapters 6, 7, 8 and 9 must make up the main course of a boulder climber's training "feast."

As in all training programs described in this book, the workout should begin with a warm-up period and then progress to climbing, climbing-specific exercises, and antagonist exercises, concluding with a cool-down of light stretching. In designing the climbing and climbing exercise portion of the workout, it's best to train either limit strength and power (together) or strength/power-endurance on any given day (see table 11.7 for sample workouts). Training both in a single workout is not ideal; in fact, you will obtain the best training results by concentrating on a single facet—either maximum strength and power or strength/power-endurance—for a week or two at a time. Two possible approaches would be to alternate your training focus every week (that is, a week training maximum strength and power followed by a week of strength/power-endurance training) or to follow a 3-2-1 Cycle or Daily Undulating Periodization (DUP) program, described earlier in the "Periodization Training Strategies" sidebar on page 199.

Table 11.7 Sample Advanced Workouts for Bouldering Specialists

Maximum-Strength/Power Workout (1.5–2.5 hours)
• 10–15 minutes of general warm-up activity including a few mobility exercises.
• 30–60 minutes maximal bouldering and hypergravity bouldering.
• 30–45 minutes maximum-strength and power-training exercises. Select appropriate finger flexor exercises (7–10 total sets) and pull-muscle exercises (7–10 total sets) from chapters 7 and 8, respectively.
• Conclude with 4–8 sets of total core, per chapter 6.
• 20–40 minutes of antagonist/stabilizer-muscle training (chapter 5), doing an aggregate of 8–12 sets— ideally, do these exercises on a rest day from climbing.
• 5–15 minutes cool-down—foam rolling and mild stretching.

Strength/Power-Endurance Workout (1.5–2.5 hours)
• 10–15 minutes of general warm-up activity including a few mobility exercises.
• 45–60 minutes interval training composed of bouldering 4x4s, near-limit rope routes, Treadwall intervals, or similar. You should get deeply pumped, yet strive to avoid complete muscle failure until late in the session.
• 30–45 minutes strength/power-endurance exercises. Select appropriate finger flexor exercises (7–10 total sets) and pull-muscle exercises (7–10 total sets) from chapter 9.
• Conclude with 3–6 sets of core exercises.
• 20–40 minutes of antagonist/stabilizer-muscle training, doing an aggregate of 8–12 sets—ideally, do these exercises on a rest day from climbing.
• 5–15 minutes cool-down—foam rolling and mild stretching.

Allowing adequate rest between workouts is essential for reaping the full benefits of your training and for avoiding overtraining. Use one of the weekly microcycles in table 11.4 or the DUP microcycle shown in table 11.8 as a template for creating a weekly schedule with adequate rest days. If regularly climbing for performance outside, favor the DUP cycle; the microcycles in table 11.4 and use of a 3-2-1 periodization cycle is better if training for gains, off-season, or between trips.

Most important for hard-training boulderers is getting enough rest. Fatigue can accumulate to the point of a performance drop-off over the course of a few weeks of extensive limit strength, power, and strength/power-endurance training. To avoid diminished performance (and reduce injury

Table 11.8 Sample Advanced Workouts for Bouldering Specialists

Sample DUP Microcycle for Boulderers						
Monday	Tuesday	Wednesday	Thursday	Friday	Saturday	Sunday
S/AA*	Anaerobic Climbing (4x4s, etc) & CE (S/P End) & TC	Aerobic Climbing & CE (AeEnd) & TC	S/AA*	R	Hard Bouldering Outside	Hard Bouldering Outside
KEY: C=Climbing; CE (S/P End)=Strength/Power-Endurance Climbing Exercises; CE (AeEnd)=Aerobic Endurance Climbing Exercises; S=Stabilizer & Antagonist Training; TC=Total Core & Leg Exercises; AA=Nonspecific Aerobic Activity; R=Rest (*Optional)						

Steep sport routes demand both a strong anaerobic and aerobic energy system, which are best trained via targeted workouts and training blocks. Here Audrey Sniezek cruises up steep Gold Coast terrain at the Red River Gorge, Kentucky.

risk), strive to maintain three nonclimbing days per week—you can do some antagonist training or generalized aerobic training on these days, but nothing that weights your fingers in a climbing-specific way. Take additional days off if you feel like you are training tired or getting weaker (a sign of under-resting).

An occasional four- to seven-day break from rigorous training and climbing is another good investment for hard-training climbers. Taking such a break every month or two will not only help you avoid the black hole of overtraining, but also create a peaking effect—that is, after this four- to seven-day rest (or training taper), you will be at your strongest for attempting a personal best route or major project. Similarly, it's advantageous to utilize a training macrocycle to integrate your workout program and rest breaks with dates of climbing trips or competitions. Make copies of the blank macrocycle in appendix B, and use it to keep track of your weekly training and to schedule a long-term program for optimal results.

Training for Sport Climbers and Multipitch Climbing

Sport climbing and traditional cragging are nearer the middle of the climbing continuum (see figure 11.1), and therefore demand a comprehensive training program for developing limit strength and power, strength/power-endurance, and local and generalized aerobic endurance. The training strategy here is not unlike the comprehensive plan detailed for the intermediate-level climber on page 197. The primary difference is that advanced climbers have higher tolerances for both training and climbing—with more years of experience and a higher level of conditioning, these experts must train and climb with higher intensity and greater volume to experience further gains in conditioning.

The 4-3-2-1 Cycle (or modified 3-2-1 Cycle) described earlier is an excellent framework by which to periodize training for optimal results.

While such a ten-week (or seven-week) schedule may be difficult to abide by during peak climbing season, it would be wise to implement it during an off-season period or between major trips. When possible, however, you want to vary the focus of your climbing every few workouts (or weeks) so as to work each of the three physical demands shown in the climbing continuum.

Planning your weekly workout schedule should be done at least a week in advance, so that you can schedule three or four days of climbing and at least three rest days. Supplemental targeted training for upper-body strength, power, and strength/power-endurance should always be performed on your climbing days, not on the rest days from climbing. Exposing yourself to more than four days of climbing-specific activity per week is a prescription for overtraining and negative results.

The details for individual workouts will depend heavily on whether you are climbing outdoors, training on an indoor wall, or just strength training on a given day. Ideally, you want to do some form of climbing on each of your three or four workout days per week—a home climbing wall is an invaluable resource if access to a commercial gym or local crag is impractical on weekdays. As shown in table 11.9, your workouts should begin with a warm-up period, followed by an extended session of climbing. Pick problems and routes that will target the physical demand of the day—limit strength and power, strength/power-endurance, or aerobic endurance.

After an hour or so of climbing, transition into your targeted training exercises for the day. Consult chapters 7, 8, 9, and 10 to select a variety of exercises that match the training theme of the day. For example, if strength/power-endurance is your training focus du jour, you'd want to execute several of the finger and upper-body exercises that work strength/power-endurance, such as fingerboard repeaters, bouldering 4x4s, power pull-up intervals, Frenchies, and ladder laps on the campus board. Use

Table 11.9 Advanced Climber Workout Guidelines for Sport and Multipitch Climbers

Visit www.TrainingForClimbing.com for detailed workouts available as downloads.
Maximum-Strength/Power Workout (1.5–2.5 hours)
• 10–15 minutes of general warm-up activity including a few mobility exercises.
• 30–60 minutes maximal bouldering and hypergravity bouldering.
• 30–45 minutes limit-strength and power-training exercises. Select appropriate forearm exercises (7–10 total sets) and pull-muscle exercises (7–10 total sets) from chapters 7 and 8, respectively.
• Conclude with 4–8 sets of total core.
• 20–40 minutes of posterior chain and antagonist/stabilizer-muscle training, doing an aggregate of 8–12 sets—ideally, do these exercises on a rest day from climbing.
• 5–15 minutes cool-down—foam rolling and mild stretching.
Strength/Power-Endurance Workout (1.5–2.5 hours)
• 10–15 minutes of general warm-up activity including a few mobility exercises.
• 45–60 minutes interval training on near-limit rope routes or a Treadwall, or bouldering 4x4s or similar. You should get deeply pumped, yet strive to avoid complete muscle failure until late in the session.
• 30–45 minutes strength/power-endurance exercises. Select appropriate finger flexor exercises (7–10 total sets) and pull-muscle exercises (7–10 total sets) from chapter 9.
• Conclude with 3–6 sets of core exercises.
• 20–40 minutes of posterior chain and antagonist/stabilizer-muscle training, doing an aggregate of 8–12 sets—ideally, do these exercises on a rest day from climbing.
• 5–15 minutes cool-down—foam rolling and mild stretching.
Aerobic Capacity Workout (2–4 hours)
• 10–15 minutes of general warm-up activity including a few mobility exercises.
• 90–180 minutes of intermittent climbing (submaximal, no-fall) routes. Build up to 1,200 feet of climbing; if the gym's routes average 30 feet in length, you'll need to climb 40+ routes (or up and down 20+). Alternatively, climb large holds on a Treadwall for 3–5-minute intervals at an intensity of between 5 and 8.5 out of 10. Do up to eight intervals with approximately a 1:1 climb-to-rest ratio.
• 3–5 sets pull-muscle aerobic endurance exercises (chapter 10).
• 15–30 minutes of antagonist/stabilizer-muscle training, doing an aggregate of 8–12 sets—ideally, do this on a rest day from climbing.
• 5–15 minutes cool-down—foam rolling and mild stretching.

the rest breaks between sets to perform a couple of the core-conditioning exercises, such as Windshield Wipers, mountain climber planks, reverse planks, and crunches.

As stressed throughout this book, two days of antagonist and stabilizer training is mandatory for all climbers. Depending on the length of your workout and energy reserves, you could close out your workout with a few antagonist muscle exercises or, better yet, schedule a time to do these non-specific exercises on a rest day from climbing. Either way, consider two sets of dips, push-ups, shoulder presses, rotator cuff internal and external rotations, and reverse wrist curls the absolute minimum requirement. See chapter 5 for details of these and other antagonist exercises.

Table 11.10 Example of DUP Microcycle for Sport and Multipitch Climbers

Monday	Tuesday	Wednesday	Thursday	Friday	Saturday	Sunday
S/AA*	Bouldering & TC/CE (Str/ power)	Aerobic Climbing, CE (AeEnd) & TC	S/AA*	R	Hard Route Climbing	Hard Route Climbing
KEY: C=Climbing; CE (Str/Power)=Strength & Power Climbing Exercises; CE (AeEnd)=Aerobic Endurance Climbing Exercises; S=Stabilizer & Antagonist Training; TC=Total Core & Leg Exercises; AA=Nonspecific Aerobic Activity; R=Rest (*Optional)						

A final training element that's often overlooked by multipitch climbers is generalized aerobic training to build stamina and enhance recovery ability. If you frequently climb full days outdoors, striving to climb several routes near your limit, then you can benefit from a modest amount of nonspecific aerobic training. While putting in frequent long days (or sessions) at the crags (or gym) is the most specific way to train climbing stamina, this is not an option for many folks with limited access to the crags (or a gym with good lead routes). Chapter 10 provides several options, including running and rowing intervals, tempo runs, and a two-a-day approach to training. By engaging in two or three generalized aerobic workouts of moderate duration and intensity each week, you'll grow your stamina and gain uncommon ability to recovery at mid-climb rests and between climbs.

Conditioning for Big-Wall and Alpine Climbing

The physical demands of big-wall and alpine climbing are as different from those of bouldering as running a marathon differs from the 100-meter dash. As shown in figure 11.1, strength/power-endurance and specific and generalized aerobic endurance are the primary physical constraints for big-wall and mountain climbing, whereas limit strength and power are essential for bouldering. Therefore, an effective training program for big-wall and alpine climbers will be vastly different from the programs described on the preceding pages.

As an advanced climber, you likely have a few big-wall or alpine ascents already under your belt. Ask yourself the question: What were the constraints on these previous climbs that prevented me from climbing faster, harder, and longer? As in all forms of climbing, such limitations are commonly a complex blend of mental, technical/tactical, and physical issues. Constantly remind yourself that taking your game to the next level requires acute attention to improving in all these areas. Since the focus of this book is the physical domain, let's examine how you can get into better shape for future ascents and expeditions.

First, you need to consider what aspect of your physical conditioning is most likely to inhibit you on upcoming climbs. If your goal is climbing a big wall in a day, then muscular endurance would be your primary constraint (being able to pump through many strenuous pitches in short order), with stamina a definite secondary limitation (having the aerobic capacity to keep moving for 12 to 18 hours). Given the goal of mountain climbing, however, these physical constraints are likely reversed. Hiking and climbing for several days at elevation is largely a matter of aerobic capacity, although there will certainly be sections of climbing (or even steep hiking) that will test your muscular endurance.

Designing the most effective program for reaching your goals, therefore, requires that you train as you will climb. If you are a big-wall climber, however, you obviously can't train on big walls every day, nor could an alpine climber live and climb in the mountains year-round. Still, you can train in a way that mimics the physical demands of these endeavors. Here's how.

CONDITIONING FOR BIG WALLS

If big-wall climbing is your passion, you would do best by improving strength/power-endurance and local aerobic endurance. Training two to four days per week with a variety of climbing-specific endurance-training exercises from chapters 9 and 10 would hit the mark. Of course, the exercise of sending many hard pitches in a half or full day is the ultimate method of training muscular endurance, so you should never pass up an opportunity to go climbing (up to four days per week) in place of exercise training.

In terms of training aerobic capacity (stamina), nothing surpasses the benefit of frequent dawn-to-dusk days of climbing. You may only be able to log a few of these marathon-climbing days per month,

however, so use the training alternative: two-a-day workouts as described in chapter 10 (see the "Aerobic Training for Multipitch and Big-Wall Climbers" sidebar on page 189).

The most effective two-a-day strategy is to combine a long run in the morning with a couple of hours of afternoon or evening climbing. Alternatively, you could engage in two aerobic workouts or two climbing workouts in the same day. Regardless, both the morning and evening workouts must be of sufficient duration to tap your reservoir of stamina. Going bouldering for 30 minutes or jogging a couple of miles won't do it. As a guideline, consider 45 minutes of aerobic exercise and 1 hour of actual climbing time to be the minimum investment. Twice this amount would be ideal for a highly conditioned climber training for elite-level ascents.

Table 11.11 presents two microcycles for integrating weekday training and weekend climbing. Given the high demands of your program, quality

Table 11.11 Big-Wall Climber Weekend-Only Climbing Schedules

Big-Wall Climber Weekend-Only Climbing—Schedule #1							
	Monday	Tuesday	Wednesday	Thursday	Friday	Saturday	Sunday
AM Workout	R	AA	AA	R	R	Climb All Day (or repeat Tuesday)	Climb All Day (or repeat Wednesday)
PM Workout	S	C/TC CE (S/PE)	C CE(AeEnd)	S/TC	R		

KEY: C=Climbing; CE(S/PE)=Climbing Exercises (Strength/Power-Endurance); CE (AeEnd)=Aerobic Endurance Climbing Exercises; S=Stabilizer & Antagonist Training; TC=Total Core & Leg Exercises; AA=Nonspecific Aerobic Activity; R=Rest (*Optional)

Big-Wall Climber Weekend-Only Climbing—Schedule #2							
	Monday	Tuesday	Wednesday	Thursday	Friday	Saturday	Sunday
AM Workout	R	AA	R	AA	R	Climb All Day (or repeat Tuesday)	Climb All Day (or repeat Thursday)
PM Workout	S	TC CE (S/PE)	S/AA	TC CE(AeEnd)	R		

KEY: CE(S/PE)=Climbing Exercises (Strength/Power-Endurance); CE (AeEnd)=Aerobic Endurance Climbing Exercises; S=Stabilizer & Antagonist Training; TC=Total Core & Leg Exercises; AA=Nonspecific Aerobic Activity; R=Rest (*Optional)

rest and nutrition (see chapter 13) play a significant role in determining your rate of recovery and absolute gains in physical conditioning. Regular antagonist-muscle training is another indispensable part of your program, as are warm-up and stretching activities. And given the full-body rigors of big-wall climbing, a commitment to training the total core and posterior chain muscles (hips and legs) will pay big-time dividends—use a broad selection of exercises from chapter 6 at least twice per week. Remember, excelling as an advanced climber requires an excellent training program and the discipline to not overlook or skip any detail, no matter how subtle or seemingly unimportant.

On a much larger scale, the magnitude of your year-to-year gains in conditioning and success on the rock will be a function of how well you plan your seasonal training, as well as your ability to remain uninjured. Incur a finger, elbow, or shoulder injury and you may lose a few months of climbing and experience a setback in your overall level of conditioning. The planned rest days each week and the occasional planned week off from serious training and climbing are invaluable for keeping your mind and body in good working order. Use the blank macrocycle in appendix B to schedule your training and rest days around climbing trips, recovery periods, and other important life events.

CONDITIONING FOR ALPINE ASCENTS

Outside of the immense technical and logistical demands, success on alpine climbs often comes down to physical and mental stamina. Whether the goal is a one-day, base-camp-to-base-camp ascent of an alpine wall or a multiday summit push up a major peak, you can never possess too much stamina and confidence in your physical capabilities. Like an ultramarathoner running a 50- or 100-mile race, knowing that you've done it before and that you are in condition to do it again is a powerful realization that will carry you through to completion. Consequently, possessing a high level

of conditioning as you set off on your expedition is as important as possessing the right equipment and climbing partners.

Although all-around fitness is a necessity, excelling on long climbs at elevation comes down to the master skill of economic movement combined with a massive reservoir of stamina. Frequent practice at the types of climbing you will be faced with in the mountains—crack, face, mixed, and such—is critical for developing the movement and tactical skills needed for fast, efficient climbing. Physically, your capability to perform at a high level will be a function of aerobic capacity and your ability to persevere through brief periods of hard climbing that require muscular (anaerobic) endurance. While the big-wall climbing program described above is certainly useful for the alpine climber, you also have a great need to grow stamina with some ultradistance conditioning (see chapter 10, page 190).

In the case of a major climb or expedition upcoming in a few months, you could begin with six weeks of the big-wall program (above) followed by six weeks of targeted ultradistance conditioning. Taper back the training volume at least three weeks before the trip, and do no strenuous training for the final week before you are to begin the actual ascent. Use the training macrocycle in appendix B to plan your training between major climbs and trips. For example, schedule a three- to four-month pre-expedition training program ending with a two-week taper period that concludes with five to seven days of complete rest leading up to your first climbing day. Then after the expedition, schedule a rest period of a length equal to at least one-half the duration of your expedition. While this may seem like an excessively long break from training, it's a demonstrable fact that high-altitude and ultramarathon expeditions take a tremendous toll on the body that requires weeks, not days, to recover from.

*Craig Demartino cruising at
the Red River Gorge, Kentucky.*
MIKE WILKINSON

CHAPTER 12

Special Training Considerations

The beauty of climbing is that anyone can experience the wonder of the sport. Simply by moving over stone, you tap into a life force that transcends ability, gender, and age. That's the power of climbing!

While climbing used to be an activity dominated by 20- and 30-something men, it is now popular among women, teenagers, and even the over-50 crowd as well. The beauty of climbing is that anyone can experience the wonder of the sport—in fact, each of the above-mentioned special groups possess unique mental and technical gifts that can be leveraged for extraordinary success! Still, women, youths, and more "senior" participants do have some special considerations to account for, mostly relating to strength training and potential for injury. If you are a member of one of these demographic groups, this chapter will touch on a few key issues that you should be aware of in planning and executing an effective conditioning program.

Training for Females

The unique physiological traits of female climbers result in both assets and liabilities when it comes to climbing performance. On the plus side, females possess shorter fingers, a lower center of mass, and better flexibility than males, which enhances grip of small finger holds, more favorably positions weight over the feet, and facilitates a greater range of footholds and body positions, respectively. In terms of liabilities, females possess a higher average percent

body fat and less natural upper-body strength than their male counterparts.

Fortunately, these physical limitations can be largely erased via an effective training program. The serious female climber must then embrace the general and climbing-specific strength-training exercises described in chapters 4 through 10. In fact, such strength training is imperative for female climbers looking for high-level performance, since lack of muscular strength, power, and local endurance is a common limiting constraint. Specifically, training should focus on increasing maximum strength in the upper-body pulling muscles and finger flexors, the antagonist and stabilizer muscles, and the core muscles of the torso. In the formative stage of conditioning, it's vital to leverage less-than-body-weight exercises such as aided pull-ups and bench dips, described in chapter 4. As strength-to-weight ratio increases, there's no reason why the female climber can't "train like a man" with all the advanced techniques such as fingerboard training, bouldering 4x4s, campus training, and such.

Female climbers would also be wise to engage in some generalized aerobic conditioning as a means of reducing percent body fat. In most cases, positive adaptations will result from a modest investment of 20 to 40 minutes of running, three or four days per week. Of course, improved dietary surveillance combined with regular aerobic activity will bring about the fastest changes in body composition. For more information on this, see the section on weight-loss strategies in chapter 4.

Tips for Female Climbers

- Fall in love with strength training! Engaging in regular training of the pull muscles, finger flexors, antagonists and stabilizers, and core will have a profound effect on your climbing.

- Engage in regular aerobic activity. In particular, running for 20 to 40 minutes a few days per week will favorably change your body composition and improve stamina.

- Go bouldering. Even if roped climbing is your preference, committing just 1 to 2 hours per week to bouldering will foster greater strength and power, as well as a more aggressive approach to attacking crux sequences.

- Work routes just like men do. Occasionally working on a climb at your limit—via toprope or hangdogging on lead—is a great physical workout, as well as a powerful way to develop technical and mental skills.

Training for Juniors

It's undeniable that junior athletes learn complex sports skills more rapidly than adults, and in recent years we've seen many wunderkinder take the climbing world by storm with their V10 and 5.14 ascents, in some cases before becoming a teenager! These featherweight prepubescent climbers can hang on to small holds with little effort and can pull through steep terrain with high efficiency. Still, it's crucial to recognize that these young climbers naturally lack the maturity, self-awareness, and life experience to transfer their sport-climbing prowess to a wide range of climbing pursuits. They are also not physically prepared for the full rigors of serious, climbing-specific training as outlined in this text.

The best training for preteens is simply to climb three or four days per week. Additionally, they can safely engage in some basic training such as body-weight exercises (pull-ups, push-ups, dips, abdominal crunches, and such) and basic dumbbell exercises to train major muscle groups for more strength and balance. Disregard any old wives' tales you've heard that "strength training is not for kids." The American Academy of Pediatrics and the American College of Sports Medicine both support supervised strength training for kids.

A junior climber entering puberty can gradually introduce some of the climbing-specific exercises detailed in chapters 7 and 9, but the most stressful—such as double-dyno campus training,

Tips for Junior Climbers

- Focus on climbing over training. Climb up to four days per week with an emphasis on skill development and having fun!

- Favor general training with body-weight exercises. Youth climbers (under age 13) should train primarily with pull-ups, push-ups, dips, and core-training exercises. Well-conditioned teenage climbers can add more advanced exercises such as the beginner and intermediate exercises described in chapters 7 and 9.

- Engage in regular training of the antagonist and stabilizer muscles. The rapid strength gains that come with puberty can result in significant muscular imbalances and a predisposition to injury. Training the antagonist/stabilizer muscles two or three days per week will greatly reduce injury risk.

- Strive for high-quality nutrition and abundant sleep. Youth climbers should not engage in strict dieting and must have 8 to 10 hours sleep per night.

hypergravity bouldering, and weighted fingerboard hangs—should not be used until near the end of puberty (age 16 or 17). Throughout the preteen and early teenage years, it's vital that the primary training focus remain on improving climbing efficiency through mastery of the mental and technical skills. Given this approach, many junior climbers will advance to extraordinary levels without an excessive commitment to strength training.

The most common setbacks for teenage climbers are overuse injuries in the tendons, joints, and bones of the fingers, including stress fractures and damage to the growth plates. Juniors experiencing chronic pain in the fingers (or elsewhere) should cease climbing for a few weeks (or more) and consult a doctor if the pain continues. As a hard-and-fast rule, climbing and training for climbing must be limited to an aggregate of four days per week. The guidance of an adult climber or coach is extremely beneficial both in helping structure workouts and in monitoring rest and nutritional habits. Consult my book *Training for Climbing* for a much more detailed youth-training program.

Training for Over-50 Climbers

As adult climbers age, numerous physiological changes combine to form an increasing constraint on performance, especially beyond the age of 50. A few of the unfortunate changes include reduced VO_2 max (aerobic capacity), decreased muscle mass, lower proportion of fast-twitch muscle fibers, and slower recovery. Despite these inevitable life changes, you can still climb at a very high level given a renewed focus on the mental and technical aspects of climbing and a commitment to a year-round strength-training program. I know of more than a few 50- and 60-somethings who climb 5.12 and 5.13, ascend big walls, and trek in the mountains. You can, too, given a three-pronged approach of injury avoidance, physical training, and mastery of technical and mental skills.

Injury Avoidance

Unlike the resilient teenage body, older climbers are susceptible to injury during every single workout and climb. Common injuries range from muscle pulls to a subluxed shoulder, torn tendons, and a variety of other joint and spinal problems. Fortunately, you can significantly reduce your risk by engaging in a comprehensive warm-up before every training and climbing session. While a younger climber might rush through a warm-up with just a few minutes of stretching, older climbers would be wise to complete a full 30-minute warm-up of general aerobic activity, foam rolling and stretching, and easy climbing. Such a progressive warm-up will markedly decrease injury risk by warming and lengthening the muscles and spreading synovial fluid to lubricate the tendons and joints. While 30 minutes of warm-up activity might not be your idea of a good time, it will enhance the quality of your climbing and reduce the risk of a muscle or joint injury that might lay you up for months or even knock you out of climbing completely.

Another way the mature, disciplined climber can avoid injuries is simply by avoiding potentially injurious moves while climbing. The goal is to foster a level of kinesthetic awareness where you can assess—or often intuit—the risk potential of a given move. Whether it is an awkward-feeling drop-knee, a tweaky-feeling pocket, or an improbable-feeling lunge, your discipline to heed the sensory feedback and rapidly evaluate the situation before forging onward can save you. Ultimately, you will need to make a quick decision as to whether you should retreat from the risky-feeling move, test the move once to see how it feels, or just push onward with the belief that you will succeed without incident. As a rule, the older you get, the more you should view such a risky-feeling move as a stop sign instead of a caution sign.

Physical Training

Physical training for over-50 climbers is not all that different from the program I prescribe for the mass of climbers. You can safely employ most of the exercises contained in this book. Most of your limitations relate to dynamic, forceful exercises, which become increasingly dangerous with advancing age. Climbers over 50 years of age would be wise to not engage in the most dynamic forms of campus training, one-arm lock-offs or one-arm pull-ups, frequent lunging, and steep V-hard bouldering. Of course, every climber possesses different genetic encoding, experience, and physical capabilities, so there are surely a few senior climbers who prevail through the most stressful training exercises and climbing endeavors. But for the vast majority of older climbers, dynamic training is dangerous training.

Otherwise, your fitness-training goals are similar to those of every other climber: Optimize body composition, improve aerobic capacity and stamina, and increase limit strength and strength/power-endurance. Use the self-assessment test in chapter 2 to provide a focus to your training, then follow either the beginner-, intermediate-, or advanced-level workouts outlined in chapter 11.

Preplanning workout and rest days is of great importance for the older climber. Too many back-to-back workout (or climbing) days, too little rest, and poor nutrition over just a few consecutive days will crack open the door to possible injury or illness. Compound this over several weeks and it will open the door wide. Once injured or sick, the reduced immune efficiency and changing hormone levels of an older climber means slower recovery and a faster drop-off of physical conditioning than for a younger climber. The bottom line for over-50 climbers: Train, rest, and eat on a calculated schedule that will increase strength and stamina, reduce injury risk, and do nothing to tempt injury.

Technical and Mental Mastery

The best older climbers are usually Zen masters who leverage the fact that climbing performance is two-thirds technical and mental and only one-third physical. By exploiting superior skill and wisdom, and bringing many years of experience to the table, older climbers can become true masters of rock by climbing very near their maximum capability.

Calvin Landrus climbing Spank the Monkey (5.12a), Smith Rock, Oregon. JULIEN HAVAC

Tips for Over-50 Climbers

- Always warm up thoroughly before training and climbing. Engage in at least 20 to 30 minutes of warm-up activity, mobility and stretching exercises, and easy climbing.

- Avoid wildly dynamic exercises and climbing moves. Strive to climb statically and with great prudence when encountering severe body positions and moves.

- Engage in a comprehensive training program. Commit to a wide range of training, including aerobic activity, antagonist and stabilizer training, and climbing-specific exercises for developing strength and endurance.

- Leverage your wisdom and skill to prevail on hard routes despite physical limitations. Make improving mental and movement skills a lifelong endeavor, and you will be a climber for life!

Whether that top capacity is 5.9 or 5.13, you can spot these elder masters by their measured approach, smooth sailing through scary terrain, and even the occasional calculated lunge or grunt that shows they are still willing to pull out all the stops to send.

Developing such mastery takes many years; in fact, in a complex sport such as climbing, you can still acquire and refine mental and technical skills even after ten or twenty years' experience. So while your physical capabilities may be plateaued or waning, you can often compensate for this by improving mentally and technically. While describing skill practice methods and mental strategies is beyond the scope of this book (see *Training for Climbing*), it's important to point out that the only pathway to improvement in these areas is to actually go climbing! Consequently, you should strive to strike a balance between fitness training—still an important part of the equation—and going climbing at any of the myriad wonderful crags around the world. And, after all, isn't that the bottom line? Simply by moving over stone, you tap into the life force that climbing provides, which transcends ability, gender, and age. That's the power of climbing!

Jonathan Hörst climbing his age on the first ascent of Valkyrie (5.14a), Ten Sleep Canyon, Wyoming.

Nutrition, Workout Recovery, and Injury Prevention

As a largely self-directed activity, climbing neces-sitates that you play the roles of both coach and athlete—you must compel yourself to do the right things right. That's the essence of an effec-tive training program.

The final facet of an effective training-for-climbing program relates to workout recovery and injury prevention. While the act of working out provides the stimulus for elevating physical performance, neuromuscular adaptations and growth occur pri-marily during nonworkout recovery periods. There-fore, becoming the best-trained climber you can be requires a conscious effort to eat and rest in ways that optimize recovery and lower injury risk.

Unfortunately, many climbers give little thought to these nonworkout aspects of effective training—after all, it's what you do in the gym and on the crags that really matters, right? Of course, this couldn't be further from the truth, as nutrition and rest habits are the obverse side of the training-for-climbing coin. Not only will poor rest and nutritional habits slow recovery and limit strength gains, but chronic under-resting and malnutrition will eventually suck you into the overtraining syndrome with its telltale decline in overall strength and performance.

Given this perspective, view this chapter on nutrition, rest, and injury prevention as the linchpin that binds this book's many aspects into a complete program for achieving stellar results. First, I'll out-line the basics of optimal sports nutrition, includ-ing a cutting-edge strategy to accelerate recovery

after a workout. Next, we'll examine the minimum requirements for rest days and sleep, since it's dur-ing these times that you literally grow stronger. Finally, we'll take a look at five rules for avoiding injury due to overuse and overtraining, as both will rob you of the very thing you want—to become a stronger, better climber!

Optimal Sports Nutrition

For some readers, the subject of optimal sport nutrition will require a paradigm shift away from the understanding of nutrition learned through gimmicky diet books or the hokum of TV info-mercials. Fortunately, optimal sports nutrition is not that complex a subject, and I provide a primer on the critical elements here. For more information on weight-loss strategies, turn to page 65 in chapter 4; for an in-depth study on this subject, I encourage you to read *Training for Climbing*, which includes a full chapter on performance nutrition.

Carbohydrate

First, let's discard the four-food-groups and three-square-meals-a-day nutritional models that many of us learned in school—these are antiquated concepts and not ideal for a serious athlete. The new model is the Food Guide Pyramid (see figure 13.1), which places more emphasis on fruits, vegetables, bread, rice, pasta, and cereal. These carbohydrate-rich foods form the foundation of the pyramid, as they should of your diet.

Figure 13.1 Food Guide Pyramid

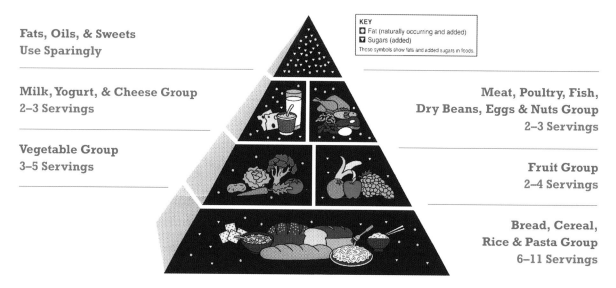

Fats, Oils, & Sweets
Use Sparingly

Milk, Yogurt, & Cheese Group
2–3 Servings

Vegetable Group
3–5 Servings

KEY
☐ Fat (naturally occurring and added)
☑ Sugars (added)
These symbols show fats and added sugars in foods.

Meat, Poultry, Fish,
Dry Beans, Eggs & Nuts Group
2–3 Servings

Fruit Group
2–4 Servings

Bread, Cereal,
Rice & Pasta Group
6–11 Servings

In my opinion, the USDA's Food Guide Pyramid is still the best model for proper eating. The agency has developed My Pyramid Plan, which suggests adjusting the amounts of these foods according to your age, sex, and physical activity. To develop a personalized eating plan, see www.choosemyplate.gov. COURTESY OF USDA AND DHHS

Carbohydrate, which is converted to glucose and glycogen in the body, is the ultimate fuel for intense physical exercise such as climbing and training for climbing, so it's best to consume five or six small meals or snacks containing carbohydrate throughout the day. This eating strategy supports steady blood sugar levels, and thus steady energy and mental focus, as well as a constant supply of substrate to resynthesize muscle glycogen. Conversely, going too long between meals or eating the wrong foods (more on this in a minute) will lead to spikes and troughs in blood sugar level and corresponding vacillations in energy and mental sharpness. Furthermore, too small of a total number of calories per day from carbohydrates will hinder supercompensation and slow recovery from exercise.

Determining the optimal amount of carbohydrate to consume in a day can be difficult, but it is something you can suss out with some experimentation and heightened awareness of your energy levels. A few classic signs that you are consuming too little carbohydrate are unusual tiredness or weakness while training or climbing, strangely weak and tired muscles despite a one- or two-day rest, and poor mental alertness. Use the calorie calculator on page 67 to estimate your daily caloric needs according to your body weight, metabolism, and activity level.

In choosing foods for your snacks and meals, it is important to understand that not all carbohydrate-based foods are created equal. While all forms of carbohydrate contain 4 calories per gram, the rate at which they are digested and transformed to blood glucose varies greatly. As mentioned above, dramatic changes in blood sugar level affect your energy level, mood, and focus, so it's best to consume mainly the types of carbohydrate that

Table 13.1 Glycemic Index of Common Foods

High (>70)	Medium (50–70)	Low (<50)
Sports drinks 70–85	Banana 55	Balance Bar 30
Clif Bar 70+	PowerBar 65	Peanuts 14
Bagel (plain) 72	Raisins 64	Apple 38
Carrots 71	Granola bars 61	Orange 43
Corn chips 73	Macaroni 64	Pear 36
Cornflakes 77	Shredded wheat 58	Grapefruit 23
Doughnut 76	Sweet potato 54	Yogurt (w/fruit) 30
Honey 73	Bran muffin 60	All-Bran 42
Jelly beans 80	Oatmeal 61	Whole wheat 37
Potatoes 83	Wheat crackers 67	Spaghetti 41
Rice (instant) 91	Cookies 60	Beans 48
Rice cakes 82	Orange juice 57	Lentils 28
Cracker (soda/water) 76	Soft drinks 68	Milk (skim) 32
Glucose 100	Sucrose 65	Fructose 23

elicit only small changes in blood sugar. Fortunately, there's the glycemic index (GI) to help you select the right carbohydrate sources (see table 13.1). Foods with a high GI cause a rapid increase in blood sugar and often a subsequent insulin release with the telltale energy trough (and sometimes even sleepiness) that soon follows. Medium- and low-GI foods produce more subtle changes in blood sugar and hence sustain stable energy levels, mood, and concentration. Consequently, it is best to consume mainly low- to medium-GI foods during rest days and in the hours leading up to exercise. Only during intense exercise and the 2 hours following exercise do you want to consume high-GI foods, since the resultant rise in blood sugar level will help sustain fatiguing exercise and best initiate recovery immediately afterward.

Protein

Nearer the top of the Food Guide Pyramid are the protein-rich food groups such as animal and dairy products, beans, and nuts. Since many foods in these groups also possess high amounts of fat, serious athletes tend to avoid them. The result is often insufficient protein intake, which is counterproductive in the quest to build stronger muscles, tendons, and connective tissues. The bottom line: Short-change yourself on protein and you are shortchanging your muscles and not recovering optimally.

So how much protein does your athlete's body really need? Furthermore, how can you consume enough protein without overdosing on saturated fats? A good estimate of the minimum daily requirement for protein is 1 gram per kilogram of body weight, with a more liberal estimate being 1.5 grams per kilo. Applying these ratios to my 160-pound (73 kg) body means I should consume between 73 and 110 grams of protein per day. This amount would certainly be fattening and unhealthy if I tried to eat all my protein in the form of red meat and high-fat dairy products. I rarely consume these foods, however, yet I never fail to consume my personal target of 100 grams of protein per day. I can easily reach this goal with four servings of skim milk (a total of 32 grams of protein), several servings of vegetables (5 to 10 grams), a serving of lean meat or beans

Pausing to eat healthy snacks and hydrate throughout the day plays a subtle, yet important role in performance on long climbs. ERIC J. HÖRST

(15 to 25 grams), and a small whey protein shake at breakfast and before bedtime (40 grams of total protein). You could certainly replace the protein shakes or some of the skim milk with yogurt or an extra serving of lean meat and still consume an adequate amount of protein without taking a huge calorie or fat hit. Speaking of fat . . .

Fat

Fats have a bad name among athletes—I admit that I've dissed them more than a few times over the years!—yet not all types of fat are bad. In fact, you may be surprised to learn that you need a steady diet of certain fats to build tissue, lubricate joints, and help combat inflammation, among other things. The problem is that average Americans consume more than 40 percent of their daily calories from fats and oils, and a large portion of these fat calories come from unhealthy nonessential and refined fats.

Note in figure 13.1 that fats and oils form only the tip of the Food Guide Pyramid. Therefore, a climber serious about training and performance must limit fat consumption to just 20 percent of total daily calories (carbohydrate and protein should make up 65 percent and 15 percent of total caloric intake, respectively). Let's run the numbers for an average climber (like me) who weighs about 160 pounds and consumes around 2,500 calories per day. Twenty percent of 2,500 calories is 500 calories, and at 9 calories per gram of fat, I must limit myself to 55 grams of fat per day. This might seem like a lot or a little, depending on your perspective—I have known climbers who swore they'd never eat more than 25 grams of fat per day, while others consume more than 55 in a single meal at McDonald's! Clearly, neither approach is ideal.

The approach I advocate is to not obsess over fat (in either way), and to let your fat intake "just happen" as you consume your planned, healthy meals throughout the day. Certainly it's advisable to avoid fast foods, fried foods, and all snack foods packaged for maximum shelf life (which surely contain a high amount of dangerous trans fats). However, fats ingested in eating lean meats such as grilled chicken, fish, or a small piece of red meat are mainly good fats, as are most fats contained in nuts, beans, olive-oil-based salad dressing, and many nutrition bars. If these foods are regular staples of your current diet, while the aforementioned fast foods are a rare treat, then you are with the program already!

Water

Whether you are training indoors, climbing outdoors, or just taking a rest day, sustaining proper hydration is essential for optimal performance, injury prevention, and accelerating recovery. Studies have shown that even slight dehydration (a 1 to 3 percent loss of water) results in reduced concentration, enhanced fatigue, and a drop in maximum strength. Furthermore, dehydration makes you more susceptible to cramps, muscle pulls, and even joint and tendon injuries. Clearly, sustaining proper hydration throughout the day is as important as any other aspect of your optimal sports nutrition program.

How much water do you need to consume? Well, this depends on a number of factors including your body weight, your level of activity, and the ambient temperature and humidity. As a rule of thumb, however, it's a good idea to pre-hydrate 1 hour before training or climbing by drinking 2 cups or more of water. Throughout your workout or day of climbing, you want to consume a minimum of 1 cup (an 8-ounce serving) of water or sports drink every hour. Double or triple this amount in hot weather, as your perspiration rate will be substantially higher.

Vitamins, Sports Drinks, and Other Supplements

Food supplements are ubiquitous these days, with countless sports drinks, vitamins, protein shakes, and other "performance boosting" concoctions and functional foods filling the shelves at health food and grocery stores alike. As a rule, these products—especially the most hyped—provide little benefit and therefore are a colossal waste of money. That said, there are a few products valuable for a serious athlete working to enhance performance and accelerate recovery.

Given the streamlined diet of a serious athlete, I feel it's a wise investment to take a daily multivitamin each morning. Supplemental protein is also a good investment, especially if you consume little meat or dairy. Whey protein powder mixed into a glass of water, juice, or skim milk is the ideal source of extra protein. Drinking a whey protein shake before bedtime and first thing in the morning will provide high-quality protein before and immediately after your 6- to 9-hour daily fast (very important!).

Lastly, I'm going to tell you about some exciting research in the area of recovery drinks. While sugar-laced sports drinks have been around since the advent of Gatorade in the 1970s, recent research shows that consuming a sports drink (immediately following a workout) containing both carbohydrate and protein triggers a faster recovery rate than does a conventional carbohydrate-only sports drink. Two popular drink mixes with an effective blend of carbohydrate and protein are Accelerade and PowerBar Recovery. A tasty alternative to these recovery drinks is lowfat chocolate milk, which contains a near-perfect ratio of protein to carbohydrate. In the case of a hard workout or full day of climbing, you would want to consume about 100 grams of liquid carbohydrate along with 25 grams of liquid protein. Research has shown that you can accelerate recovery by as much as 50 percent if you consume a drink with a four-to-one carbohydrate-to-protein ratio within 2 hours of completing your workout—the sooner, the better.

Sleep and Recovery Requirements

The act of physical training doesn't make you stronger; it merely stimulates gene expression and the body's other growth mechanisms into motion. It's during periods of rest and sleep that your body actually recovers and supercompensates to a level higher than before the workout. Therefore, your workouts must be balanced with adequate periods of rest in order to produce the adaptations that will enhance your physical capabilities and climbing performance.

There are two categories of rest to consider: your hours of sleep per night and the number of rest days you take between workouts or days of climbing. In terms of sleep, it's important to recognize that the body repairs itself and new growth occurs primarily during your sleeping hours. Therefore, the amount of sleep you get the night following a hard workout is as important as your use of proper training exercises and consumption of sufficient nutrients. The bare minimum amount of sleep per night is 6 hours, with 8 or 9 hours being optimal after an especially hard day of training or climbing. If you are like most people, that kind of free time is hard to come by, but you might be able to pull it off by giving up some nighttime activities (TV and such) in favor of going to bed earlier. Remind yourself that sleep is an essential part of your training program. What are your priorities?

Specifying the optimal number of rest days between workouts or days of climbing is harder to pin down. There are many factors that contribute to rate of recovery, such as the quality of your diet, hours of sleep, rest-day activity, level of fitness, age, and genetics. Another major factor is workout intensity. Complete recovery from a low-intensity stamina workout such as moderate climbing or jogging often takes less than 24 hours, whereas recovery from a rigorous limit-strength and power or a strength/power-endurance workout could take as much as three to five days. Ultimately, you need to be aware of your body's signals and continue with your next workout only when you feel recovered enough to make it a quality effort.

If you ever sense that you are getting weaker, despite your dedicated training, there's a good chance that your workout-to-rest ratio needs

Sending your hardest-ever project demands you get everything right: training, nutrition, sleep, and game-day warm-up and psych. Here's B. J. Tilden on his soon-to-be-sent mega-project, Mutation (5.14d).

adjustment. Overtraining is a covert (and surprisingly common) cause of frustrating performance plateaus and injury among enthusiastic, hard-training climbers. If you frequently arrive at the gym or crags feeling tired and unmotivated, or if you feel weak and out of whack on the rock, then you may be suffering from overtraining. Although you may get away with this for a while, the practice of constantly climbing weak and tired will eventually lead to overtraining, a decline in performance, and perhaps injury or illness.

The antidote to overtraining is over-resting! Begin by taking three to seven days off from training and climbing activities. After this break you can ramp back up into your return to a schedule of regular exercise over the course of the next

week—but at a frequency reduced by one day per week. For example, if you previously climbed and trained a total of five days per week, reduce this to four. Increasing your quantity of rest will begin a new growth phase with corresponding gains in conditioning and climbing performance!

Injury Prevention Tips

In concluding this text on exercises for climbers, I will provide you with five tips for reducing your injury risk and hopefully remaining on-route to reaching your climbing goals. The recent escalation in chronic injuries of the fingers, elbows, and shoulders is alarming, so the wise climber will be proactive in mitigating injury risk. Remind yourself frequently that an injury is the single greatest barrier between you and your climbing goals. Here's what you can do to prevent this.

Limit Climbing and Training to Four Days a Week—or Less

As a rule, it is counterproductive to climb and train specifically more than four days per week, in aggregate. For example, if you are climbing four days a week on the rock, in the gym, or a combination, you should do no other climbing-specific training during the three remaining days of the week. Even with three days' rest out of seven, your body will struggle to repair the stressed tendon and muscle tissues that results from your four climbing days. For this reason, it is wise to utilize a training cycle that provides a four- to seven-day training taper or rest week every month or two.

Don't Skip the Warm-Up and Cool-Down

I'm always surprised by the number of climbers I observe who arrive at the gym or crag and just start climbing without any warm-up activity whatsoever. No serious athlete in any other sport would ever consider jumping into full-speed training or competition without warming up, yet many climbers do. This probably has to do with the fact that, unlike participants in other sports, most climbers don't have a coach to direct warm-up drills and workout strategy. As a largely self-directed, self-coached activity, climbing necessitates that you play the roles of both coach and athlete—you must compel yourself to do the right things right. That's the essence of an effective training program.

All you need by way of a good warm-up is to break a light sweat for 5 to 15 minutes by jogging, hiking, or riding, or at the very least climbing around on large holds and easy terrain to elevate your heart rate. This prepares you to then engage in some of the mobility and stretching exercises described in chapter 3, after which you are ready to start climbing on a series of progressively more

difficult boulder problems or roped climbs. The entire warm-up process will take anywhere from 15 to 30 minutes, but it will leave you ready to execute your most difficult exercises, limit bouldering, or project rope climbing with the least risk of incurring an injury.

A brief cool-down is also beneficial to loosen up tight muscle groups and enhance the recovery process. In particular, stretching and a few minutes of light aerobic activity will sustain elevated blood flow to the muscles and thus speed dispersion of metabolic by-products and a return of homeostasis.

Regularly Train the Antagonist and Stabilizer Muscles

As explained in chapter 5, training the antagonist and stabilizer muscles is one of the most overlooked—and vital—parts of an effective training-for-climbing program. Muscle imbalances in the forearms, shoulders, and torso are primary factors in many of the overuse injuries experienced by climbers. If you are serious about climbing your best and preventing injury, then you must commit to training the antagonist muscles twice per week.

The time investment is minimal—about 20 to 40 minutes, twice a week, is all you need to adequately strengthen the various opposing muscle groups. I prefer doing these exercises on my rest days between climbing workouts, although you could also engage in this push-muscle training at the end of your climbing session. Either way, I advise doing most of the antagonist and stability exercises described in chapter 5, as well as several of the core-training exercises detailed in chapter 6.

Leverage Periodization

In chapter 1 you learned about the principle of variation and how a periodization scheme will supercharge your training program. As explained, periodization involves a premeditated variation in workout focus, intensity, and volume, which in the long term produces a maximal training response.

Periodization also reduces the risk of overuse injury since the training focus and intensity change every few days or weeks.

In a highly stressful sport such as climbing, the most valuable aspect of periodization may be the intermittent rest phases or breaks away from all sport-specific activity. Chapter 11 promoted use of a training cycle such as the 4-3-2-1 Cycle (or similar) for most intermediate and advanced climbers. This training cycle provides one full week of tapered training or rest out of every ten-week cycle for systemic recovery and to blunt long-term accumulation of overuse stress. In the yearlong macrocycle, it is similarly advisable to take an entire month off from climbing-related stresses. These breaks away from climbing go a long way toward allowing the slow-to-adapt tendons and ligaments to catch up with the more quickly occurring gains in muscular strength. Be wise—periodize!

Strive for Optimal Rest and Nutrition

This final tip completes the circle of knowledge for this final chapter of *The Rock Climber's Exercise Guide*, since it underscores the importance of proper rest and nutrition. I encourage you to reread the section on optimal sports nutrition on page 219, and then internalize and apply this information. No matter your age or ability, improving your nutrition and recovery habits is essential to reaching your training and climbing goals.

Since you have now read this book to its end, it's clear that you are a climber passionate about reaching your true potential. This book has covered the many facets of effective training for climbing that must be interlaced to form a superlative and uncommonly effective program. Remember that the chapters relating to self-assessment, mobility and stability, and recovery are as important as those dealing with developing greater strength, power, and endurance in the climbing muscles. Becoming the best climber you can be takes many years of dedicated, comprehensive effort, and I hope this book will be your constant companion on this wonderful adventure.

Be safe, be strong, and always have fun, whether you are climbing or training for climbing!

Appendix A

Muscular Anatomy

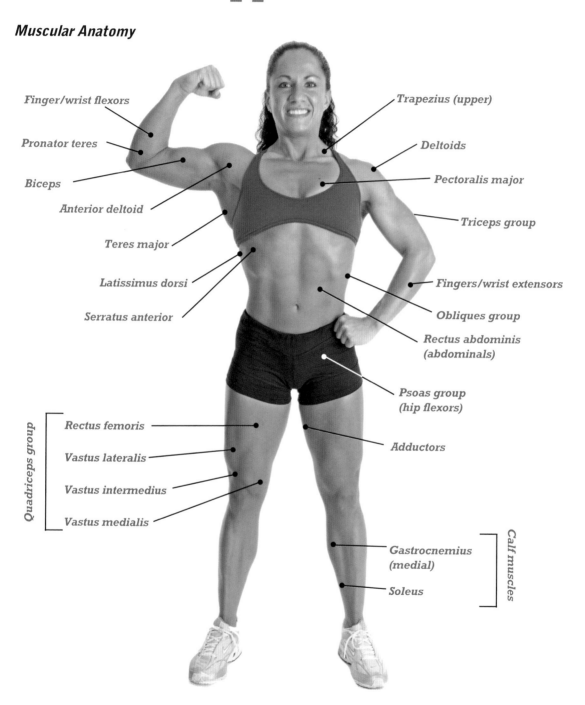

Finger/wrist flexors

Pronator teres

Biceps

Anterior deltoid

Teres major

Latissimus dorsi

Serratus anterior

Trapezius (upper)

Deltoids

Pectoralis major

Triceps group

Fingers/wrist extensors

Obliques group

Rectus abdominis
(abdominals)

Psoas group
(hip flexors)

Quadriceps group

Rectus femoris

Vastus lateralis

Vastus intermedius

Vastus medialis

Adductors

Gastrocnemius
(medial)

Soleus

Calf muscles

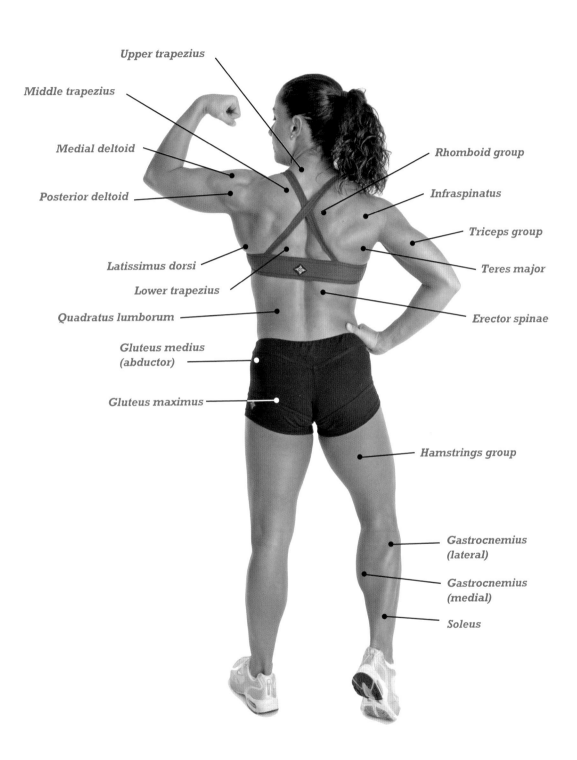

Upper trapezius

Middle trapezius

Medial deltoid

Posterior deltoid

Rhomboid group

Infraspinatus

Triceps group

Latissimus dorsi

Lower trapezius

Teres major

Quadratus lumborum

Erector spinae

Gluteus medius
(abductor)

Gluteus maximus

Hamstrings group

Gastrocnemius
(lateral)

Gastrocnemius
(medial)

Soleus

Appendix B

Training and Climbing Macrocycle

Name/Year																																																				

Training Objectives and Seasonal Climbing Goals

Month	Jan					Feb				Mar				Apr				May				Jun				Jul					Aug				Sep					Oct				Nov				Dec			
Week	1	2	3	4	5	6	7	8	9	10	11	12	13	14	15	16	17	18	19	20	21	22	23	24	25	26	27	28	29	30	31	32	33	34	35	36	37	38	39	40	41	42	43	44	45	46	47	48	49	50	51	52

Training Focus
- Stamina/skill
- Max. strength and power
- Anaerobic endurance
- Taper/Rest

Total number of days per week of climbing and climbing-specific training
- 7
- 6
- 5
- 4
- 3
- 2
- 1

Benchmark achievements and notes

Glossary

The following is a compilation of some of the technical terms and climbing jargon used throughout this book.

active recovery—Restoration of homeostasis following vigorous exercise that involves continued light-intensity movement; facilitates faster recovery by enhancing lactate removal from the blood.

acute—Having rapid onset and severe symptoms.

adaptive response—Physiological changes in structure or function particularly related to response to a training overload.

aerobic—Any physical activity deriving energy from the breakdown of glycogen in the presence of oxygen, thus producing little or no lactic acid, enabling an athlete to continue exercise much longer.

agonist—A muscle directly engaged in a muscular contraction.

anaerobic—Energy production in the muscles involving the breakdown of glycogen in the absence of oxygen.

antagonist—A muscle providing an opposing force to the primary (agonist) muscles in action.

atrophy—Gradual shrinking and deconditioning of muscle tissue from disuse.

basal metabolic rate—The minimum level of energy required to sustain the body's vital functions.

campus (or campusing)—Climbing an overhanging section of rock or artificial wall with no feet, usually in a dynamic left-hand, right-hand, left-hand (and so forth) sequence.

campus training—A sport-specific form of plyometric exercise developed by Wolfgang Güllich at the Campus Center (a weight-lifting facility at the University of Nuremberg, Germany).

capillary—The tiny blood vessels that receive blood flow from the arteries, interchange substances between the blood and the tissues, and return the blood to the veins.

concentric contraction—Any movement involving a shortening of muscle fibers while developing tension, as in the biceps muscle during a pull-up.

detraining—Reversal of positive adaptations to chronic exercise upon cessation of an exercise program.

dynamic move—An explosive leap for a hold otherwise out of reach.

dyno—Short for "dynamic."

eccentric contraction—Muscle action in which the muscle resists as it is forced to lengthen, as in the biceps during the lowering phase of a pull-up.

epicondylitis—Inflammation of the tendon origins of the forearm flexors (medial) or extensors (lateral) near the elbow.

ergogenic—Performance enhancing.

extension—A movement that takes the two ends of a jointed body part away from each other, as in straightening the arm.

flash pump—A rapid, often vicious, muscular pump resulting from strenuous training or climbing without first performing a proper (gradual) warm-up.

flexion—A movement that brings the ends of a body part closer together, as in bending the arm.

glycemic index (GI)—A scale that classifies how the ingestion of various foods affects blood sugar levels in comparison with the ingestion of straight glucose.

glycogen—Compound chains of glucose stored in the muscle and liver for use during aerobic or anaerobic exercise.

homeostasis—The body's tendency to maintain a steady state despite external changes.

hormone—A chemical secreted into the bloodstream to regulate the function of a certain organ.

Hypergravity Isolation Training (HIT)—A highly refined and specific method of training maximum finger strength and upper-body power by climbing on identical finger holds (isolation) with greater than body weight (hypergravity). Also known as Hörst Isolation Training.

hypergravity training—A highly effective method of training maximum strength that involves climbing or training with weight added to the body (simulates hypergravity).

hypertrophy—Enlargement in size, as in muscular hypertrophy.

insulin—A hormone that decreases blood glucose levels by driving glucose from the blood into muscle and fat cells.

isometric—Muscular contraction resulting in no shortening of the muscle (no movement).

ligament—Fibrous connective tissue that connects bone to bone, or bone to cartilage, to hold together and support the joints.

limit strength—The peak force of a muscular contraction, irrespective of the time element.

lunge—An out-of-control dynamic move; an explosive jump for a far-off hold.

macronutrients—Basic nutrients (carbohydrates, fat, and protein) needed for energy, cell growth, and organ function.

micronutrients—Noncaloric nutrients needed in very small amounts, as in vitamins and minerals.

motor learning—The set of internal processes associated with practice or experience leading to a relatively permanent gain in performance capability.

motor skill—A skill where the primary determinant of success is the movement component itself.

open-hand grip—A less stressful finger grip involving only slight flexion of the finger joints.

overhanging—A wall surface that angles outward beyond vertical, so that the top of the wall overhangs its base.

overload—Subjecting a part of the body to greater efforts (intensity or volume) than it is accustomed to in order to elicit a training response.

overtraining—Constant severe training that does not provide adequate time for recovery; symptoms include increased frequency of injury, decreased performance, irritability, and apathy.

overuse—Excessive repeated exertion or shock that results in injuries such as inflammation of the muscles and tendons.

plyometric—An exercise that suddenly preloads and forces the stretching of a muscle an instant prior to its concentric contraction, as in dynamic up-and-down campus training.

power—A measure of both force and speed (speed = distance x time) of a muscular contraction through a given range of motion. Power is the explosive aspect of strength.

pronation—The inward turning of a body part, as in turning the forearm inward and the palm facedown.

pumped—When the muscles become engorged with blood due to extended physical exertion.

recruitment—Systematic increase in the number of active motor units called upon during muscular contraction.

schema—A set of rules, usually developed and applied unconsciously by the motor system in the brain and spinal cord, relating how to move and adjust muscle forces, body positions, and so on given the parameters at hand, such as steepness of the rock, friction qualities, holds being used, and type of terrain.

send—Short for "ascend."

skill—A capability to bring about an end result with maximum certainty, minimum energy, and minimum time.

slow-twitch fibers—Muscle fiber type that contracts slowly and is used most in moderate-intensity endurance activities, such as easy to moderate climbing or running.

sport climbing—Refers to any indoor or outdoor climbing on bolt-protected routes.

spotter—A training partner who assists you in executing an exercise safely and effectively. Also, a person designated to slow the fall of a boulderer, with the main goal of keeping the boulderer's head from hitting the ground.

supercompensate—The body's recovery process of adaptation and overcompensation to the stress of exercise.

supination—The outward turning of a body part, as in rotating the forearm outward and the palm upward.

synovial fluid—A viscid fluid secreted by the membrane lining joints, tendon sheaths, and bursae to lubricate and cushion them during movement.

tendinitis—A disorder involving the inflammation of a tendon and synovial membrane at a joint.

tendinosis—Chronic tendon pain due to an accumulation of microscopic injuries that don't heal properly; the main problem, then, is failed healing, not inflammation.

tendon—A white fibrous cord of dense connective tissue that attaches muscle to bone.

toprope—The most secure roped climbing setup in which the rope passes through an anchor atop the route.

vein—A vessel that returns blood from the various parts of the body to the heart.

visualization—Controlled and directed imagery that can be used for awareness building, monitoring and self-regulation, healing, and, most important, mental programming for good performances.

VO$_2$ max—Maximal oxygen uptake, as in the measurement of maximum aerobic power.

wired—Known well, as in a wired route.

working—Practicing the moves on a difficult route via toprope or hangdogging.

Suggested Reading

Bechtel, Steve. *Strength: Foundational Training for Rock Climbers*. Lander, WY: Elemental, 2014.

Erikson, Lisa. *Climbing Injuries Solved*. 2014.

Hörst, Eric J. *Training for Climbing: The Definitive Guide to Improving Your Performance*. Guilford, CT: Globe Pequot/FalconGuides, 2016.

———. *Maximum Climbing: Mental Training for Peak Performance and Optimal Experience*. Guilford, CT: Globe Pequot/FalconGuides, 2010.

———. *How to Climb 5.12*. Guilford, CT: Globe Pequot/FalconGuides, 2003.

Matros, Patrick, Dicki Korb, and Hannes Huch. *Gimme Kraft*. Nuremberg, Germany: Café Kraft GmbH, 2013.

Schöffl, Volker, and Thomas Hochholzer. *One Move Too Many*. Ebenhausen, Germany: Lochner-Verlag, 2016.

Stricker, Lauri. *Pilates for the Outdoor Athlete*. Conifer, CO: Fulcrum, 2007.

Index

About the Author

Eric J. Hörst (pronounced "Hurst") is an internationally renowned author, researcher, climbing coach, and accomplished climber of four decades.

A student and teacher of climbing performance, Eric has coached hundreds of climbers, and his training books and concepts have spread to climbers in more than fifty countries. He is widely recognized for his innovative training techniques and equipment, and he has been a training products design consultant and Training Center editor for Nicros, Inc. since 1994. Eric is author of eight books (with many foreign translations) with worldwide sales of over 300,000 copies. Eric's popular texts include *Maximum Climbing, Training for Climbing, How to Climb 5.12*, and the gym climbing book *Learning to Climb Indoors*.

Eric has written more than one hundred magazine articles and appeared on numerous TV broadcasts, and his techniques and photos have appeared in many publications including *Rock & Ice, Climbing, Outside, DeadPoint, Men's Health, Fortune, Men's Journal, Muscle Media, Muscle & Fitness, Paddler, Urban Climber, Parents, Wall Street Journal, Experience Life, Outdoor 4X*, and *National Geographic Adventure*, as well as European magazines such as *Desnivel, Alpen, Climax*, and *Climber*. He has coauthored one research paper ("Behavior Analysis and Sport Climbing," *Journal of Behavioral Health and Medicine*, 2010), with Dr. Richard Fleming. Eric is a member of the International Rock Climbing Research Association (IRCRA) and the National Strength and Conditioning Association (NSCA).

A self-professed "climber for life," Eric remains active at the cliffs, traveling widely with his wife, Lisa, and sons, Cameron and Jonathan. Driven by his passion for adventure and challenge, he has established over 400 first ascents, primarily on his home cliffs in the eastern United States. Still pushing his personal climbing limits in his early 50s, Eric's focus is now on R & D of new training techniques, traveling and sharing his knowledge with new climbers, and coaching the next generation of elite climbers. Eric's website is www.TrainingForClimbing.com.

Other Books by Eric J. Hörst

Maximum Climbing (FalconGuides, 2010) presents a climber's guide to the software of the brain, based on the premise that you climb with your mind—your hands and feet are simply extensions of your thoughts and will. Becoming a master climber, then, requires that you first become a master of your mind. In this breakthrough book, Eric Hörst brings unprecedented clarity to the many cognitive and neurophysical aspects of climbing and dovetails this information into a complete mental-training program.

How to Climb 5.12 (FalconGuides, 2011) is a performance guidebook to attaining the most rapid gains in climbing ability possible, and it's written specifically for intermediate climbers looking to break through to the higher grades. It provides streamlined instruction on vital topics such as accelerating learning of skills, training your mind and body, and becoming an effective on-sight and redpoint climber.

Learning to Climb Indoors (FalconGuides, 2012) is the most complete book available on indoor climbing. Topics covered include beginning and advanced climbing techniques, tactics, strategy, basic gear, safety techniques, self-assessment, and a primer on mental training and physical conditioning. This guide includes everything you need to know from day one as a climber through your first year or two in the sport.

Training for Climbing, 3rd edition (FalconGuides, 2016), is the most comprehensive and advanced text ever published on the subject of climbing performance. Building on decades of experience and the latest climbing research, this voluminous tome presents a unique synthesis of leading-edge strength and power-training methods, tried-and-true practice strategies, and powerful mental-training techniques that will empower you to climb better, regardless of your current ability. Now in its third edition, TFC remains an international bestseller!

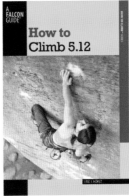

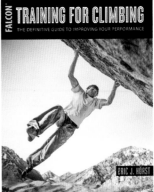

PROTECTING CLIMBING **ACCESS** SINCE 1991

ACCESS FUND

| JOIN US |
WWW.ACCESSFUND.ORG

Jonathan Siegrist, Third Millenium (14a), the Monastery, CO. Photo by: Keith Ladzinski